Canada's National Parks

A Visitor's Guide

Revised and Updated
Marylee Stephenson

0 57812 16468 0

Canada's National Parks

A Visitor's Guide

Revised and Updated
Marylee Stephenson

*(Photos by the author
unless otherwise noted)*

Prentice-Hall Canada Inc., Scarborough, Ontario

YUKON
TERRITORY

☐12

☐11

● Whitehorse

☐13 Fort
Simpson
●

NORTHWEST TERRITORIES

● Yellowknife

Fort Smith
☐14 ●

☐1

BRITISH
COLUMBIA

ALBERTA

☐9

☐10
Edmonton
●

SASKATCHEWAN

MANITOBA

☐5

☐15

☐3 ☐4 ☐8

☐2 ● Vancouver

☐6

● Calgary

Saskatoon
●

Victoria
●

☐7

☐16

Regina
●

☐17

Winnipeg
●

Thu

UNITED STATES

Canada's National Parks

1 South Moresby/
   Gwaii Haanas
2 Pacific Rim
3 Mount Revelstoke
4 Glacier
5 Yoho
6 Kootenay
7 Waterton Lakes
8 Banff
9 Jasper
10 Elk Island
11 Kluane
12 Northern Yukon
13 Nahanni
14 Wood Buffalo
15 Prince Albert
16 Grasslands
17 Riding Mountain

18 Pukaskwa
19 Bruce Peninsula
20 Fathom Five
21 Georgian Bay Islands
22 Point Pelee
23 St. Lawrence Islands
24 La Mauricie
25 Auyuittuq
26 Mingan Archipelago
27 Forillon
28 Kouchibouguac
29 Fundy
30 Prince Edward Island
31 Kejimkujik
32 Cape Breton Highlands
33 Gros Morne
34 Terra Nova
35 Ellesmere Island

BAFFIN ISLAND

25 Pangnirtung

NEWFOUNDLAND

QUEBEC

33 Corner Brook
34 St. John's

Sept Iles 26

27 Gaspé

PRINCE EDWARD ISLAND 32 Sydney

Moncton 30 Charlottetown

NEW BRUNSWICK 28 NOVA SCOTIA

Quebec

24

29 Halifax

Saint John 31

18

NTARIO

Sault Ste. Marie

North Bay

Ottawa Montreal

19 23

20 21 Kingston

Toronto

Windsor 22

Canadian Cataloguing in Publication Data

Stephenson, Marylee, 1943-
    Canada's national parks : a visitor's guide

Rev. and updated.
Includes bibliographical references.
ISBN 0-13-116468-6

1. National parks and reserves - Canada - Guide-books.
2. Canada - Description and travel - 1981-
I. Title

FC215.S86 1990   917.104'647   C90-093648-7
F1011.S86 1990

Prentice-Hall Inc., *Englewood Cliffs, New Jersey*
Prentice-Hall International, Inc., *London*
Prentice-Hall of Australia, Pty., *Sydney*
Prentice-Hall of India Pvt. Ltd., *New Delhi*
Prentice-Hall of Japan, Inc., *Tokyo*
Prentice-Hall of Southeast Asia (Pte.) Ltd., *Singapore*
Editora Prentice-Hall do Brasil Ltda., *Rio de Janeiro*
Prentice-Hall Hispanoamericana, S.A., *Mexico*

Editor: William Booth
Design: Gail Ferreira Ng-A-Kien, Olena Serbyn
Maps: Julian Cleva
Composition: Olena Serbyn
Manufacturing Buyer: Lisa Kreuch

ISBN: 0-13-116468-6

Printed and bound in the U.S.A. by R.R. Donnelley & Sons Company

1 2 3 4 5   RRD   95 94 93 92 91

Contents

Acknowledgements

In revising this book, I have drawn on the assistance of many people, at the parks, in the administration of the Canadian Parks Service, at the publishers, and among friends and associates. Those listed below, park by park, made corrections and suggestions for the materials on their parks, and I am particularly grateful for their promptness and thoroughness. Also, I visited Banff, Fundy, Fathom Five, Georgian Bay Islands, and Bruce Peninsula National Parks, and received a great deal of on-the-spot help from those cited here. They are very busy people, but they found the time to show me around and answer my questions—and see a few birds along the way.

I went on these visits with Sharon Kelly, and her help and patience were great assets. Also, the hospitality of Susan and Peter Clark, in Halifax, was most appreciated. This is the second round for them in the history of this book.

Tanya Long, at Prentice-Hall, has been very patient throughout this process, which always takes longer than one thinks.

Jeannie McIntosh was invaluable in preparing the materials for final submission to the publisher.

And, finally, I would like to thank again Scott Meis, the person who first introduced me to the outdoors of Canada. He was instrumental in the completion of the first edition of this book, and his continued encouragement of all my work continues to be of great importance to me.

Even though the people listed below were very careful in their reviews of the chapters, the responsibility for any errors is my own.

Fundy National Park   Rob Walker

Grasslands National Park   W.J. Masyk

Prince Edward Island National Park   Paul De Mone

Gros Morne National Park   Anne Marceau

Kouchibouguac National Park Barry Spencer

Kejimkujik National Park Peter Hope

Mingan National Park Reserve Marc Pagé, Daniel Rosset

Cape Breton Highlands National Park Elaine Wallace

Georgian Bay Islands National Park Greg Gemmell

Bruce Peninsula and Fathom Five National Parks Donald Wilkes

South Moresby National Park Reserve Ron Hooper, Steve Suddes

Riding Mountain National Park Celes Devar

Prince Albert National Park Merv Syroteuk

Wood Buffalo National Park Mike Rosen

Nahanni National Park Reserve Sean Meggs and Sheila Michaelis (NWT Economic Development and Tourism)

Waterton Lakes National Park Duane Barris

Auyuittuq National Park Reserve and Ellesmere Island National Park Reserve Jack Ricou (Winnipeg CPS)

Kootenay National Park Larry Halverson

Kluane National Park, North Yukon Phil Bastien

Canadian Parks Service, Winnipeg Jack Ricou, Michael Cobus

Canadian Parks Service, Ottawa Gary Sealey, Bruce Amos

Banff National Park Rob Harding, Donna Pletz, Jeff Waugh, Mike Kerr, Colin Brander and visitor Heather F. Crane

Pacific Rim National Park Bill McIntyre

Yoho National Park Kevin Van Tighem

Jasper National Park Jim Todglam

Elk Island National Park Murray Christman

Pukaskwa National Park Donna Rykma-Rooney, Michael Jones

Point Pelee National Park R.A. Watt

St. Lawrence Islands National Park Dave Warner

La Mauricie National Park Jacques Pleu

Forillon National Park Marc Trudel

Terra Nova National Park G.F. Marsh

Mount Revelstoke and Glacier National Parks Pat Dunn

Map Legend

Highway ▬

Secondary Road ▬

Marsh

Information Centre (?)

Administration (A)

Trails - - - -

Camping Λ

Group Camping ΛΛ

Primitive Camping* Λ

Viewpoint

Warden Station (W)

Park Gate/Entrance ⊓

Accommodation 🏠

Mountain ▲

Shelter Λ

Railway ┼┼┼┼┼

Icefield/Glacier

Lake/River/Creek

Interpretive Centre/Exhibit (E)

*This designation means there are no flush toilets, kitchen shelters, hook-ups or waste disposal units for trailers. These campgrounds usually have pit toilets and well or fresh stream water.

Readers should note that conversions from metric to imperial measure in the text are not exact. They are intended to provide a rough guide.

Introduction

Canada's national parks are simply splendid. One is as far south as the border of northern California, and several are above the Arctic Circle. You can side-step a buffalo in the baking prairie sun, or listen to beavers chewing their evening meal beside a Rocky Mountain stream. Kayaking, walking, swimming, rolling along in a wheelchair, driving in your car, or bumping along on horseback—there's no end to the ways you can get close to the natural wonders encompassed by our national parks. And, it has to be said, the shopping and restaurants, ski lifts and tour boats, can add a lot to your enjoyment, as well. Given this vast natural richness and the multitude of possibilities for fun, learning, and what might be called spiritual renewal, that our parks provide, this book is designed to help you match your interests as a potential visitor with what Canada'a national parks have to offer. In planning a trip, or having arrived at your destination, this book should be treated as a friend who has been there before you, and who continues to walk along with you, chatting about what you're seeing now, and mulling over what to do next.

Canada's thirty-four national parks and park reserves protect some of the most precious natural resources of our country and, in many cases, of our world. The stated goal of the park system is

> To protect for all time representative natural areas of
> Canadian significance in a system of National Parks, and to
> encourage public understanding, appreciation, and enjoyment
> of this natural heritage so as to leave it unimpaired for future
> generations.

It would be naive to think that this protection is complete, or that this system could not be improved upon, but what we have is truly marvellous.

1

The national system began in 1885, with the creation of what is now Banff National Park. The establishment of Banff and its successors, such as Yoho, Glacier, and Waterton Lakes, came about largely because the federal government acted in conjunction with the railroad companies, or other commercial interests, to set aside for tourism the spectacular scenic areas through which the railroads passed. In some cases, there were a few local people who were aware that the environment was being threatened by the rapid encroachment of settlement, hunting, mining, or logging, but this was not the primary impetus for very early park establishment. In fact, hunting, mining, and logging continued in a number of parks for decades, and town-based commercial development remains a major feature of a number of the parks today, as any visit to Banff, Riding Mountain, Prince Edward Island or Fathom Five national parks readily reveals.

Gradually, however, there has been a shift in the balance between protecting resources for commercial exploitation and protecting natural resources for their own inherent values. Now the primary rationale for establishing parks is to set aside forever at least one significant segment of each of Canada's types of natural regions. Thirty-nine of these regions are terrestrial—like the Northern Yukon Region or the Northwestern Boreal Uplands, and twenty-nine are marine—like the Labrador Sea or Queen Charlotte Sound. In terms of the establishment of parks in terrestrial regions, twenty-one of the thirty-nine regions are represented by national parks. Of the twenty-nine marine natural regions, two are represented in existing parks, and three more will be represented when the boundaries of two more parks are finalized. (One of these marine parks, South Moresby, has two distinct marine natural regions.) So much has been done to preserve at least some part of a number of natural regions, but there is a long way to go before the national park system has met its goals for representation and protection.

One example of the application of this rationale for park establishment was the designation, in 1981, of Grasslands National Park in Saskatchewan. This park has been created to preserve some of what little is left of Canada's true short-grass prairie. Grasslands is also an example of the relative weighting of commercial against conservation interests: while it is true that it has been declared a national park to preserve part of our prairie grasslands region, its final boundaries will not be drawn until gas and oil interests have had a number of years to explore. Boundaries then will be fixed, to exclude any extraction operations. What will happen if gas or oil is found, and if it is found in prime antelope-wintering grounds, or in the home territory of a rare form of prairie dog? This would present another of the many agonizing conflicts the parks system and the Canadian public have to resolve about resource use.

2

Of course, the struggle over the establishment of South Moresby National Park Reserve is internationally known. And, with all the effort that went into setting this marvellous maritime area aside as a reserve, there are many years to go before competing claims for its use will be resolved. Visitors can come to the area, and planning for park facilities and services is being done, but, here again, there is no simple or clear path to national park status.

Similar conflicts exist in established parks, as well. Will there be a dam near Wood Buffalo, more condominiums in Banff, should cottages remain in several parks with a long history of cottage use, when they've been removed in others, like Point Pelee? It's never an easy decision. If you would like to participate in resolving these issues, see the list of national and provincial organizations in the chapter entitled **Conservation and Natural History Associations**.

This book has two purposes. The first is explicit: to make a visit to a national park an easier thing to do. This book should help in the planning of a visit and, once you're in the park, the book should help in understanding and enjoying the natural aspects around you.

The second purpose is implicit: it relates to the conservation/exploitation conflicts mentioned above. Whatever perspective a person has (and mine is strongly conservationist), surely the more people know about the national park system in particular, and the natural environment in general, the more informed and responsible they can be in participating in public debates on these crucial issues. If this book can help you have a wonderful and informative visit to any national park, this second goal will have been met.

Readers need to know the basis of the information given here. I am a sociologist by training, but I've been a natural history enthusiast for over twenty years. For the first edition of this book, I worked sporadically over nearly four years, visiting twenty-five of the twenty-nine parks, excluding only Wood Buffalo, Nahanni, Auyuittuq, and the newly-established Grasslands. For these last four, I interviewed people who were very familiar with them, and I read widely. For the twenty-five I visited, I spent an average of five days and four nights in each. I interviewed staff, went to most of the interpretive events, hiked most major trails, camped in at least one or two of the campgrounds, and visited virtually all the rest to see what their location and facilities were like. I checked commercial facilities near the parks, where possible. Though I was usually alone in my visits, I based my evaluations on my idea of what visitors, such as retired couples, or families with kids, or keen hikers, might look for in a park. In preparing the revisions, I re-visited Banff, Fundy, and Georgian Bay Islands National Parks, because so much had changed in them. I also visited

South Moresby National Park Reserve, Bruce Peninsula and Fathom Five National Parks. These visits were from two to five days, and I was able to interview staff and explore what areas could be covered in this more limited time. Of course, there is a lot of written material to draw on for describing the parks, and I have used it, as well.

The parks all have interpretive programmes. An imaginative, well-planned and interesting interpretive programme can greatly increase the enjoyment and appreciation of a park. I always planned my visits around the schedule of interpretive events and recommend that all visitors do the same.

Given the value of interpretation, I find it particularly regrettable that government cutbacks, over the last five years or so, have eroded the number of staff who are available for this key service. It is amazing what the park management and interpretive staff are able to do, in the face of this shrinkage of resources. You will still receive an excellent service, but the person-to-person experience, which adds so much to the enjoyment of a visit, just isn't there, as it used to be. That is a loss that should be made good at a national level.

The interpretive and visitor-services staff, at the parks and at several regional offices, reviewed the revised chapters and, therefore, the materials are as up-to-date and accurate as possible. But circumstances can change and, if you're planning a long trip far from home, do write to the parks in the area you plan to visit, and get the latest information. Addresses and phone numbers are listed at the end of each chapter.

This book is full of advice about what to do, or how to do it, in each park. But there are several suggestions that I'd like to make, which cover any or all visits to parks. One is to contact, not only the park or parks you plan to visit, but also the provincial or regional tourism departments. Canada's tourism industry is becoming more and more sophisticated, and there is a great deal of effort made to help visitors get the full benefit of a given area. The national park(s) may be your primary goal, but there are very likely to be other interesting and important places for you to visit on your way there, or in the surrounding area. The amount and quality of information available to you is staggering. Just call Information, in the province you plan to visit, and ask for the tourism bureau for the province, and the equivalent for the nearest town of any size.

Another word of advice in planning your visit: if you can, plan to come in the "shoulder seasons." These are late spring, before school lets out, and the autumn, after Labour Day. These are wonderful seasons in themselves, with the added benefit that the parks are much less likely to be crowded, yet most of the facilities are open and staff are readily available to assist you. In some parks, interpretive programming is already underway, or continues as winter approaches. Some parks, it's true, are too far north to be visited comfortably in spring or fall. However, Banff in October, or La Mauricie in May, seem to be all yours. Of course, winter is an opportunity in itself, and the parks, in general, have greatly expanded their winter visitor use. This isn't only true for the famous downhill-ski sites, such as Banff. Many of the parks, right across the country, have become very active focal points of winter action for their whole areas.

Also, the parks have been making significant efforts to increase access for handicapped people. Wheelchair access is much more widespread, and some parks have special interpretive programming for people with visual or other impairments. Again, write or call, and ask about the status of these services in the park.

Canada's national parks are surely one of the greatest treasures of our world. It may seem a contradiction to write a book that encourages more people to visit these parks, when great numbers of people can destroy the physical environment and intrude on the peace and quiet. But I believe that, if people will cherish their parks by encouraging the establishment of new areas of preservation and by supporting the protection of existing ones, if they will treat the parks carefully when visiting them, then people and the parks can enrich each other's existence. This book is written with that hope in mind.

SOUTH MORESBY/ GWAII HAANAS

NATIONAL PARK RESERVE

This is the most recent park area added to the national system and, already, it may be one of the most famous of them all. There was a struggle, of at least ten years' duration, to set aside the southern part of the Queen Charlotte Islands as a national park, and it will still take a long time for issues about ownership, management and access to be settled. The Haida have already designated this area as a Haida Heritage site. The Canadian Parks Services and the Haida are forging a unique partnership to share in its planning, management and operaton of the area.

South Moresby/Gwaii Haanas (Haida for "Islands of Wonder") encompasses the lower third of the Queen Charlotte Islands, with South Moresby Island itself being the main land mass. There are 138 islands, and uncounted islets, in the reserve. The larger or better known islands include Moresby Lyell (famous for attempts by Haida people and environmentalists to halt logging, in the final days before the park reserve status was declared), Hotsprings, and Anthony (or "Sgan Gwaii"—home of the village of Ninstints, the location of a hauntingly beautiful group of totem poles. Anthony Island has been selected as a UNESCO World Heritage Site.

South Moresby/Gwaii Haanas is both a terrestrial and a marine park. The land mass is mountainous, with the San Cristoval Range dominating Moresby Island itself. The wildlife is very rich, from the puffins and sea lions in the sea, to the bears and eagles feeding on salmon in the many rivers and streams.

There are no roads, trails, or visitor facilities in the park reserve. Access is by chartered plane, boat, or kayak. In time, there will be development of trails and minimal visitor facilities, to prevent the deterioration of the land and waters, which can come if there are no sanitary facilities, or if visitors are not encouraged to use those areas that can best tolerate increasing human use.

Meanwhile, visitors continue to come, some on their own, and many in organized tours. Sea-kayaking is a favourite way to see much of the area, but you must be very experienced or be with a well-run and experienced tour group—who will help you learn the basics before you venture out. Canoeing is not considered to be safe for visitors, because of the rough and unpredictable sea conditions. The hiking that is done in the reserve is very rugged, because there are no trails, and all you can do is bushwhack, often in very difficult, wet and slippery terrain. People camp wherever they find suitable places, but it is very important that absolutely no traces of their visit remain.

In planning to visit South Moresby/Gwaii Haanas, it is especially important to find out about the status of any kinds of visitation, what tours are available, and about other services and facilities there are in the islands. In the towns and villages of the Queen Charlottes as a whole, there are a number of fascinating visitor sites, many of which reflect the Haida heritage and the rich natural history of the whole archipelago. Write to the superintendent of the park reserve, who can give you information both on the park reserve, and on where else to write or call for information about the visiting opportunities throughout these islands.

Further Reading

Chiefs of the Sea and Sky by George F. MacDonald (University of British Columbia Press, 1989)

Islands for Discovery by Dennis Horwood and Tom Parkin (Orca Book Publishers, 1989)

Ninstints: Haida World Heritage Site by George F. MacDonald (Museum Note No. 12, University of British Columbia Press, 1983)

Islands at the Edge by the Islands Protection Society (Douglas & McIntyre, 1984)

Guide to the Queen Charlotte Islands (Observer Publishing Co. Ltd., P.O. Box 9, Tlell, B.C. V0T 1Y0) Published yearly.

A Guide to the Queen Charlotte Islands by Neil G. Carey (Alaska Northwest Books, Edmonds, Washington, 1989/90)

FOR FURTHER INFORMATION

The Superintendent
South Moresby/Gwaii Haanas
National Park Reserve
P.O. Box 37
Queen Charlotte City, British Columbia
V0T 1S0

Phone: (604) 559-8818
Fax: (604) 559-8366

PACIFIC RIM

NATIONAL PARK

The Pacific Ocean has shaped much of the natural and human history of the west coast, and Pacific Rim National Park is the place to go to experience the ocean's powerful, ever-changing nature.

Pacific Rim is a thin strip of land along the southwest coast of Vancouver Island. There are three segments of the park. The most accessible is the northern, or Long Beach, area, which has an interpretive theatre, marked trails and kilometres of uninterrupted beach. From Victoria, you can drive there in four to five hours, along good but winding roads.

Southeast of the Long Beach section are the Broken Group Islands. This second segment is located in Barkley Sound, and is made up of about one hundred islands, covering an area of about fifty-eight square kilometres (twenty-two square miles). Some of the islands are tiny exposed rocks with a bit of vegetation clinging to them, and some are several hundred hectares in area—big enough for people to land their boats, to hike or to camp on. The Broken Group can be reached by boat, though users of any kind of watercraft should take care not to end up in that cold, often-stormy sea.

The third segment of the park is managed as a wilderness area. It lies at the southern tip, a narrow, seventy-two-kilometre (forty-five-mile) strip from Bamfield to Port Renfrew, along which runs the West Coast Trail. The trail was originally laid out in 1891 as a telegraph line route, and later, between 1908 and 1915, as a "lifesaving trail." This trail was needed because so many lives were lost in shipping disasters off the coast. The forest was so dense, it was impossible to make any attempts from shore to rescue shipwrecked people. Also, some shipwrecked people did manage to get to the land, but found the forest impenetrable. They died from exposure on the shore! The park has restored sections of the trail to make it a little safer and easier. Park wardens patrol the trail in the summer season, to protect it from misuse and to help any hikers who run into difficulty.

To understand the natural and human history of Pacific Rim, it is best to picture it as a series of long, thin strips of water and land, running from north to south, parallel to each other. These strips are the sub-tidal zone of deep water; the intertidal zone, which lies between the highest and lowest reach of the tides; the foreshore zone of gravel bars, drift logs and patchy plant life; and, finally, the forest zone, with its own successive bands of plant life.

The location of Pacific Rim, its relatively mild climate, and its rich marine life and forest growth have made it a place with a long human history. The Nuu-Chah Nulth (West Coast) people lived, fished, hunted and gathered here for thousands of years. The Spanish, Russians and English hunted sea otter in the teeming waters. The area was on major shipping lanes to and from Victoria and Vancouver. People came as fur traders, then as loggers and gold miners, and finally as settlers.

In the late 1960s, before Pacific Rim was established as a national park, the Long Beach area became a celebrated refuge for young people who wanted to live awhile unfettered by the demands of modern city life. I was there briefly, years ago. Today, this environment is a little more developed, and park operations are in place to manage and protect it. It doesn't look very different, and I'm glad it's now a national park.

How to See the Park

The Long Beach Area

Much of the Long Beach segment can be experienced independently. Good maps and informative brochures show the hiking trails, or describe the plant and animal life found in the forests or in the ocean, and I would suggest participating in the interpretive programme. It is one of the most varied, well-coordinated and pleasing programmes in the national park system. It is such a good way to complement your own ramblings and observations. For learning about the sub-tidal zone it is more than a complement, it is the only way possible for the non-diver to explore this otherwise-inaccessible place.

The **sub-tidal zone** covers an underwater area, including the Continental Shelf. Conditions are ideal for kelp, which grows here in rafts, some as deep as 30 metres (100 feet). These rafts are frequented by grey whales, who feed off the bottom life in and near kelp beds. The whales migrate along the west coast from their summer feeding grounds in the Bering Sea and the Arctic Ocean, and their winter grounds off the Baja

Peninsula in Mexico, where the calves are born. People come to Pacific Rim from afar, in the hope of glimpsing the grey whales puffing out clouds of vapour as they surface from their dives to the bottom. It's not unusual to see sea lions basking on islands, or swimming in the surf in the intertidal zone.

Tide pool at Wya Point

For a closer view of the life of the sub-tidal zone, you can scuba dive or snorkel in the park and get out to relatively deep waters. The underwater life is very rich, but the water is extremely cold, often rough, and the currents are hazardous. Unfortunately, most good dive sites are in exposed locations. Braving this problem, some of the staff have used their own diving skills to bring the sea life back to the visitor. They take beautiful pictures underwater, and present them at the evening interpretive programme in the theatre at the Green Point Campground.

On special occasions, there is a "Scuba Special," when the divers go out and bring back all kinds of undersea plant and animal life from the sub-tidal zone. They put their treasures in portable aquaria for safekeeping, and then interpreters guide a large troop of visitors on a short hike to the dive site. As the divers paddle around in the cove, the interpreter takes out each plant or animal and explains how it is suited to its deep, cold home. The samples are passed around, but the more fragile ones are protected in water-filled plastic bags. Eventually everything is returned to its original place by divers.

To explore the **intertidal zone,** you must get a copy of the Tofino tide tables for the Long Beach area. They are available at the Park Information Centre, and are posted on bulletin boards throughout Long Beach. Wherever there are sandy beaches, you can walk at high or low tide. But where it is rocky, you can scramble out on little headlands. You should know which way the water is going, in order to avoid having to beat a hurried and damp retreat.

Rocky areas harbour the beautiful tide pools. At low tide, they are a marvel of brightly-coloured anemones, starfish, barnacles and nearly invisible little fish darting to avoid your shadow.

My favourite place for observing the intertidal zone was **Wya Point,** at the south end of **Florencia Bay.** Four trails lead to Florencia Bay, and then there's a pleasant walk to Wya Point itself. The southernmost, the

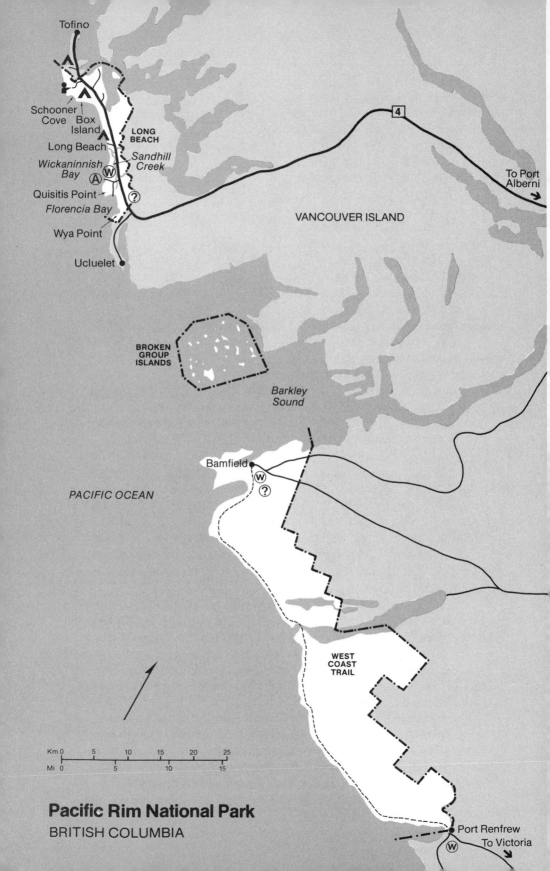

Tofino

Schooner
Cove   Box
Island

Long Beach

*Wickaninnish
Bay*

Quisitis Point

Florencia Bay

Wya Point

Ucluelet

**LONG
BEACH**

*Sandhill
Creek*

Ⓐ Ⓦ

?

4

To Port
Alberni →

VANCOUVER ISLAND

**BROKEN
GROUP
ISLANDS**

*Barkley
Sound*

Bamfield

Ⓦ

?

PACIFIC OCEAN

**WEST
COAST
TRAIL**

Km 0   5   10   15   20   25
Mi 0   5   10   15

Pacific Rim National Park
BRITISH COLUMBIA

Port Renfrew
To Victoria

Ⓦ

Willowbrae Trail, actually starts outside the park but emerges nearest the point. The walk takes perhaps a half-hour, and it goes through several forest zones to narrow foreshore to intertidal zone.

Another excellent place for sandy beach, tide pools and islets is the area just west of the Schooner Walk-In Campground. There you'll see Box Island, with its striking layers of rock, which give the effect of rows and rows of circular saw blades packed together and resting in an upright position.

The interpretive programmes concentrate on the intertidal zone. There are a number of guided walks a week, and several related evening slide shows that shouldn't be missed.

For the wilderness visitor, the **Broken Group Islands** and the **West Coast Trail** provide marvellous opportunities to experience firsthand the intertidal zone. There's no formal interpretation, but there are a number of books or pamphlets on intertidal life, which are published by the British Columbia Provincial Museum and other local publishers. You can usually buy these publications in good bookstores in Victoria, Vancouver, on the ferries and in shops in Tofino or Ucluelet.

The Foreshore: A Transition Zone

Any walk about the beaches bordering the forest reveals the log-strewn upper beach, with its fine, wind-blown sand and its sparse plant life struggling to take hold.

The foreshore area at **Florencia** is very different, in that it is bounded by gravel cliffs, pitted with the small holes made by nesting rough-winged swallows. The birds swoop and chatter over the beaches, gathering the insects that swarm in swathes of rotting debris, stranded high up on the shore by storms.

At the northern end of Florencia Bay, a little lagoon has been formed by the entry of **Lost Shoe Creek** into the ocean. The gulls love it, and I saw several black oystercatchers washing themselves in the stream water where it met the ocean. It's particularly easy to get to from a parking lot at Florencia Bay. The road goes off to the left, from the Wickaninnish Road.

The Forests

Most of the land area of Pacific Rim is forest, with the occasional break where there are burned-out sections now recovering, or shorepine bogs, or the marsh as at **Grice Bay**. There are at least three excellent places in the park to see the sequence of forest growth, from the shrubs at the edge of the beach through the Sitka spruce band up to the dominant cedar/hemlock growth. Off Highway 4, toward the Tofino end, there is the trail down to **Schooner Cove**. It is only 0.8 kilometres (0.5 miles) long, but it descends by a winding, stairstepped trail from the cedar/hemlock forest through the Sitka spruce fringe to the open camping area on the beach.

Another short trek is down the cliffs at **Green Point**. Near the top of the cliffs, you can see what has happened to some of the tallest cedar trees when they are constantly exposed to the salty winds from the sea. The salt eventually kills them but, before it does, the trees send out major branches that are almost second or third trunks. These branches spread out horizontally for a few feet and then take an upward turn. When the tree finally dies and the greenery has fallen away, the remaining trunk, with its offshoots, looks like a ghostly candelabra. At the trail edge, as you walk down, notice how the salal has occupied the open space, growing well over head height.

As the trail flattens out at the bottom of the cliffs, there are pit toilets which, in effect, mark a branch of the trail that runs behind the gnarled wall of Sitka spruce *krummholz* that borders the foreshore. This very short trail branch goes to another opening onto the beach and, at several places along the way, there are picnic tables. Being so close to the ocean, but completely screened from it, demonstrates very clearly how effective the gnarling and overlapping of the trees is, as an adaptation to the constant wind. Be sure to look away from the sea, to the trees overhead, and then up the shore. I was there on a grey day and the damp tree silhouettes stood out like stage flats against the featureless sky.

The third place to appreciate the temperate rainforest is on either section of the **Rain Forest Trail**. There are two short loop trails, one on either side of Highway 4, about sixteen kilometres (ten miles) north of the Park Information Centre. Here the amabilis fir grows, along with the cedar and hemlock, as the dominant trees in a fully mature, climax rain forest. The trail winds along over streams, up and down gentle hillsides. Often there are boardwalks or staircases to ease the way.

Park Services and Facilities

The Park Information Centre is located just inside the park boundary, on the main highway. Up-to-date information, relating to camping, naturalist programmes and other items of interest, such as displays and brochures, are available. The centre is open daily from Easter to Thanksgiving.

Interpretive Programme

The most outstanding service the park provides is its interpretive programme. The presentations are very well planned and, while each stands on its own, they are so well-coordinated that, after a few days of going to

Parks Canada/G.E. Tayler

Broken Group Islands

the various walks and talks, you can get a really good idea of how the various parts of the marine environment interrelate. To be comfortable on the walks, take a raincoat or windbreaker, and wear rubber boots or shoes with good traction. A variety of programmes cover the human history of the area. They range from guided hikes to see Indian petroglyphs, to slide talks on native uses of the region's plants, on the history of logging, mining and the ships that, too often, met their doom on the rocky coast. The interpretive theatre at Green Point offers free interpretive programmes each night, from late June through Labour Day. The theatre is wheelchair accessible, as is Wickaninnish Centre, a beautiful interpretation facility, open from March to Thanksgiving each year.

Camping

There are two campgrounds in the Long Beach unit of the park. **Green Point** is the main one for people who are car-based. There are ninety-four sites in a wooded area at the top of bluffs. The beach is a five-minute walk down a well-kept trail. The washrooms have hot and cold water, faucets every few sites for cooking water, picnic tables and fire grates at each site; firewood is provided. There are no kitchen shelters or showers, no electricity or trailer hook-ups, but there is a trailer-waste disposal system and bear-resistant garbage containers. There is a seven-day stay limit. Note that this campground is extremely popular and it fills every day. There is a wait-listing system to smooth access. However, you may have to camp first at the commercial campground down the road.

Trail trhough the rain forest at Florencia Bay

Schooner Walk-In Campground is at the north end of Long Beach. There are pit toilets and fresh water from faucets. An attendant on duty collects the small fee and makes sure the environment is protected. Sites are not specifically designated, but there is a limit of eighty tents. The walk down to the campsite from the parking lot is about one kilometre (half a mile). It is lovely, a bit winding and steep, although rough places have stairs.

Primitive Camping

There are eight designated sites with pit toilets on Broken Group Islands, on **Clark, Dodd, Gilbert, Hand, Willis, Benson, Turret** and **Gibraltar** islands. Water is usually available, but may run dry in late summer, so consider bringing your own.

There is wilderness hiking on the **West Coast Trail**. Campers must be fully provisioned and capable of self-reliant camping for as long as a week. Campers usually pick places near streams. Drinking water is obtained from these streams, so dispose of personal wastes carefully and far from fresh water. Driftwood is used for small fires, which should be built only on sand or rock, below the high-tide line.

Other Camping

A few kilometres north of the park (near Tofino), there is a 500-site commercial campground, **Pacific Rim Resort**. It is rather densely populated, but it is on the beach, has showers, a small store for snacks or supplies, a game room for kids, etc. The mailing address is Box 570, Tofino, B.C. V0R 2Z0. Phone (604) 725-3202. You can phone ahead and reserve. There are also five other smaller commercial campgrounds in the area.

Other Accommodation, Gas, Food and Supplies

Tofino, Ucluelet and surrounding areas have a number of motels of varying quality. They fill quickly, so it is important to phone or write ahead for reservations. For further information, consult B.C. Tourism's *Travellers' Handbook*.

Victoria, Port Alberni, Ucluelet and Tofino all have a full range of groceries, restaurants, service stations and supply stores. They also have shops with local arts and crafts.

Recreational Services

Swimming   There is supervised swimming at North Long Beach in summer, but the water is cold and often rough. Extreme care should be taken, even when wading, because of currents, usually near any rocky headlands.

Scuba Diving, Kayaking, Surfing   You can do all these in park waters, but cold water, high winds and strong currents require skill and experience— keep away from rocks and keep an eye on the weather. These sports are not recommended in this area unless you are trained and experienced.

Fishing   Fishing is allowed from the shore. A federal salt-water fishing licence is required. Information and licences are available from the Department of Fisheries and Oceans, 1090 Pender Street West, Vancouver, B.C. Licences are available in several stores and marinas in Ucluelet and Tofino. Fresh-water fishing requires a B.C. licence.

Shellfish Gathering   Scuba divers may catch a few crab or abalone, but the gathering of clams, mussels or oysters for food is often prohibited, because of the presence of highly toxic "red tide." Ask at the park or confirm with Federal Fisheries offices, before attempting to collect any of these molluscs.

Boating   Rentals and charters operate out of Tofino and Ucluelet for sightseeing, bird-watching or fishing. Check the B.C. *Travellers' Handbook* or write to Visitor's Services at the park, for a list of operators. There are complete marine facilities at Ucluelet and Tofino, and boat-launching facilities in the park at Grice Bay.

*Naturalists explain the survival strategies of animal and plant life of
the sub-tidal zone.*

Canoeing   You can canoe at Grice Bay, Kennedy Lake, Clayoquot Sound,
Clayoquot Arm and in sheltered areas of the Broken Group Islands. There
is limited canoeing in the Nitinat Triangle area of the West Coast Trail.

Hiking   Get the *Hiker's Guide* pamphlet from the park, for Long Beach unit trails. The West Coast Trail is for experienced hikers. Write for the park brochure on it.

How to Get There

Write to the Visitor's Services for a detailed brochure. Note that you can reach the Broken Group Islands by boat only. In the summer, there is a passenger ferry between the Broken Group Islands unit and Port Alberni, which will drop off those with canoes and kayaks at Gibraltar Island. This is a ten-hour round trip. Access to the West Coast Trail is from the northern trailhead and information centre, at Camp Ross, Pachena Bay, five kilometres (three miles) from Bamfield. Bamfield is ninety kilometres (fifty-six miles) by car from Port Alberni, along a gravel logging road. The *Lady Rose* also carries passengers to and from Port Alberni and Bamfield, several times weekly.

Further Reading

The Pacific Rim Explorer by Bruce Obee (Whitecap, 1986)

FOR MORE INFORMATION

The Superintendent
Pacific Rim National Park
Box 280
Ucluelet, British Columbia
V0R 3A0

Tourism B.C.
1117 Wharf St.
Victoria, British Columbia
V8W 2Z2

Phone: (604) 726-7721/726-4212

Phone: (604) 387-6417

MOUNT REVELSTOKE AND GLACIER

NATIONAL PARKS

Because of their natural and human history, Mount Revelstoke and Glacier National Parks are best considered as two segments of the same park, with Mount Revelstoke as the "little sister" of Glacier. These two parks preserve essentially the same habitat—sections of the Columbia Mountains, in eastern British Columbia.

The Columbias lie to the west of the Rockies, and can be subdivided into four mountain groups: the Purcells, Selkirks and Monashees extending in narrow north-south strips from east to west, and the Cariboos forming a steep triangle at the northern end of the system. The Columbia River forms a low valley border that runs directly north-south between the Monashees and Selkirks. Mount Revelstoke National Park lies in sight of the Columbia River, and Glacier National Park, less than fifty kilometres (thirty miles) east, includes parts of both the Selkirks and the Purcells.

The Columbias differ from the Rockies, in being an older mountain system and in being composed of much harder rock. Hard rock in mountains means that the forces of erosion grind exceedingly slowly, even over eons. Most mountains start out jagged and rough-edged, but wind, rain, freezing and thawing pare them down. However, the Columbias resist erosion. This is an area of sharp, angular mountains, with narrow, steep-walled valleys.

Location and climate, too, contribute to the rugged natural character of these mountains. Vast quantities of moist air blow into the area, over the lower coastal mountains and across the Columbia River Valley. The air rises naturally when it hits the Columbias; it begins to cool rapidly, leading to heavy, persistent rainfall in summer and massive snowfall in winter. However, the cloud cover retains the relative warmth of the mild Pacific air masses. As a result, temperatures in the area are fairly mild compared with those in the higher altitudes of the Rockies.

The combination of steep mountain walls, huge collections of snow and near-freezing or even warmer-than-freezing temperatures creates ideal conditions for avalanches. Avalanches roar down mountain slopes at speeds of up to 325 km/h (200 mph), and little can resist their momentum. In Glacier National Park, avalanche slopes are so numerous and extensive that they cover a considerable portion of what would otherwise be forest areas. You can see how avalanches have created a whole new habitat for plants and animals, by clearing paths for a new cycle of growth.

Huge amounts of snow have also created a multitude of glaciers. Glacier National Park has over four hundred of them, making up ten percent of its area.

The ruggedness of the Columbias posed enormous problems in the late nineteenth century, when there was great interest in finding a southern transport route through the western mountains to the sea. The first problem was to find a pass and the second was to make the passage safe for train travel. Rogers Pass was discovered in 1881, but steep grades, avalanches and climate would all work together to tear apart in seconds what had taken weeks, or even years, to build. Over two hundred people were killed in avalanches in the Rogers Pass area between 1885 and 1911. Finally, construction began on the eight-kilometre (five-mile) Connaught Tunnel under Mount Macdonald. The tunnel shortened the route and avoided Rogers Pass.

Today, new techniques have resulted in a fairly good method of predicting when and where avalanches are likely. Then the park gets there first. Along Rogers Pass, seventeen circular emplacements have been built, where 105 mm howitzer cannons can be rolled up, aimed, and fired on the danger spots. The potential avalanche is released before too much snow builds up, or the slides move safely across one of the numerous snow sheds that bridge the road and carry the snow harmlessly further down slope. It's a big, complicated operation that interrupts traffic, which must be turned back or stopped in safe places, but tragedy has become a virtual stranger to Rogers Pass.

Even though Mount Revelstoke and Glacier National Parks are very close to each other and have the same type of habitat, the facilities and services of each are designed for different use. Glacier is a multi-use park, with campgrounds, many trails and daily interpreter-led hikes. Mount Revelstoke is primarily for day use, with a road to its summit, and a series of shorter trails leading from there to the alpine meadows.

However, in both parks the narrowness of the valleys and the steepness of the mountains means the different life zones are compressed. Both parks have three major zones—interior rain forest, sub-alpine forest and alpine forest—succeeded by the windswept, harsh tundra and the glacier-laden mountain tops. The compactness intensifies the experience of the

Columbias, even from a car, though the guided walks greatly enhance the feeling of intimacy.

How to See the Parks

In Glacier, the interpretive programme concentrates on introducing visitors to the life zones and human history, through guided hikes. Visitors to Mount Revelstoke are more on their own: two short, self-guiding walks start just off the highway, and a twenty-six-kilometre (sixteen-mile) drive leads up to the summit plateau and a network of trails there. There are also trails at the base of the mountain, and it is possible to hike quite a direct route up to the summit area.

Glacier lily

Glacier National Park

The interpretive programme at Glacier National Park is like no other in the park system. There are some night-time slide shows, but the focus is on quite lengthy guided walks. Here they take you by the hand—sometimes literally—and lead you up a different mountainside. The hikes usually take three to five hours, starting at mid-morning. You always need to pack a lunch and have warm clothes and rain gear, just in case the weather turns cold or wet. Guided hiking opportunities vary according to staffing levels. All start at the Illecillewaet Campground, which seems to be the most popular place to stay. Check the bulletin boards for schedules.

On the hikes, the interpreter makes frequent stops to point out the characteristic plant life at each level. Bird songs are identified, and the relationship of the birds to each zone is described. Avalanche slopes are scanned for grizzlies, but probably all you'll see are the glacier lilies, whose blossoms and roots the bears feed on. Most of the hikes reach as far as the timberline, if the snow has retreated that far (which means July at the earliest). You can see the cushions of moss campion, as it protects itself from cold and wind by forming low-lying tufts of roots and foliage. Hoary marmots bask on rock outcrops. Many trails overlook glaciers. Check the bulletin boards and read the hiking brochure to see where each trail goes, but most will take you to the upper habitat zones.

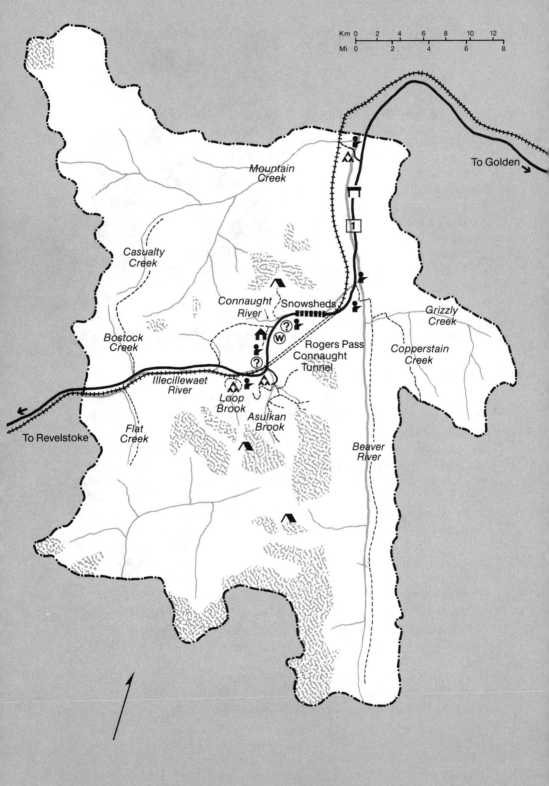

Glacier National Park
BRITISH COLUMBIA

Km 0   2   4   6   8   10   12
Mi 0   2   4   6   8

To Golden

Mountain Creek

Casualty Creek

Connaught River

Snowsheds

Bostock Creek

Grizzly Creek

Copperstain Creek

Rogers Pass Connaught Tunnel

Illecillewaet River

Loop Brook

Asulkan Brook

Flat Creek

Beaver River

To Revelstoke

The programme of personalized hikes is the ideal way to visit this environment. In an area with radically varying weather, fairly steep terrain (though the paths are wide and well maintained), and the occasional grizzly, it is good to go with experienced hikers. Don't worry that it may be too rigorous, because people of all ages and conditions went on each hike. One naturalist told me that he'd recently taken a four-year-old and an eighty-four-year-old on the same hike, and they'd gone all the way. I went on hikes several days in a row, and I cannot recommend this programme too highly.

I would suggest going on two or three of the guided hikes, before striking out on your own. Even though the hiking brochure is excellent, you'll be better prepared to understand what you see, to deal with the erratic weather, and to evaluate potential grizzly encounters.

Human History at Glacier

You can see the evidence of the building of the railway at **Rogers Pass** from the road or near the campgrounds. Just behind Mountain Creek Campground, at the northern end of the park, is **Trestle Trail**, a short trail to the creek, which runs through a very steep canyon. The canyon is crossed by a towering cement-and-steel railroad bridge. In the old days, the trestle was wooden and it was the largest structure in the Canadian Pacific Railway. An interpretive sign explains its history.

The **Loop Trail** follows the route of the old railway line, starting at the Loop Brook Campground. It's an easy half-hour through the thickest of rainforests, full of ferns and fungi, cedar and hemlock. In places, you pass the huge stone pillars that once supported the train trestles. There is also what's left of one of the wooden snow sheds built to protect the railroad, long ago crumpled by age and avalanches. Self-guiding signs along the way add to the experience of the dramatic past.

Another trail that touches on the railroad history of the park is called **Meeting of the Waters**. It starts at the rear of the Illecillewaet Campground, and loops over a rustic footbridge across the Illecillewaet River and back past the remains of the Glacier House hotel, which was a tourism centre in the late 1800s. The trail is mostly very level, and it stays in the forest. It leads past a footbridge, to a point where the creek from the Asulkan Glacier meets the Illecillewaet River. The Asulkan Brook is usually much milkier from glacial debris than the Illecillewaet and, for a little while, at the "meeting of the waters," they flow side by side, each retaining its distinctive colour.

The final railroad history trail is called **Abandoned Rails**. It starts near the Summit Monument in Rogers Pass, at the Visitor Centre, and is self-guiding. A very level trail, it will take about a half-hour, one way. It follows the route the railroad took, before the Connaught Tunnel was built.

Mount Revelstoke National Park

Mount Revelstoke is mostly a place of dense forest, rushing streams, and sub-alpine meadows, which lead to tundra and its major glacier and ice-field. However, it also has one small place that is reminiscent of the quiet river valleys meandering across the inland trench, to the east of the Columbias. Where the Illecillewaet River is slow and wide enough for a marshy area to have formed, there is a beautiful self-guiding trail, inelegantly named **Skunk Cabbage**. It runs behind the Skunk Cabbage Picnic Area, about eight kilometres (five miles) east of the park entry kiosk. This short trail is almost entirely boardwalk. The richness and variety of plant life there makes it the best area for bird-watching in the park. The most noticeable marsh plant near the boardwalk is the skunk cabbage, which, in the west, is different from the plant of the same name in the east. They are both early spring plants, but the western one grows to mammoth proportions. When I was on this walk, in early July, the leaves were the size of banana-tree leaves, sticking directly out of the water. About 2 kilometres (1.2 miles) further east, up the highway from Skunk Cabbage Trail, is one of the most spectacular short trails in the whole park system. **Giant Cedars Trail** provides an intimate experience of the interior rainforest of the Columbias. A parking lot and picnic area have been cleared next to the trail. The trail is a gently sloping and winding boardwalk, marvellously designed, and carefully banked for walking ease. Even if you're only driving through the park, even if it's raining, take a few minutes to enjoy this trail.

To experience the full transition of life zones in Mount Revelstoke, take the road that starts at the edge of the City of Revelstoke and then winds its way up to the peak of the mountain. The road is free of snow only from mid-July into September, and is paved as far as Balsam Lake. As it progresses, the road has a number of picnic areas and viewpoints from which you can see the great sweep of the **Columbia River Valley** and of the Monashees, the westernmost mountains in the Columbias. There are several hiking trails that cross the road, and some have their start at pull-off areas part way up the road.

The road is one of the few places in the park system where it is possible to drive to the summit of a mountain high enough to reach alpine meadows. You can picnic at **Balsam Lake**, below the summit. At the summit, you can stroll around in the immediate area, take any of a number of short trails that lead to vista points, or start off on longer hikes to several of the alpine lakes that are scattered 5 or 6 kilometres (3.5 miles) farther

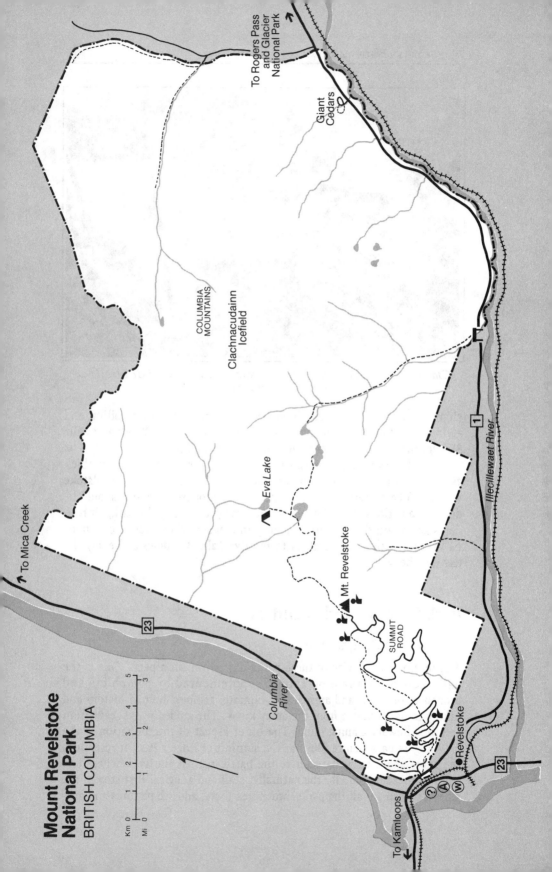

Mount Revelstoke National Park
BRITISH COLUMBIA

To Mica Creek

COLUMBIA MOUNTAINS

Clachnacudainn Icefield

Eva Lake

Mt. Revelstoke

SUMMIT ROAD

Columbia River

To Kamloops

Revelstoke

Illecillewaet River

To Rogers Pass and Glacier National Park

Giant Cedars

23

1

Km 0   1   2   3   4   5
Mi 0   1   2   3

Glaciers like this one can be seen from many of the hiking trails at Glacier National Park

along the crest of this mountain range. These trails are gently rolling, and go in and out of sub-alpine forest and alpine tundra. The **Meadows in the Sky** (formerly **Mountain Meadows**) trail is self-guiding.

Wildflowers are abundant here in late summer; they grow as thick as grass. It was this beauty in particular that the residents of Revelstoke wanted to be preserved when, in 1914, they proposed the area should be declared a national park. An annual pilgrimage is held by the park, for residents and visitors, on the first Monday in August, when everyone is invited to walk with the naturalists to the **Eva Lake Meadows** and enjoy the day together.

Park Services and Facilities

Interpretive Programme

The interpretive service of these parks has two main aspects. One is the daily guided-hiking programme, supplemented by pamphlets and brochures on plant and animal life, climate, geology, human history and hiking trails, available from the entry kiosk. The guided walks leave from the Illecillewaet Campground. The other aspect of interpretation is the new Rogers Pass Centre. Built at the summit of Rogers Pass, it resembles the snow sheds that characterize the battle against the avalanches. The centre is headquarters for the naturalist staff and a logical first stop in the park. You can get all the parks' brochures there, and see pictures and artifacts illustrating the Columbias and their natural and human history. The theatre, where evening programmes are offered, and exhibit areas are also located here. Visitors should check with park staff, or at the bulletin boards in the campgrounds, for a schedule of walks and programmes.

Camping

There are camping facilities in Glacier National Park only. There are three campgrounds, all just off the Trans-Canada Highway. The northeastern-most is **Mountain Creek Campground**. It is just inside the park, about five kilometres (three miles) before the entry gate, so you have to keep a close eye out for the sign. It is a large, heavily wooded campground, with swathes of flowers in the understory. There are over 250 sites, with 3 loops that have drive-through strips for long trailers. There are flush toilets, cold water in the washrooms and at outdoor faucets, kitchen shelters with stoves, and firewood depots. There are no trailer hook-ups, but a waste disposal station is provided. This campground rarely fills, so consider it if you come into the park on a Friday evening in August.

In the summer of 1989, the campground was closed, due to an epidemic of fungal infections in the trees. The fungi, which occur naturally in the park's old-growth forests, cause extensive rotting of the heartwood and roots of the trees; the trees become unstable and create a potential falling hazard. In the interest of public safety, the campground is to remain closed until there is no further hazard. Campers should check with the park superintendent before making plans to stay here.

Illecillewaet Campground is not a large campground, having only fifty-nine sites, but it is centrally located and is the starting point for most hiking. It is moderately wooded and is beautifully situated along the narrow Illecillewaet River. There are kitchen shelters, washrooms with flush toilets and cold running water, depots for water and wood, picnic tables and fire grates at each site.

Loop Brook Campground is the smallest campground, with only twenty sites. It is very similar to Illecillewaet, being situated by a river, and has identical facilities. The Loop Brook Trail starts here, and should not be missed.

Since both these campgrounds are small and popular, campers are advised to arrive early in the day to get a site.

Primitive Camping

There are no established back-country campsites in either park. The ruggedness of the terrain makes it unreasonable to establish the looping trails that are favoured for most back-country hiking. Hikers are permitted to make overnight trips in Glacier National Park, but they must register

Giant Cedars Trail

with the warden first. Some excellent, but little-known, backpacking opportunities exist in both parks, notably **Copperstain/Bald Hills** in Glacier and **Eva Lake** and **Jade Lakes** in Mount Revelstoke. Be sure to enquire first about fire regulations, bears, feasible routes, etc.

Other Accommodation, Gas, Food and Supplies

There is a large hotel at Rogers Pass. Otherwise, the nearest accommodation is in the City of Revelstoke, sixty-eight kilometres (forty-two miles) from Rogers Pass and right at Mount Revelstoke. The city is not large, but has a reasonable number of motels and small hotels. Golden, B.C., is eighty-two kilometres (fifty-one miles) from Rogers Pass, and also has motels and hotels.

The only place in the parks for gasoline is at Rogers Pass, at the hotel. I suggest filling up elsewhere, if possible, since gas can be particularly expensive here. The Rogers Pass hotel has a large restaurant and a small general store. Revelstoke and Golden have a full range of gas stations, grocery and supply stores.

Recreational Services

Hiking   This is the most popular use of the parks. There are 140 kilometres (93 miles) of established trails in Glacier, and 65 kilometres (40 miles) at Mount Revelstoke. Often the elevation gain is considerable, but the trails are well maintained and the scenery is magnificent. There is an excellent hiker's guide, *Footloose In the Columbias*, supplied by the park. Topographical maps of the area are available as well, at a modest cost.

Fishing   Fishing is poor in the rivers, because they are glacially fed. However, in some of the lakes on the summit area of Mount Revelstoke, you can fish for trout. A national parks licence is required, and is available at the Rogers Pass Centre or the park administration office in Revelstoke, at 313-3rd Street West.

Winter Use   In Glacier Park, the conditions are usually too rigorous for light cross-country skiing, but the park has a lot to offer for the experienced touring skiier. If you are interested in alpine ski touring, you must be well aware of avalanche hazards. You must register at the administration office for any off-highway travel. The Illecillewaet Campground is open for winter camping. The washrooms and kitchen shelters are maintained. Snowmobiles are not allowed in Glacier.

In Mount Revelstoke, there are several groomed cross-country skiing trails. At the base of the mountain, near Revelstoke, there is one trail 2 kilometres (1.2 miles) long and another 5 kilometres (3 miles) long. There are trails at Maunder Creek and the Summit Road, too.

Further Reading

Roads and Trails of Waterton-Glacier National Park by George Ruhle (Douglas & McIntyre, 1976)
Glacier Country: A Guide to Mt. Revelstoke and Glacier National Parks by John G. Woods (Douglas & McIntyre, 1987)

FOR MORE INFORMATION

The Superintendent
Mount Revelstoke and Glacier National Parks
Box 350
Revelstoke, British Columbia
V0E 2S0
Phone: (604) 837-5155

YOHO

NATIONAL PARK

Yoho is the more northern of the two Rocky Mountain parks situated in British Columbia. Bordered on the east by Banff and Kootenay National Parks, it is bisected from north to south by the Trans-Canada Highway. Yoho is the second-smallest of the Rocky Mountain parks at 1,313 square kilometres (506 square miles), and perhaps it is this fact that gives the visitor such a sense of intimate contact with steep mountains and powerful rivers, and their natural and human history.

Yoho's most impressive peaks are those near its eastern boundary, adjacent to the Continental Divide. These mountains are part of the Eastern Main Ranges of the Rockies. Their dramatic cliffs and lofty heights result from the nature of their rocks—limestones and erosion-resistant quartzose sandstone. During the mountain-building process, these sturdy rocks were heaved up in great chunks, producing the massive blocks of mountains we see today. Of course, glaciers and erosion have since had their way in softening the valley contours.

Farther west, approximately even with the village of Field, the character of the mountains changes. Here, in the Western Main Ranges of the Rockies, the mountains are not based on the resistant sandstone. The limestones are interspersed with softer rocks, such as shales. Over time, these mountains have weathered more than the peaks along the continental divide, as you can see by their less-jagged shapes.

Yoho's famous Burgess Shale fossils outcrop in the rocks between the Eastern and Western Main Ranges. About 530 million years ago, living sea creatures were buried in catastrophic mudslides. Their remains were preserved with incredible detail, and now give scientists an excellent record of life at that time. The Burgess Shales are an important part of Yoho's contribution to the selection of the four mountain parks as a World Heritage Site. These parks join an international list of locations, including the Egyptian pyramids and other famous sites, that evidence humanity's natural and cultural heritage. Yoho's fossils are now heavily protected. The fossil beds are now closed to the public, except for guided walks. There are guided hikes to the trilobite beds on Mount Stephen in the summer, but you have to register in advance and it's first-come, first-served, to a maximum of fifteen people on each walk. For a less strenuous way of learning about the fossils, there is an exhibit in the Field Information Centre, and also an interpretive exhibit at the base of Mount Field, adjacent to the Kicking Horse Campground.

The location of the park and the shape of the mountains had considerable consequences for its human history. One of the two train routes through the Rockies runs through Yoho National Park. The Canadian Pacific Railroad was stymied for years by the height of the Rocky Mountain passes and by the steepness of the western slopes. Eventually, the Kicking Horse Pass was chosen as the route across the Great Divide. Work began on the line through Yoho in 1884. The gradient from west of Lake Louise to Field, the small railroad town at the centre of Yoho National Park, was 4.5 percent; that is, 4.5 feet descent per 100 feet of distance (almost 1.4 metres descent per 30 metres distance).

The steepness limited the number of train cars that could be pulled up the grade or that could safely be run down the slope towards the west coast. The answer to this problem was the construction of the Spiral Tunnels. In 1907, 9 kilometres (5.5 miles) of tracks were looped out from the main direction of the line, to pass through two mountains that sit astride the route. This reduced the gradient to 2.2 percent. The Spiral Tunnels Viewpoint is one of the most visited interpretive sites in the park.

The railroad played a considerable role in the mining of lead and zinc in Yoho. These metals were discovered in two areas at the head of the Kicking Horse Valley, just before the railroad was completed. One mine entrance that can be seen from the road is on the side of Mount Field, next to Kicking Horse Campground.

It was not until 1927 that a car road was built through the Kicking Horse Pass. It has been upgraded with time, and now is part of the Trans-Canada Highway. It is the primary means for visiting the park, though it is still possible to take the daily passenger trains from Lake Louise to Field.

How to See the Park

There are four main sections of the park with easy visitor access. Starting from the north they are: the Lake O'Hara area, which is accessible by reservation only, even for day-users; the Yoho Valley road, which starts at the Kicking Horse Campground and leads along a beautiful and very winding drive to Takakkaw Falls and the back-country trail system beyond; the Emerald Lake and Natural Bridge area to the south of Field; and the Trans-Canada Highway, in particular the Spiral Tunnel Viewpoint, and the quiet trails and campgrounds at the west end of the park.

Round-leaved orchid

Lake O'Hara

The **Lake O'Hara** section of Yoho is almost a separate park in itself. The core is Lake O'Hara, a small lake backed by magnificent castellated mountains. There are twenty-five other lakes or ponds within a five-kilometre (three-mile) radius of Lake O'Hara. Within an eight-kilometre (five-mile) radius there are eighty kilometres (fifty miles) of trails.

This zone of interconnecting trails, running through alpine meadows and past icy blue lakes is, to my mind, one of the most beautiful and exciting areas in the entire park system. The extreme fragility of the alpine meadows, and the great popularity of the place, have made it necessary to control access to it. This not only protects the area from damage, but allows hikers to enjoy scenery without crowds. A few people hike along the trail to the lake, but most people reserve a place on the bus that goes there two or three times a day. You can visit for the day only, or you can stay at the Parks Canada campground or at the luxurious, privately-run Lake O'Hara Lodge. The Lake O'Hara Trails Club has erected a day shelter here. It is quite popular with hikers, who can buy hot drinks, snacks and souvenirs, as well as come in out of the rain during bad weather. There is also an Alpine Club of Canada hut here for the use of members. There is a small fee for the bus ride in and out. Space on the bus is reserved for campers, lodge visitors and a specified number of day-use visitors each day. Park naturalists offer programmes at the lodge for all visitors.

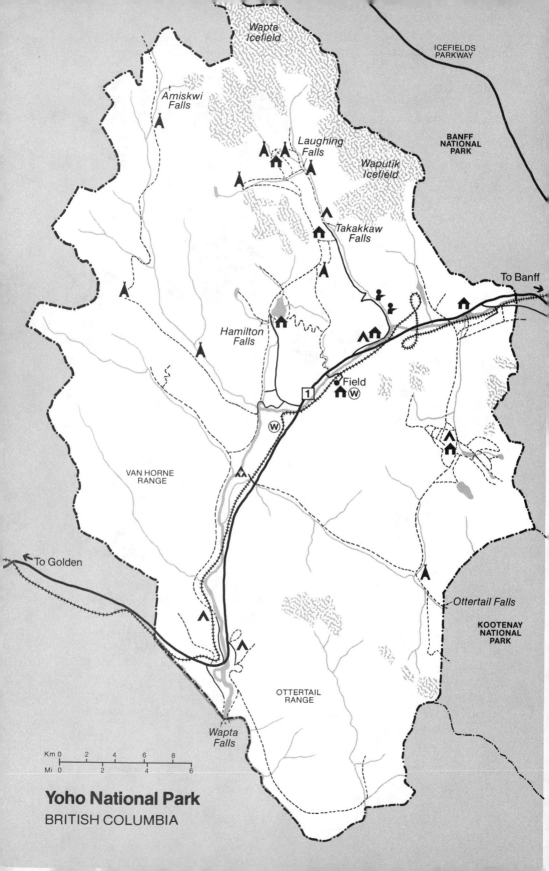

Yoho National Park map, British Columbia. Locations shown include Wapta Icefield, Amiskwi Falls, Laughing Falls, Waputik Icefield, Takakkaw Falls, Hamilton Falls, Field, Van Horne Range, Ottertail Range, Ottertail Falls, Wapta Falls, with Banff National Park and Kootenay National Park adjoining. Routes To Banff, To Golden, and the Icefields Parkway are indicated.

Yoho Valley and Takakkaw Falls

This combination drive and walk takes you from the broad valley of the **Kicking Horse River** steadily upward, as it follows the more sharply descending and turbulent **Yoho River**. The Kicking Horse was dedicated, on Canada Day 1989, as a Canadian Heritage River—the first ever within the boundaries of British Columbia. This designation recognizes its unique place in Canada's history, its beauty, and its significance as a classic example of a glacially-fed mountain river. The drive to **Takakkaw Falls** is narrow and winding. Trailers or large motor homes cannot negotiate some of the turns. There is a drop-off area for trailers near the beginning of the road. It is marked and should be used. The road takes you through subalpine forest areas, which are periodically stripped of tree growth by avalanches. The vegetation that survives or first recurs is low, supple and bushy, and full of flowers and berries. Along the side of the road, you can frequently see mountain goats and marmots; it's important not to feed them. The thirteen-kilometre (eight-mile) road ends in a parking area at Takakkaw Falls. This is among the highest waterfalls in Canada. There is a viewpoint at the river's edge, with interpretive signs along the short walk to the base of the falls. There is also a picnic area and flush toilets near the parking lot.

From the viewing area, you can begin your walk up the Yoho Valley. The usual destination is **Twin Falls**, or a good view of the falls from the **Twin Falls Chalet** below. This hike is ideal for seeing the interplay of the faulting patterns of these mountains and the power of water. From Takakkaw Falls, the trail passes four more falls of varying shapes and sizes. They have wonderfully descriptive names: **Laughing Falls**, **Point Lace Falls**, **Angel's Staircase Falls** and, more prosaically, **Twin Falls**.

This is the most popular walk in the Yoho Valley. It is about nine kilometres (six miles) long, but it is easy and rolling with only two steep parts, one just beyond Point Lace Falls and one just before the Twin Falls tea house. There is a primitive campsite on the river, just before that final ascent. The trail does continue beyond the chalet, though many people turn back after a rest. You can go up to the **Yoho Glacier** or join a very large network of rigorous back-country trails, before returning to Takakkaw Falls. There is a primitive campsite at the top of Twin Falls, on a rock ledge just a few metres from the rather precipitous drop.

But for me, the highlight of the hike was the destination—the tea house. This rustic chalet was built in 1900 by the Canadian Pacific Railroad for the tourists who came into the area by pack horse. It is privately run, but seems entirely in keeping with the natural protection of the area. There is no electricity or running water; all supplies are packed. The visitor can have hot tea and light lunches.

Travelling slowly, the whole trip took about 6 hours—2^1/$_2$ up, an hour at the chalet and 2 hours back.

A new trail, completed in 1987, the **Iceline Trail**, has become very popular. It was designed to replace the eroded **Highline Trail**, and offers spectacular views of Takakkaw Falls, hanging glaciers and the alpine terrain overlooking the Yoho Valley.

Emerald Lake, Natural Bridge and Hamilton Falls

The eight-kilometre (five-mile) road into this area begins just three kilometres (two miles) south of Field. Two kilometres along the Emerald Lake road is a large parking area for visiting the **Natural Bridge**. The keystone of the bridge has collapsed, but you can still see very well the vertical faulting that is characteristic of the mountains here, and how the enormous force of rivers cuts through them.

Emerald Lake is a major day-use area, and an access point for a number of back-country trails. There is also a short trail leading from the large parking lot to another of the park's major waterfalls, **Hamilton Falls**. This is an easy, quick trip, which complements the walk around Emerald lake. You can go another 4.5 kilometres (3 miles) of trail, quite steep above the falls, to **Hamilton Lake** itself. It is nestled in a cirque, the characteristic bowl shape that glaciers gouge out of mountainsides.

Emerald Lake is another beautiful, glacially-formed lake. There is a parking lot near it, restrooms and a level, self-guiding trail around its five-kilometre (three mile) perimeter. Park staff try to offer a guided canoe trip once a week. You can rent a canoe at the lake or bring your own.

Our group, which included toddlers, and which stopped often for the interpreter's explanations of the environment, took three hours on this trail. It could take a lot less with a more mobile group, or on your own.

The Trans-Canada Highway

The Trans-Canada follows closely the route of the railroad. There are several signed points of interest and park facilities along the way. The main park brochure has a map on which each of the points is marked and coded with brief descriptions. A note of caution here. Because of the number of injuries and deaths that occur on the Trans-Canada in Yoho each year,

Twin Falls from near the Chalet tea house

due to the mixing of through traffic with pleasure traffic, use extreme care when turning onto and off the highway, and when slowing or stopping for any reason. At the north end of the highway is the **Old Bridge on the Big Hill**, where trains would go out of control and plunge off the tracks on this steepest railroad grade in North America. Just down the road is the **Lower Spiral Tunnel Viewpoint**. The park has built a viewing platform in the style of the old wooden trestles that once supported the tracks. There is a fascinating interpretive display, which tells why and how the spiral tunnels were built. You can take the popular short train ride from **Field** to Lake Louise, spend part of the day there, and return. This will give you first-hand experience of the tunnels at a moderate cost.

At the southern edge of the highway, just off the Hoodoo Creek Campground, **Deer Lodge Trail** leads to the home of the first warden of the park. The Deer Lodge is just a small cabin that has seen better days, but it's set on a lovely beaver pond between deep forest and a marsh.

The trail to the **Hoodoos** begins at the northeast corner of Hoodoos Campground. Hoodoos occur in a number of places where there are steep slopes composed of glacial debris. Over time, water cuts downward

Elk browsing in the stillness of early evening

through soft layers, which underlie more resistant flat rocks, and carries away the soft material. The flat rocks form a cap, or umbrella, which protects the material directly below, so columns are left, towering over the gutted ravines or valleys around them.

The trail to the Hoodoos is three kilometres (two miles) long. The first half of it is through level forest. After crossing the footbridge over the **Hoodoos Creek**, the trail climbs quite steeply. There are switchbacks, and the trail surface is level, but it can be wearing, depending on how fit you are. There are several good views along the way, of the river below you and the mountains on the opposite side. The walk is not self-guiding but, at the river crossing, there is a sign explaining how hoodoos are formed.

Park Services and Facilities

Interpretive Programme

The park's active interpretive programme is well worth attending. Evening slide shows or campfire talks are given in at least one of the campgrounds every night, in the summer. There are interpreter-led walks, six days a week. The weekly canoe paddle on Emerald Lake is an interesting feature. (Frequency and scheduling of events may change from year to year.) A number of park publications—self-guiding trail brochures, a newspaper, back-country trail booklet, hiking maps, etc.—are available at the new Travel Information Centre at the Trans-Canada Highway junction for Field, operated by staff of Yoho National Park and Travel Alberta. Also at the Information Centre, the park cooperating association, Friends of Yoho, has a sales outlet where you can buy topographical maps, field guides and various books and souvenirs. The Centre has orientation exhibits to help you plan your travels in Yoho, the four-parks block, or Alberta, and interpretive exhibits on the Burgess Shales and Alberta's Dinosaur Provincial Park—both of which have been recognized as World Heritage Sites.

Camping

Kicking Horse Campground is five kilometres (three miles) from Field. In late July and August, it fills quite early in the afternoon and on weekends. Tent areas are lightly wooded, and the trailer area is a lawned space. The campground is dominated by Mount Stephen, and some sites lie by the river. There are ninety-two sites, kitchen shelters, flush toilets, showers, trailer sewage disposal, but no hook-ups. Water is provided at washrooms, and from faucets every few sites. Each site has fire grates, picnic tables and firewood. There is an outdoor interpretive theatre here, and a play area for children. A small grocery store is located just outside the entry kiosk.

     Hoodoo Creek Campground, near the southern end of the park, is densely wooded. It is the most peaceful and least crowded campground in the park, popular with those who want an old-style forest-camping experience. It has 106 sites, flush toilets and kitchen shelters. There is trailer-waste disposal, but no hook-ups. Each site has a picnic table and fire grate, with firewood provided. There is an outdoor theatre, and the campground is near the Deer Lodge and Hoodoos Trails.

     Chancellor Peak Campground is the southernmost of the campgrounds. It is more primitive than the other two car-based ones. It is self-registering: you fill out an envelope and deposit your fee. It is in a lightly treed area, right on the Kicking Horse River. The train runs behind it. There are sixty-four sites, with pit toilets, kitchen shelters, water from faucets, and each site has a fire grate and picnic table.

     The walk from the parking lot to **Takakkaw Falls Walk-in Campground** takes about three minutes, along a gravel path. The sites are in very lightly wooded or open areas. Because of the rocky terrain and sparse plant growth, the tents go on large wooden pallets. There are thirty-five sites. There are pit toilets, an enclosed kitchen shelter, and fire grates and picnic tables at each site. This self-registering campground has a spectacular location, with a great view of the falls. Because it is at the start of the numerous Yoho Valley trails, it is very popular with hikers.

Lake O'Hara Campground is close to 2,135 metres (7,000 feet) elevation, so it can get snow or sleet at virtually any time of the year. There are thirty-two sites, kitchen shelters, pit toilets, picnic tables and fire grates. You must reserve at the Information Centre (phone 604-343-6433 for Lake O'Hara reservations) in Field, and most people reserve a seat on the bus, rather than walk in eleven kilometres (seven miles). Bus reservations are made automatically for campers, when they reserve sites. The campground is just a few steps from the bus drop-off point. There is a fee for the bus.

Primitive Camping

There are a number of back-country campgrounds. All sites have pit toilets. Fires are prohibited—plan to use a backpack stove. Water is from lakes or streams. I visited the Twin Falls and Laughing Falls Campgrounds. They were well maintained and had wooden bars high up between two trees, for suspending food away from bears. Laughing Falls had about eight sites; Twin Falls had places for about ten tents. There are a number of other back-country campgrounds. Free overnight permits are required to control overuse and for safety. These can be obtained from the Information Centre at the Field turnoff.

Other Accommodation, Gas, Food and Supplies

There are a few commercially-operated bungalows, the Cathedral Mountain Chalets, next to the Kicking Horse Campground. The West Louise Lodge is a large motel/restaurant at Wapta Lake, at the north end of the park. There are approved accommodation (bed and breakfast) facilities and a small hotel in Field. There is a Lodge at Emerald Lake, too. Write the Superintendent for lists of all this accommodation. Golden, B.C., is 25 kilometres (15.5 miles) from the south gate. Phone (604) 344-7125 for the Golden Information Centre. Lake Louise is only a twenty-minute drive from the north end of the park. Both offer accommodation.

The Twin Falls Chalet has rustic accommodation for a maximum of fourteen people at a time, in three-bed rooms or four-bed rooms. The cost includes all meals and bedding supplies. After 4:30 p.m., day-visitors are no longer served and the cosy dining room becomes the dining and living room for overnight guests. Hot water is supplied in jugs and basins for each room, and the pit toilets are a one-minute walk from the chalet. Phone (403) 269-1497 for reservations. The chalet is open in summer only; book early.

Lake O'Hara Lodge provides luxury accommodation. Guests stay in the upstairs of the main lodge, or in small cabins near the lakeshore. Prices vary, but all include sumptuous breakfasts and dinners, afternoon tea and a huge packed lunch. The lodge is open in summer and winter. There are daily bus services from Lake Louise, Calgary and Banff. Phone (604) 343-6418 in summer, (403) 762-2118 after September; reservations are required. Book early, as much as a year ahead for summer reservations.

Members of the Alpine Club of Canada can reserve the hut in the Lake O'Hara area or the Little Yoho Valley. Phone (403) 762-4481; book several months ahead for summer.

Gas and groceries are available at a small grocery store and service station just outside the Kicking Horse Campground. Field has a gas station, and a small combined restaurant and grocery store. West Louise Lodge has gasoline and some camping supplies and groceries. For a larger selection of camping supplies and of groceries, you must go to Golden, Lake Louise or Banff, all within an hour's drive from the park.

Recreational Services

Hiking   Yoho has 360 kilometres (225 miles) of hiking trails, from the very easy, short, self-guiding ones, to ones in the back-country, which can be travelled for days. Overnight campers must obtain a back-country use permit. The Friends of Yoho sell trail maps for each of the major areas, and topographic maps may be purchased at the Information Centre in Field. Snow remains on the higher trails into July. Always inquire as to snow levels, trail conditions, bear sightings, and availability of back-country campsites. Park interpreters lead hikes of several hours duration to different locations each week.

Fishing   There is fair fishing for several varieties of trout in the streams and lakes that are not too close to glacial sources. A national park fishing permit is required, and is available for a moderate fee from the Information Centre.

Boating   Non-motorized boats are allowed on all waters in the park. People canoe at Lake O'Hara and Emerald Lake. Canoes can be rented at both lakes. Ask at the Information Centre for the best places on the Kicking Horse River. The river is canoeable (Grade II water) between the confluence of the Amiskwi River and the Trans-Canada Highway bridge near Chancellor Peak Campground.

Horseback Riding   There is a stable at Emerald Lake, where rides from an hour to all day can be arranged.

Winter Use   There are several designated cross-country ski trails in the park. Ask for the small, free, descriptive booklet. Back-country camping is allowed, but a permit (free) is required. The trails are of varying length and difficulty. The longer ones require considerable skill and endurance, the ability to deal with rigorous winter conditions, and the ability to judge avalanche hazards. Current snow and avalanche condition information is available at the Information Centre.

Further Reading

The Wonder of Yoho: A Trail Guide by Don Beers (Rocky Mountain Publications, 1989)

The Canadian Rockies Access Guide by J. Dodd and G. Helgason (Lone Pine, 1985)

Handbook of the Canadian Rockies by Ben Gadd (Corax Press, 1986)

Wonderful Life by Stephen Gould (Norton, 1989)

Birds of the Canadian Rockies by Rick Langshaw (Summerthought, 1988)

Parkways of the Canadian Rockies: An Interpretive Guide to Roads in the National Parks, Revised Edition by Brian Patton (Summerthought, 1988)

Canadian Rockies Travel Guide by Gail Starr and Beverly Graf (Sojurn Press, 1988)

94 Hikes in the Northern Canadian Rockies by Dee Urbick and Vicky Spring (Douglas & McIntyre, 1983)

FOR MORE INFORMATION

The Superintendent
Yoho National Park
Box 99
Field, British Columbia
VOA 1G0

Phone: (604) 343-6324

Friends of Yoho
Box 100
Field, British Columbia
VOA 1G0

KOOTENAY

NATIONAL PARK

Kootenay National Park has much in common with other Rocky Mountain parks, with which it shares the distinction of being a World Heritage Site. But it is also very distinct in important ways. It is located in southern British Columbia, with the eastern park boundary following the Continental Divide. Thus, Kootenay runs along the west side of the Rockies, sloping to the Rocky Mountain Trench, a valley that separates the Rockies from the Columbia Mountains in the interior of British Columbia.

The Rockies are made up of three ranges of mountains roughly parallel to each other, running north-south; the Front Ranges, the Main Ranges and the Western Ranges. The divisions between each run along deep faults, or cracks, in the surface of the earth, which have formed large, wide valleys.

The extensive faulting in the Rockies makes a fascinating story of the shaping of the mountains. Take advantage of the park's interpretive programmes and brochures, to learn about their formation. At Kootenay, you can enjoy a close-up view of some of the smaller-scale results of faulting, too. There are two places of particular interest. The first is Radium Hot Springs, at the southern edge of the park. Hot springs are fairly common all along the geologically-active western edge of our continent. They have an intriguing origin. I thought that they must start very deep in the hot core of the earth, and then steam upward, but this is not so. The water drains *down* from the rainfall run-off at the earth's surface. It then finds its way down interconnected faults, which must go at least 2415 metres (7920 feet) below the surface, to a zone where the earth's temperature is hot enough to heat the water to the vaporizing point. The steam changes back into water as it rises and, by the time it reaches the surface through other faults, it is usually about 30° to 40°C (85° to 102°F). The surface water may take quite a while to make its journey deep into the earth, and then out to its surface spring. Experiments have shown that, at Banff, the time may be three months. (At Yellowstone National Park, it takes fifty years!)

While in the bowels of the earth, the water often acquires chemicals and gases that become dissolved in it. Sometimes, they show up as deposits at the edge of the spring, or they can be smelled, like the rotten-egg odour in the pools at Cave and Basin in Banff. The Kootenay Hot Springs have a component of radium that's about as radioactive as a luminous watch dial. But, in the prepark days at the turn of the century, there were many claims for the restorative effects of bathing in the hot springs of Kootenay. I think the relaxation of lolling in a hot pool after a chilly hike is justification enough for a long soak.

Faulting is easy to see at another place, the Redwall Fault, just a few steps from the Radium Hot Springs. This fault forms Sinclair Canyon, the walls of which are vertical cliffs rising directly above the highway. Redwall Fault is very well named, because the oxidation of the iron in the rock has resulted in a brilliant reddish colour. Much of the exposed rock in the southernmost end of the park has this same red: it looks like sunset colours all day long.

Paint Pots is another very special place in the park. Here an active spring (this time a cold one), with a great deal of dissolved iron in its water, bubbles to the surface, forming muddy beds of reddish ochre.

The Native people felt that the area had considerable spiritual significance, and used the ochre for paint pigments and, at the turn of this century, the ochre beds were claimed for commercial mining. When Kootenay became a park, in 1920, the mining leases were terminated and the mining sites abandoned, though a few rusting hulks of machinery still remind us of the past.

Kootenay National Park has significant differences between its north and south, because of the effect of the topography of the land to its west. In the south, the air currents are relatively dry. They descend to the Rocky Mountain Trench, having already released a lot of moisture, as rain or snow, on the Columbias. Thus, the forest is predominantly dry interior Douglas fir, and rather patchy, at that. But, as you go north in the park, following the Kootenay River to the McLeod Meadows, there is a distinct transition to a much moister environment. The forest here is characteristically sub-alpine, with a mixture of Engelmann spruce and sub-alpine fir trees.

These two environments make Kootenay particularly rich in plant and animal life. Good grazing on the slopes of the mountains, particularly Mount Wardle and around Sinclair Canyon, and a relatively warm and dry winter, mean that the animals can get down below the snow to food (unlike Glacier National Park, which is nearby, but has such a heavy

snowfall that grazing animals cannot survive). Kootenay has a large
population of bighorn sheep, especially in the southern part of the
park, and of mountain goats that
live year round at Mount Wardle.
These animals are often seen from
the road: I saw lots, as well as a
cow moose with her calf, and a bear
digging furiously at the edge of the
forest by the road. Keep your camera ready!

Labrador tea blosoms

How to See the Park

The Park is "organized" by the
Banff-Windermere Highway, which
stretches its full length. Everything to see and every place to visit starts at
the highway. The first thing to do is get the main park brochure and map
at the entry in Radium Hot Springs, or at the Marble Canyon Information
Centre, if entering from the north. The brochure gives an excellent
overview of the park, and locates and briefly explains thirty-one places of
interest along the highway.

There is a very busy interpretive programme in the park, as well.
There are naturalist-led walks or other events at least twice a day in summer, and nine different evening programmes presented over any week-long
period at the campgrounds. The park has many excellent pamphlets on its
wildlife and history.

There are three self-guiding trails in the park, and several short and
fairly easy non-guided ones around the Radium Hot Springs and the
Redstreak Campground.

The Mountains - East and West

Marble Canyon Trail is a beautiful walk, guided by interpretive signs that
tell you more about what you're seeing. It is an easy walk, a little uphill,
always along the river on one side of the canyon, and then back down the
other. It starts just about 6 kilometres (3.5 miles) from the Banff border.
The trail takes twenty minutes, or so, to walk.

As you go up, crossing from bridge to bridge, you learn from signs
that the outlines of the canyon are angular because limestone and related
rocks crack in a characteristic block fashion. Limestone is easily shaped by

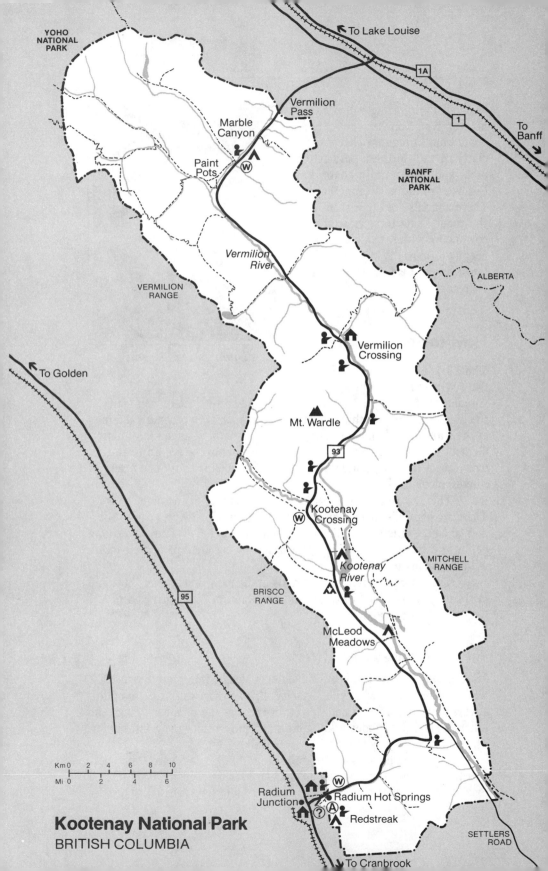

Kootenay National Park
BRITISH COLUMBIA

flowing water, and it is fascinating to see the scoops and swirls carved in the canyon walls, many metres above where the water now flows.

Plants have taken hold wherever they could in the moist, chill environment of the canyon walls. My favourite place was a big bowl shape, reamed out by an earlier whirlpool, which now provides a catchment for dust and debris. Mosses and arctic flowers have found a haven here. It's damp; the little soil that collects is undisturbed. Since it is many metres below you, just a big shelf on the canyon wall, nothing and no one nibbles on it or tramps across it.

The Marble Canyon area has a large parking lot, washrooms equipped for handicapped use, and a picnic area.

The **Paint Pots Self-guiding Trail** is just south of Marble Canyon. There is a parking lot from which you start the 1.5-kilometre (1-mile) round-trip walk on asphalt. (This artificial surface seems to be the best way to minimize wear and tear on this fragile area. Without it, the trail would be a complete mire.) The first few hundred metres takes you over a long, low suspension that crosses the **Vermilion River**. The flowers on the far side of the river are very thick. To my amazement, I saw dozens of butterwort, an insectivorous flower I'd last seen in the harsh environment of the Tablelands in Gros Morne National Park in Newfoundland. Look for it to your right as the trail winds on, before you get to the **Ochre Beds**. The flower is purple, reminiscent of violets, on a stalk only seven centimetres (three inches), or so, tall. In a rosette at ground level, are the buttery-yellow leaves with their sticky, slightly hairy surfaces, which trap tiny insects.

The Ochre Beds are a flood plain or spillover area of the springs that bring up the iron-laden water and spread it over the surrounding area. The beds are bright brownish-orange, dotted here and there by small islands of grass and small trees. Interpretive signs explain the Indian people's attitude toward the beds and **Paint Pots** and their use of the ochre. Not far from here, there are the remains of mining equipment used before Kootenay became a national park.

As you go further up the slight hill, you reach the Paint Pots themselves. Several exit holes for the springs have been formed into "pots," because the iron is naturally deposited in a circle around the spring outlet. Eventually, the rim gets so high that the weight of the contained water forces the spring water to follow a less resistant route, and to form another outlet nearby. Thus, there are a number of pots, some active and some just collecting spring water and surface drain-off. The mixture of underground and surface waters colours the water blue-green in one or two of the pots.

The **Hot Springs** are the centrepiece of the southern part of the park. They are no longer in a natural setting, but in a large building with a restaurant, viewing balcony, changing rooms, and a deep "cool pool" for swimming, which overlooks the "hot pool" for lazing. The hot pool is nearly Olympic size, but is not more than just over a metre (four feet) deep. There are plenty of underwater terrace steps to sit on, or you can just wander around, peering muzzily at other equally mellowed bathers. The only natural feature is that one side of the pool is bordered by a limestone cliff, which is quite crumbly; golden-mantled ground squirrels live in the chinks, quite oblivious to people. Also, where the canyon walls meet the cement retaining wall, there are small spaces where violet-green swallows nest. They flit in and out constantly, and make a beautiful sight.

Kootenay - North and South

Marble Canyon is the place to get acquainted with the moist and densely forested area north of the McLeod Meadows, along the Vermilion River.

In 1968, lightning started a fire near Marble Canyon, and it burned furiously for three days. Rain came on the fourth day and, with its help, the fire fighters were able to put the fire out—it had burned 2,494 hectares (6,162 acres). With a boost from nature's regenerative powers, the park has turned this seemingly-unwelcoming environment into a most pleasant and interesting self-guiding trail. **Fireweed Trail** begins at the parking lot at the northern border of the park. Interpretive signs guide you along your way. The trail is only 0.8 kilometres (half a mile), a gently sloping crescent. In late June, it was a riot of colour—the fireweed wasn't out yet, but the ground was amply sewn with meadow rue, yellow columbine, berry bushes of all kinds, and several species of rich green moss with bright brown fruiting bodies or green cup caps.

Signs along the way tell about the plants, and explain how a burn area becomes a perfect home for small mammals. All is not lost in forest fires, in the natural scheme of things, though a great deal is changed. This is a wonderful way to learn more about it.

For a good exposure to the drier, Douglas-fir forest of the southern part of Kootenay, a number of short, self-guiding trails wind throughout the Radium Hot Springs area. One is the **Valley View Trail**, which parallels the access road to the Redstreak Campground. A trail also descends from the campground to the back of the Hot Springs Aquacourt. Both are very short and easy.

Juniper Trail is somewhat longer, and starts just inside the park gate at the entrance to Sinclair Canyon. It is not a loop trail; it runs 3.2 kilometres (2 miles), zigzagging down to **Sinclair Creek**, up to the crest of the canyon, and then gradually down to the motel area across from the Aquacourt. It does gain a bit of altitude, so I'd suggest starting from the lower Sinclair Canyon end so that, when you emerge, you can be going downhill, back to your car. Several lookout points with benches survey

Mountain goats at roadside deposits—frequently seen and very vulnerable

the Columbia Valley. I particularly liked the sun-lit open areas, filled with many flowers, especially asters and black-eyed Susans. It was a great place for dragonflies and butterflies. I saw checkerspots, crescents, swallowtails, blues and sulphurs.

Park Services and Facilities

Interpretive Programme

The park offers well-developed interpretive programmes and excellent self-guiding trails. Pamphlets and brochures cover a lot of material and make good reading.

Camping

There are three campgrounds for car-based campers. **Redstreak Campground**, at the southern end of the park in the Douglas-fir forest, is the largest, most developed, and quickest to fill. The Valley View Trail and the trail to the Aquacourt run from here. It has two playground areas for children, with swings, slides, teeter-totters and climbers. There are 241 sites, a number of which are pull-throughs for trailers. There are seven kitchen shelters, also flush toilets, showers and trailer sewage disposal. Some sites have full hook-ups. All sites have picnic tables, and most have

New growth on the Firewood Trail

fire grates. Firewood is available at depots. An outdoor theatre presents interpretive shows in the evening.

To find Redstreak, you must enter from outside the park, off Highway 95, just southeast of the park entrance on Highway 93. Go past the junction, past a few snack bars and shops, and look for the RCMP and Redstreak Campground signs. Both are on the same road.

McLeod Meadows is a smaller campground, twenty-six kilometres (sixteen miles) north of Radium Hot Springs. There are one hundred sites in a wooded area, sandwiched between the Meadow Creek and Kootenay River. It seems not to fill quickly and it is quiet. Dog Lake Trail starts from here; naturalist-led hikes often use the trail. This is a self-registering campground; you fill out a permit, deposit your minimal fee in an envelope, and settle in. A caretaker's lodge is nearby, as well as a picnic area. All sites have picnic tables, fire grates and firewood depots. Kitchen shelters are supplied with woodstoves and wood. Flush toilets and cold water are provided. There is a trailer sewage disposal but no hook-ups. An A-frame theatre often has evening shows.

Marble Canyon is a very quiet campground, and not heavily used. It is about fifteen kilometres (nine miles) from the northern border of the park. There are sixty sites in the rather dense sub-alpine forest. Kitchen shelters provide wood stoves and firewood; flush toilets and trailer waste disposal are available, but not hook-ups. Sites have picnic tables and fire grates, with wood at depots. This campground is well-located for the Marble Canyon walks, and is near the Paint Pots and Stanley Glacier trails. In the evenings in July and August, there are interpretive programmes in the campground's outdoor theatre.

Primitive Camping

Along the back-country trails, there are a number of primitive sites for the overnight hiker. Some have fire grates and wood provided, others require self-contained pack-in stoves. All have pit privies, and most are near water. Check the back-country guide brochure, and ask park staff for information on available sites and their condition.

Other Camping

There are commercial sites at **Radium Hot Springs**, and a provincial park campground at **Dry Gulch**, just to the south of that.

Other Accommodation, Gas, Food and Supplies

Radium Hot Springs has a wide variety of motel and hotel accommodations. For information, write to the B.C. Rocky Mountain Visitor Association. Gas and supplies are also available at Radium Hot Springs.

Recreational Services

Hiking   The park has 200 kilometres (125 miles) of hiking trails, ranging from a few kilometres to hikes than can take several days to do, linking one trail with another. There is an excellent back-country trail guide available from the park. It has detailed information on elevation gain at a number of points along the trail, and provides an amazing amount of information. Topographic-map use is recommended, as well. You must register with the information centres for overnight trips. There is no charge for these permits. The park encourages spring and fall off-season use, when the park is particularly quiet. Permits can be mailed ahead of time. For further information, write the Superintendent.

Swimming   The Hot Springs Aquacourt is the most heavily used feature of the park. There is the huge, shallow "hot pool" directly from the springs, and a "cool pool" that is a regulation swimming and diving pool. There are changing and shower rooms, a snack bar and restaurants, a small gift shop area and a viewing terrace. You can rent bathing suits and towels for a small fee.

This mud is the brilliantly-coloured ochre once used by the Native people for symbolic decoration

Fishing   Fishing is not particularly good in the park, since so many streams and lakes are glacier-fed, but there are some whitefish, trout and Dolly Varden. A national park licence is required, and is available for a small fee from information centres, wardens and campground kiosks.

Boating and Canoeing   Canoes are allowed on the Vermilion and Kootenay Rivers, but no watercraft of any sort are allowed on lakes in the park. There are private river-rafting outfits outside the park, which offer trips in the area. Write to the B.C. Rocky Mountain Visitor Association.

Winter Use   There is some cross-country skiing and winter camping in the park. There are no warming huts for skiing, but the area around Dolly Varden picnic area is kept open for campers. Redstreak Campground forms part of the Radium Hot Springs Nordic trail circuit. A two-kilometre track is machine-set, and it connects with the circuits at the nearby Best Western Resort. Night skiing under lights and a warming hut are available on the Redstreak section. There are pit privies and a picnic shelter with wood stove and firewood. Bring your own water.

Further Reading

See the titles listed in the chapter on Yoho National Park.

FOR MORE INFORMATION

The Superintendent
Kootenay National Park
Box 220
Radium Hot Springs,
British Columbia
VOA IMO

Phone: (604) 347-9615

B.C Rocky Mountain Visitor
   Association
Box 10
Kimberley, British Columbia
V1A 2Y5

WATERTON LAKES

NATIONAL PARK

At Waterton Lakes, the prairies meet the mountains. This is the southern-most of the Canadian Rocky Mountain parks, but it is also a true prairie park. Nowhere else in Canada is there a place where these two ecological zones are so intermixed. Here, no transition zone of foothills intersects prairies and mountains. On the eastern side of the park, the elevation sometimes soars 1,220 metres (4,000 feet) only a kilometre (half a mile) from the prairie floor.

Waterton Lakes is located at the southwest corner of Alberta, where it borders on the United States. The American Glacier National Park was established as an extension of Waterton Lakes National Park. In the years that followed its creation, members of the Rotary Clubs of Montana and Alberta promoted the idea that, since the natural character of the Rockies here was not changed or severed by a political boundary, the two parks should not be divided, either. So, in 1932, the parks were joined in spirit as an "International Peace Park," the first in the world.

Partly because Waterton Lakes is a small park, just 525 square kilo-metres (202 square miles), it is extraordinarily accessible. Prairies fill in many of the canyon and valley floors between mountain ridges, and the three types of mountain habitat—montane, sub-alpine and alpine tundra—are reached by driving, short walks, or on trails easily covered in a short hiking day. The park has a fascinating geological history, based on the for-mation of the distinctive Lewis Overthrust.

How to See the Park

There are three main roadways in the park, and most of the trailheads, viewpoints, facilities and services are accessible from one of these routes. There is an excellent map of the park (MCR 222), which is sold at the Park

Administration office, the Information Centre at the north end of the community of Waterton Lakes, and at the Heritage Centre downtown.

For an excellent self-guided walk that introduces all the major themes of mountain-building and shaping in this area, take the **Red Rock Canyon Interpretive Trail**. The setting is breathtaking: you follow an easy incline along the top of a brilliant orange canyon. Where the creek moistens the rock, it glistens red; the sides of the canyon have greenish bands of rock sandwiched between the red strata. The colouration is due to the iron content of the rock; the reddish bands have oxidized the most. On this walk, there are places where hardened ripple marks from the shallow sea that once covered this area have etched the rock, and fossil algae are visible in rocks transported by glaciers from further west. The story of the plants and their arrival and establishment here is told by trailside signs.

The townsite area has been greatly shaped by glacial action, and there are signs of it everywhere. First, there are the three Waterton Lakes. For the most spectacular view of them (and of the townsite) take the short trail to the **Bear's Hump**, just behind the Information Centre. You can go on the trail any time, but try to go on one of the interpreter-led walks. Groups are led several times a week in the summer. The trail is one kilometre (half a mile) each way, and it is steep, though very wide and smooth.

From the hump, you see the lakes, which were carved out by glaciers and filled by remnants of ice. **Upper Waterton Lake** extends some sixteen kilometres (ten miles), south, about half of it in the United States. As the glaciers melted, they deposited a great deal of debris along their sides and at their toes, forming plateaus or terraces known as kames. The **Prince of Wales Hotel** below is on a kame terrace. **Linnet Lake**, behind the hotel, and **Lonesome Lake**, just before the Red Rock Canyon road turn-off, are also glacially formed.

There are a number of viewpoints along the roadways that have pull-offs for cars, and interpretive signs to explain topographic features. One of the best is the **Valley Viewpoint** on Highway 6, 7 kilometres (4.5 miles) east of the park entry gate. It has an interpretive display and a free high-power telescope. *Mountains and Valleys* is a very good and handy booklet on the landscape of the park, concentrating on what is seen from this viewpoint. It is available from the Information Centre.

The Prairies

There are two particularly good ways to get the flavour of the prairies. One is to drive through the **Buffalo Paddock**. Park, and walk up the path to a telescope for viewing the buffalo inside the paddock. On the paddock drive itself you cannot get out of the car, but you can, and should, drive very slowly, or even stop at times. The buffalo are often visible, and they add a strong sense of what the prairies must have once been like.

Another way to experience the prairies is to walk on them. The **Blakiston Valley/Red Rock Canyon Parkway** has good places to get out, closer to these subtly beautiful sweeps of land. A trail runs along the front of the greenish face of **Bellevue Hill**, eventually going into park back country, but the trees to the north, near the paddock, signal the limit of the prairies segment. The trail begins on the north side of the road, a few kilometres from the entry to the Red Rock Canyon Parkway. On a brief walk, I saw a

Bear-grass, found in no other Canadian national park

number of prairie flowers, the bright Gaillardia (brown-eyed Susan) being the most prominent. You could look closely at the tight tufts of grass, feel the constant wind of the high prairies, and think about how humans, animals and plants lived in this environment, past and present.

The Mountains: Three Life Zones

Mountains and their valleys make up most of the area of the park. The highest mountain is **Mount Blakiston**, at 2,920 metres (9,490 feet). Since the park has a well-developed network of walks, day-hiking and backpacking trails, most people can easily experience the two lower life zones, the montane forest and the sub-alpine forest. The alpine zone takes real hiking, but I saw a number of families with young children doing well on the shorter of the day-hike trails. Ask park staff at the Information Bureau which trail would be suitable for your party's interests, skills and energy level.

For a good overview of these three life zones, the park distributes, on request, a Forestry Service pamphlet entitled *The Trees and Forests of Waterton Lakes National Park*. It is extremely good, with lots of colour pictures, good map, informative text and specific locations for each of the major tree species.

Montane forest grows on wooded valley floors and the mountain slopes, up to between 1,350 and 1,675 metres (4,500 and 5,500 feet). The townsite is at about 1,280 metres (4,200 feet) elevation, so the forest around it, and along the lakeshores, is a blend of what is called Canadian forest and true montane forest. The predominant trees at the montane

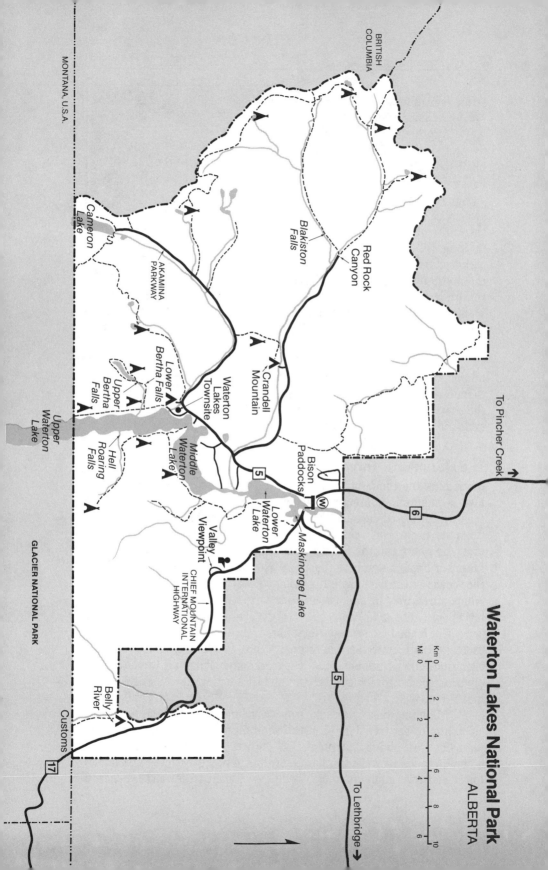

Waterton Lakes National Park
ALBERTA

BRITISH COLUMBIA

MONTANA U.S.A.

Cameron Lake

AKAMINA PARKWAY

Lower Bertha Falls

Upper Bertha Falls

Upper Waterton Lake

Hell Roaring Falls

GLACIER NATIONAL PARK

Waterton Lakes Townsite

Middle Waterton Lake

Blakiston Falls

Red Rock Canyon

Crandell Mountain

Bison Paddocks

To Pincher Creek →

Valley Viewpoint

CHIEF MOUNTAIN INTERNATIONAL HIGHWAY

Lower Waterton Lake

Maskinonge Lake

Belly River

Customs

To Lethbridge →

Km 0
Mi 0
2
2
4
4
6
6
8
10
6

5

6

17

W

level are Douglas fir, lodgepole pine and white spruce. Many flowers and shrubs grow in open spaces or on the forest floor. A talk with an interpreter will help identify them.

Two walks are excellent for learning about the montane region. One is the trail to **Lower Bertha Falls**, and the other goes the full length of Upper Waterton Lake to **Goat Haunt**, in the United States.

The **Bertha Lake Trail** starts just on the south edge of the townsite, and there is a parking lot off the road to the west. The lower falls are 2.5 kilometres (1.5 miles) away, with an altitude gain of 213 metres (700 feet). Signs all along the trail are keyed to the brochure available at the trailhead. By following the descriptions in the brochure, you learn about the growth, death and decay cycle in the forest; which trees are typical of the montane zone; how fire plays an active role in forest life; and that plants such as the devil's club and western yew are ordinarily found west of the Continental Divide.

The walk to Goat Haunt is rather long, but very interesting. It is best to take the tour boat on the return trip. A boat runs every couple of hours from the marina in the townsite at Waterton Lakes, and you can reserve your return space by purchasing your ticket before you start. If you go with an interpreter-led group, arrangements are made for you. The price per person is very modest. When I went on this walk, themes of both the montane forest and the International Peace Park were discussed by two interpreters, one from each side of the border, and they alternated their brief presentations at each pause in the walk. These walks are held on each Saturday in July and August.

The walk is almost entirely level, and it follows the lakeshore quite closely until it rounds the curve of the south end of the lake. In July, wonderful flowers cover the forest floor. If you look carefully, you may see several species of orchid, though far more common is the false hellebore, a member of the lily family. It grows well over a metre (three feet) tall, and the dense collection of pale green flowers make it a distinctive and beautiful plant.

Near the end of this walk, the trail crosses a river, and hikers go one at a time over a narrow, cable-suspended foot-bridge. Then the trail passes a marshy area, full of moose tracks, and finally curves back to the lakeshore and the Goat Haunt visitation area. There are restrooms and two display areas telling about the natural and human history of the two parks.

The walk takes perhaps three hours, depending on the group. There is a stop to eat lunch (bring your own, with lots of drinks) right at the international border, about two-thirds of the way along the trail.

The **sub-alpine zone** at Waterton Lakes is very easily reached by car. Two lakes, linked by trails, are the focal point for visiting and for interpretation of this zone. They are **Cameron Lake** and **Summit Lake**, at the end of the Akamina Parkway. The parkway is sixteen kilometres (ten miles) long, and starts just north of the townsite, near the Information Centre. The drive to the lakes actually begins the sub-alpine experience, because it ascends gradually to the sub-alpine altitude of about 1,676 metres (5,500 feet) and more. Bear-grass grows in profusion at several spots along the roadside. Keep an eye out for big horn sheep, as well, for a small herd frequents this valley. At Cameron Lake, there is a large parking lot, picnic area, fishing tackle rental, paddle boat, row boat and canoe rental, and an interpretive display. There is a brochure for a 2.5 kilometre (1.5 mile) self-guiding trail that follows one side of the shore of Cameron Lake. It points out the typical trees, such as Engelmann spruce, sub-alpine fir, white bark pine and sub-alpine larch, that grow in this relatively cool and moist environment—so moist, in fact, that it is snow-covered eight to ten months a year! This is an easy, level walk, and will take one to two hours.

During the summer, there is an interpreter available every day at the Cameron Lake day use area, to answer questions about the park. In July and August, the park conducts canoe excursions on the lake and has interpreter-led walks in the surrounding area.

By going left, past the exhibit centre, you will find the trail to Summit Lake. The brochure that describes the natural history of Cameron Lake does the same for the trail to Summit Lake. This hike is a steady ascent over switchbacks. Going slowly and peering out at the ever-more-impressive scenery, you can reach Summit Lake in an hour of moderate effort. The trail is wide and smooth, and passes through a sub-alpine forest. There are good views of surrounding mountains; the ridge that borders the lake is just at the transition to the alpine zone. When I was there, in late July, there were still patches of snow on the ground with glacier lilies popping through.

By late July much of the **alpine tundra zone** in the park is clear of snow, and there are a number of good trails to various high mountain areas. The most travelled trails, such as **Carthew Lakes** or **Crypt Lake**, are very well maintained, but they are anywhere from 5.5 to 19 kilometres (3.5 to 12 miles) one way, and often have long up-and-down stretches. Once again, get the trail guide and talk with park staff at the Information Centre, to make a trail choice. For most trails that go to the high country, hikers who take their time, start early, take a good lunch and lots of drinks, and who have sturdy shoes and layered clothing will be able to make the grade.

If you are uncertain about your legs, consider one of the horseback rides. There are a number of locations to choose from; check at the stables. The **Alderson Lake Ride** traverses montane forest at **Cameron Falls** in the

Waterton Lakes and the Prince of Wales Hotel from Bear's Hump

townsite, ascends through sub-alpine forest, decorated with the bright yellow flowers of heartleaved arnica, and emerges at the transition to the alpine zone at Alderson Lake. The round trip horseback ride, including a lunch stop at the lake, takes about five hours. The scenery is lovely, and worth the discomfort that the less-than-fit may feel, after dismounting for the day.

The other way to get to the alpine zone is to walk. The **Carthew Lakes Trail**, which goes nineteen kilometres (twelve miles) from Cameron Lake, past Summit Lake, past the Carthew Lakes, down past Alderson Lake and to the townsite, took me seven hours, including many stops for photography and a lunch break at Upper Carthew Lake. This walk was a trip highlight. First, although the goal is the alpine zone, most of these trails start at montane or sub-alpine levels, so you see a cross-section of all three mountain life zones. Seeing the changes of plant and animal life, and gradually getting better and better views of more and more of the park, is a marvellous experience. Second, the alpine zone shocks the senses with its bleakness on the large scale, and its rich, fascinating life up close. For instance, you see ahead a whole slope of what seems to be nothing but gravel, with a few patches of low vegetation here and there. Close up, these patches—no larger than door mats—are oases of tiny greenery and brilliant flowers. All the strategies of alpine survival are there: low growth; thick, waxen leaves; furriness; cushioning; tendrils, to grab hold where little bits of dust have collected and started to be soil. Without these protec-

Cable-suspension bridge on the trail to Goat Haunt

tions against dry wind, low temperatures and minimal nutrition, plants could not exist here.

Park Services and Facilities

Interpretive Programme
The park has an active and varied interpretive programme from late June through Labour Day. The Information Centre, at the north end of the townsite, has brochures, booklets, maps, etc., and the schedule of interpretive events. You can visit the exhibit on the sub-alpine area at Cameron Lake, and there are other on-site interpretive exhibits at Red Rock Canyon and at the Valley Viewpoint. Other signs and exhibits are scattered along all of the park roads, some of which have telescopes and three-dimensional casts of natural objects. Be sure to stop and look. There are indoor theatres at the townsite campground and at the Crandell Mountain Campground, where slide-show talks are given. Outdoor campfire talks are held at the Belly River Campground on weekends.

There is a very active Waterton Natural History Association, which works closely with the park in helping visitors understand and enjoy the park. It operates the Heritage Centre, with an exhibit and orientation service, including a book shop with material that will add to your stay in the park. The park and the Association also cooperate on some events, one of which is an old-time story-telling contest, held on the long weekend in August. The Association services and activities are very popular.

Camping

There are three park campgrounds for car-based campers. The one that fills first, and has three-way hook-ups for trailers, is in the **townsite**. There are kitchen shelters, flush toilets, showers and running water. There are picnic tables at each site. An interpretive theatre is close, and several trails start nearby.

Crandall Mountain Campground has a more natural setting than the townsite ground. It has 140 sites, in a mixed forest and prairie area. One of its pleasing aspects is that deer regularly browse or rest in the shrubbery between sites. The campground has picnic tables, firepits, firewood, kitchen shelters, a nearby interpretive theatre, and access to several trails.

Belly River Campground is about fifteen-minutes' drive from the townsite, south along the Chief Mountain Road to the U.S. and Glacier National Park. Its twenty-nine sites are located in a mixed tree and grassland area. This is a small, very quiet campground. Pit and flush toilets, water faucets, picnic tables and fire grates at each site, kitchen shelters, and firewood are provided. You can fish along the river.

Primitive Camping

A number of primitive campsites are set up along back-country trails. They have pit toilets; water is usually from the nearest lake or stream. Some have kitchen shelters, all have fire grates for cooking. Deadfall wood may be used, but carrying your own stove is strongly encouraged. Permits for overnight use are required. They are available free from the Administration Building in town, or the Information Centre, seven days a week in summer. Ask for the latest trail information, and for maps and brochures on back-country travel.

Other Camping

There is a large, highly developed commercial campground just north of the park on Highway 6. It is situated on the prairies, and is very windy. There is another one just east of the park on Highway 5, along the Waterton River. It is sheltered and pleasant. If you arrive at the park near or on a weekend, especially late in the day, you may well find these are the only available places to stay, at first. That happened to me, and it is a reasonable alternative.

Krummholz at the Carthew Lakes

Other Accommodation, Gas, Food and Supplies

Waterton Lakes has a small townsite, so virtually all sorts of visitor amenities are available: banks, laundromats, groceries, restaurants, gift shops, camping and outdoor supply stores, gas stations, etc. There are motels and the huge Prince of Wales Hotel, a real landmark.

Recreational Services

Hiking   The park has 183 kilometres (114 miles) of excellent trails, with a wide range of location and skill level. Ask at the Information Centre for all related information.

Fishing   Several lakes are stocked with trout, and the rivers provide good fishing. Boats are allowed in a few lakes. A National Parks fishing licence is required. It is available for a moderate fee from the Information Centre, Administration Building, some businesses in the townsite, and the fishing tackle/boat concession at Cameron Lake. Fishing tackle may be rented or purchased at the concession at Cameron Lake, and at several stores in the townsite.

Boating   There are boat rental concessions at the townsite marina, and at Cameron Lake. Rowboats and canoes are available at both lakes. There are cruises on tour boats on Waterton Lake. Visitors can take round-trip tours of Upper Waterton Lake, or be dropped off for the Crypt Lake Trail or at Goat Haunt, at the south end of the lake. Pick-up can be arranged for later in the day, or days later if you are back-country hiking.

Golfing   There is a spectacular eighteen-hole public golf course, just north of the townsite. It is open seven days a week, May through September. There is a pro shop with all services.

Horseback Riding   There is a commercially-run riding stable, just north-west of the townsite. It offers rides of various destinations and durations. Boarding of privately-owned horses is available. Horse grazing is not allowed in the park. (People bring along the food for their horses.)

Winter Use   Most park and townsite facilities close in winter, but there is some cross-country skiing and snowshoeing. An excellent booklet on cross-country skiing is available on request. Write to the Superintendent for up-to-date information.

Further Reading

Plants of Waterton-Glacier National Park and the Canadian Rockies by Richard J. Shaw and Danny On (Summerthought, 1979)
Waterton Lakes National Park by Heather Pringle (Douglas & McIntyre, 1986)
See also titles listed in the chapter on Yoho National Park.

FOR MORE INFORMATION

The Superintendent
Waterton Lakes National Park
Waterton Park, Alberta
T0K 2M0

Phone: (403) 859-2262

Waterton Natural History
  Association
Box 145
Waterton Park, Alberta
T0K 2M0
Phone: (403) 859-2624

BANFF

NATIONAL PARK

Banff is Canada's most famous national park. Its staggering natural beauty, its location as a key to east-west transportation in Canada, and its value for tourism led to its establishment as our first national park in 1885. Today, all these elements of its beginnings continue to play a vital role in the life of the park.

Banff National Park includes parts of two of the three parallel mountain systems that make up the Rocky Mountains—the easternmost Front Ranges, with their slanting table-top shape, and the castellate Main Ranges. Mount Rundle, at the Banff townsite, is the classic example of the geology that characterizes the Front Ranges, and Castle Mountain is the most obvious example of the layer-cake or castellate configuration. The park has a complex and fascinating geological history. If you are interested in geology, don't miss the presentations at the Information Centre, and look out for the books and pamphlets available in stores in Banff.

There are basically three life zones in the park: the montane forest, the sub-alpine forest and the alpine tundra. All of these are capped by the perpetually frozen world of ice and snow at the tops of the highest mountains. The montane zone is a fairly open forest of Douglas fir, white spruce, lodgepole and limber pine, with some stands of trembling aspen and balsam fir. The area is the home of grazing mammals, such as deer, elk and sheep, while the wide river valleys at the base of the montane zone provide excellent feeding and nesting areas for many kinds of waterfowl, for wading birds, such as herons, and fishing birds of prey, such as the osprey.

The sub-alpine forest is more dense and uniform than the montane forest. It is almost entirely coniferous, with two kinds of spruce, sub-alpine fir, Lyall's larch and white-bark pine. Many kinds of large mammals, including bears, wander through this zone, and seed-eating birds and small mammals, such as chipmunks and ground squirrels, are at home here. Harlequin ducks and Barrow's goldeneye breed in lakes at the border of the sub-alpine and alpine zones.

The alpine tundra area, which occurs above 2,195 metres (7,200 feet), is seen by some as bleak. However, careful inspection shows that it is a world of beautiful flowers and intriguing animals—all of which must deal with daily life in a dry, cold and windswept environment. An alpine hike in July or August can reveal many of the fascinating solutions to life's problems at this altitude.

The icefields and glaciers do not teem with life, as the forest and alpine zones do, but they are the source of much of the life-giving water in the park. They drain into beautiful alpine lakes, or tarns, some of which, like Lake Louise, are world famous. They form the streams, falls and rivers that shape the mountains and make the valleys into the rich life zones that they are. Few people actually walk to a glacier in Banff, but there are many opportunities to see them from a moderate distance.

How to See the Park

One of the first things that is evident to the visitor is that Banff National Park has a full-blown, bustling town, from which all activities seem to flow. This town has a year-round resident population of close to six thousand people, but several millions more come through in the summer and in the extraordinarily popular winter-sports season. The long history of recreational vacationing in the park has resulted also in the development of pockets of commercial activity in several outlying locations, such as Canmore. Whether the highly commercialized town of Banff and the satellite villages outside the park work against the ideals of conservation of our natural heritage, or simply help people get closer to the natural wonders of the park, is a hotly debated topic. You'll have to see for yourself.

Some visitors are perfectly happy to stroll along Banff Avenue, peering and being peered at. For these visitors, it's nature enough to be able to do customary things in a very unlikely and dramatic setting.

But, for the visitor who is more interested in peace, quiet and getting away from it all, there is no reason to be dispirited. It is usually possible to be virtually alone within a five- or ten-minute walk or drive.

The Town of Banff

A visit to the town of Banff can be an adventure all in itself, if only in trying to hold onto your money. All facilities are here for shopping of any sort, from high-fashion outdoor clothes to rugged jeans, from that axe you forgot to organic or gourmet food.

If your interests extend to learning more about the natural and human history of the park, there are a number of excellent places to do so, right downtown. First, the park itself has a natural history museum, on Banff Avenue, just south of the bridge across the Bow River. Only a couple of minutes' walk from there is the **Whyte Museum of the Canadian Rockies**, which has excellent displays of the human history of the area. It also has an art gallery, which features a permanent collection of art relating to the Canadian Rockies. Another section of the gallery has rotating shows of local, regional and national artists. The

Western anemone

Whyte Museum also encompasses archives of the Rockies, with collections of materials of both general and scholarly interest. Included in the collection is the archive of the Alpine Club of Canada, which is Canada's largest resource for historical information on mountaineering worldwide.

Another museum, this one on Birch Street, on the way to the Cave and Basin exhibit, is the **Luxton Museum of the Plains Indians**. It is a subsidiary of the Glenbow Museum in Calgary. There are dioramas and other displays, a gift shop, and special programming in the summer, designed to familiarize the visitor with the cultural activities of contemporary Native peoples. There is also a privately run museum of the geology of the area, in the Clock Tower Mall, on Banff Avenue.

Cave and Basin Centennial Centre is one of the most striking of all visitor sites in the whole national parks system, to my mind. It commemorates the one hundredth anniversary of Banff's establishment as a park and, as such, it marks the beginning of our national park system. It recreates the cave that "housed" the hot springs that put Banff on the national and international tourism map. The history of how the springs became the keystone of our first park, and the forward-thinking of the government of Canada and the Canadian Pacific Railway, which led to setting aside this segment of the Rockies as a national park, is too long to tell here. But you will be able to walk into the cave itself, smell the sulphur, peer up to the hole in the top of the cave, and picture the rough-hewn men descending into the pool that you now stand beside.

But there is much more to the Centre than the cave itself. The park has reconstructed the bathhouse and swimming pool, which were built in

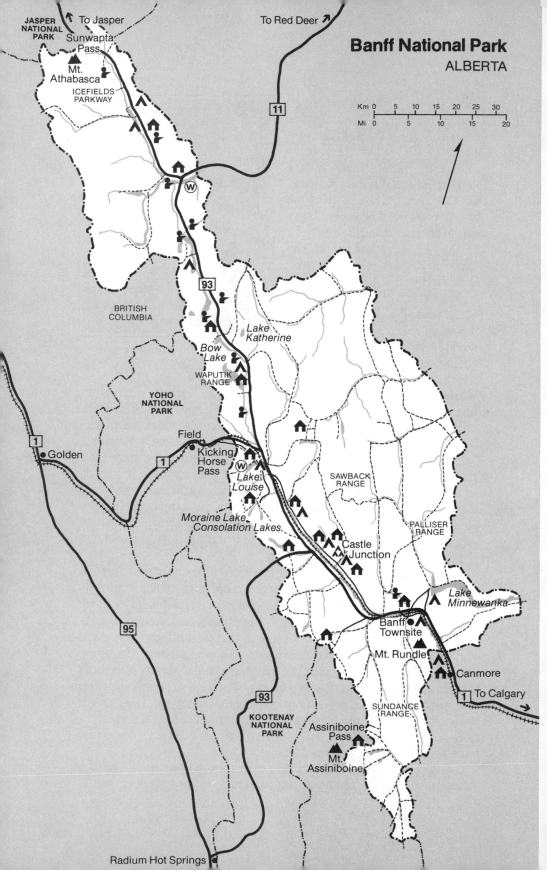

1914. There are a number of activities that you can do in the Centre, because it is designed to be a focal point for visitor activities in the park. There is an excellent interpretive section of the building, just as you come in through its twin-turreted entryway. There is a video about the national parks, and good diplays about Banff and Cave and Basin. (There used to be interactive computer games about the parks and wildlife, but the sulphur vapours rendered them inactive in very short order.) There are terraces and overlooks on the building roof, and the views are spectacular. There is a gift shop, a tea room, a picnic area on a terrace, an outdoor hot-springs pool (the "Basin" of Cave and Basin), and the very large swimming pool. There are showers and changing rooms—for a small user fee.

The Cave and Basin area is also the starting point for several trails—**Discovery Trail** (which is wheelchair accessible, as is the whole Centre), the **Trail to Sundance Canyon** (which is a walking, bicycling, and cross-country trail, in season) and the **Marsh Trail**.

The Centre is about a five-minute drive from downtown Banff, on the road past the Administrative Centre. There is plenty of parking. You can visit the Centre year-round, but swimming is in the summer only.

Of course, you'll want to get out into the very nature about which you learn so much in these interesting places. There are many trails for hiking, driving, horseback riding, canoeing and bicycling, which are all accessible from the town centre; the area around Banff Springs Hotel is a starting point for a number of them. I enjoyed two different activities from the downtown core, and both were very good for learning about the natural history of the life of a montane river valley, such as the townsite location.

I followed the **Fenland Trail**. It's only about two kilometres (1.5 miles) in a loop that is bordered, through three quarters of its length, by the rushing **Forty Mile Creek**. The trail begins at the Creek picnic area. It's marked on local maps. The walk is self-guiding, which means you should take the interpretive pamphlet available at the beginning of the trail. I was alone on the trail, and the pleasant sounds of the creek masked any noise from my footsteps. Two out of the three times I have been there, I have seen beavers carrying out their evening activities in complete peace.

Walking and Driving at Vermilion Lake

Vermilion Lake is another easily accessible drive or walk from the centre of town. There is a well-maintained road, running four kilometres (2.5 miles) along the lake, and a numbers of pull-outs where the visitor can park and then easily walk along the flat land that edges the river or lakes. You may see the Rocky Mountain sheep on the slopes leading to the lakeshore. This kind of habitat, a meandering stream widening into lakes dotted with evergreen islands, is a wonderful contrast to the rugged mountains surrounding you. Because wetlands are not common in the park, this is a great place for viewing wildlife.

Auto Tours

The auto tours you can take in the park cover a considerable distance, but are very easy to follow. Two are self-guiding. The first of these is the **Bow Valley Parkway**, Route IA, which starts approximately five kilometres (three miles) west of Banff Townsite. It is marked by the signs to Johnston Canyon. At either end of the Bow Valley Parkway, there are signs that orient you to what you will be seeing. Plan to go slowly, and take a picnic. There are a number of excellent sites, with their own tables and pit toilets.

The other self-guiding drive is along surely one of the most spectacular stretches of road in North America—the **Icefields Parkway**. The section within Banff National Park runs 122 kilometres (75 miles) from **Lake Louise** to the **Sunwapta Pass**, at the boundary between Jasper and Banff National Parks. A park brochure lists the numerous points of interest all along the parkway, and tells about their natural and human history. Every few kilometres there is another glacier to be seen, or a lookout or turquoise-coloured lake to enjoy and photograph. The road is on the east side of the Bow River and North Saskatchewan River valleys. On the western side of the rivers, the tops of icefields are visible in places, their glaciers spilling over here and there toward the valleys. It is quite stunning to see from so close the giant rivers of ice, with their massive cracks and huge overhangs. The major stops along the way are **Bow Summit Lookout** and **Peyto Lake**. There is an "auto-tape tour," prepared by a commercial enterprise, which is available to accompany you on this drive. I have not heard it, though I like the idea. Look for brochures about it in restaurants, shops, etc., in either Banff or Jasper.

It took three and a half hours to go from Lake Louise to the Banff/Jasper border, making sure to stop at each of the interpretive displays. There is a commercial rest stop at the North Saskatchewan River Crossing, about halfway up the parkway, where you can buy gasoline, go to a restaurant, or shop for souvenirs. Several of the park campgrounds are along this route, so you might consider staying in one of them, and taking some of the hikes to the east of the parkway, which would give you spectacular overviews.

The **Lake Minnewanka Loop Drive** is about twenty-four kilometres (fifteen miles) round trip. It starts from the big interchange on the main highway, where you go in and out of town. Drive as though you were heading toward the Two Jack Lake campgrounds. The road follows the base of **Cascade Mountain** and gives marvellous views of the **Palliser Range** mountains just across Lake Minnewanka. The lake is the largest in Banff National Park, and is, in fact, an artificially constructed reservoir,

Rocky mountain sheep by the road at Mt. Norquay

producing electrical power. You can drive over the earth damming the lake, on a road that attracts Rocky Mountain bighorn sheep as well as tourists. Pocked and gravelly, the road evidently has salts that the sheep love. You must drive slowly and carefully, for the sheep spend a great deal of time standing in the road, licking at the cracks in the surface. They beg for snacks, too, but this unfortunate habit absolutely should not be encouraged—and it is illegal to feed any wildlife in a national park. The animals are endangered enough by traffic already, and junk food can be equally deadly.

The natural resources of Banff haven't been used just for electrical power. Those sedimentary strata contain quite a different source of power—coal. There were two areas where coal mining took place in the park, well after it had been established. These two little towns, Anthracite and Bankhead, had brief booms in the first quarter of the century. The park has turned the remains of the town at **Bankhead** into a fascinating interpretive site. There are trails winding from old foundations to old machinery. The transformer building still remains, and contains various displays, including a life-size diorama of work at the coal face, complete with miners, tools, dim light and grime. Bankhead is just under three kilometres (two miles) from the highway interchange. Follow the Bankhead "e" (for "exhibit") signs to one of the best historical displays in the park system.

Mount Norquay Drive is a 6-kilometre (3.5-mile) drive up a very steep and winding road, just at the west exit to the Trans-Canada Highway from Banff. It takes you through the typical montane and sub-alpine forest (watch for the bighorn sheep), and then to a breathtaking view across the town and to the mountains south and east of there. At the 5 kilometre (3

Vermilion Lakes, a short walk or drive from Banff townsite

mile) point, there is a pull-off viewpoint at 1675 metres (5500 feet) in elevation. From here, the biggest mountain you see is **Mount Rundle**. It will be familiar from your stay in the town, but this view of it is far better.

At the end of the road, you can park and take the commercially-run gondola to the 2,135 metre (7,000 foot) level of **Mount Norquay**. This is where the ski lodge is located. A chair lift operates for sightseers in the summer. There are trails from the parking lot, which take you to alpine levels. It is generally open all winter, but its availability in summer varies. Ask at the Information Centre or look for brochures in shops.

Halfway There - Walking in the Mountains

If walking or driving, with the mountains towering to either side, is wonderful, but not quite enough, then it's time for some of the easily accessible trails that take you into the mountains themselves. The Bow Valley Parkway, en route to Lake Louise, offers several varied and interesting walks of no more than a half-day's duration. So does the Moraine Lake area.

Keep in mind that the walks I describe here are only a few of many similar ones. I went on these because they are in well-known areas, but also because I was in the park in mid-June, and many of the higher trails were still under snow. As the summer continues, and there are more people in the park, you may find that the trails I mention are the very ones you wish to avoid, because of crowding. The best thing to do is go to the Information Centre on Banff Avenue and ask about trails equivalent, in terms of accessibility or scenery or ease of walking, but less travelled.

From the Bow Valley Parkway, you reach Johnston Canyon, which is eighteen kilometres (eleven miles) west of the town of Banff. It is an extremely popular day-use area, with a restaurant, bungalows, picnic areas nearby, and a well-marked path up the canyon itself.

Johnston Canyon Walk takes you along the pathway of Johnston Creek, starting at a fairly low point and then moving past two major falls and several smaller ones. If you are energetic enough, you can follow the 5.5 kilometres (3.5 miles) up to the broad upper valley, which the stream winds across, as it comes from its source in the snow-laden mountains above. I went all the way up, taking a good two hours each way (though I walked very slowly and stopped frequently to take pictures). The kilometre up to the first viewpoint, at the **Lower Falls**, is the most developed form of park trail; a firm, gravelled surface, with a very gentle slope. When you reach the edge of the canyon, an extremely attractive levered walkway juts out from the sides of the gorge on your left, while the stream rushes below you and out to your right. There is a very good railing, and you never feel unsafe. It is delightful to be so close to the water, almost to be a part of it, as the mist from the cataracts and, eventually, the falls drifts over you.

Above the Lower Falls there is about another 2-kilometre (1.5-mile) upward climb to the **Upper Falls**. This is not a difficult walk, but it is nearly continuously ascending. There are interpretive signs along the trail, up to the Upper Falls. The Upper Falls are about twice the height of the Lower ones. You can climb above the Upper Falls, and it is very interesting to see how, in a number of other places, the stream is compressed to very narrow widths. At one point you can see that, even though it is only perhaps a metre wide, it must be very deep. It seems to be undercutting the rock beneath your feet.

Above the Upper Falls, the path cuts away at a right angle to the river. The first few hundred metres are a catwalk. Then the trail continues for several kilometres along a wide fire road through the forest. One of the lovely sights along the walk, in late June, was that of many calypso orchids right along the path. Eventually, after perhaps another hour's walk, the path begins to descend. Suddenly, you are in the wide, flat, high valley through which the Johnston Creek flows, before it tumbles through its canyons to the Lower Bow Valley. Just another five minutes takes you to the **Inkpots**.

The Inkpots are a most interesting example of the effect of moving water upon land, for here the runoff has occasionally seeped through underground channels in the limestone, and has created sinkholes, and then enlarged them. These sinkholes occur at a high point in the flat upper valley, and then stairstep down. The result is seven small pools, which appear to be spring-fed. They are most often a beautiful, bright and clear blue. Occasionally, however, with a sudden increase of pressure in this underground drainage system, the water stirs up black silt from below the white limestone surface. The inky darkness in the water has resulted in the name *Inkpots*. It's a wonderful place to rest or to cool your feet in the water. You can't cool them for long, however, because the water has a steady temperature of 1°C (35°F).

Beyond the large flat meadow of the Inkpots, the land rises a little toward another plateau level, where small conifers are sparsely scattered. This is the nearest of all of the primitive campsites for the back-country packer. It is Johnston Creek 6. It is five minutes from the Inkpots to this campsite, where there are four rustic picnic tables, pit toilets, and open spaces for tents. It would be an easy overnight spot to reach, and it is the entry to much more back-country camping.

No one can go to Banff and not visit **Lake Louise**. In fact, that's about all some people do—roll out of the dusty parking lot, ramble up to the lake, stare in amazement for a while, go into the Chateau for tea, and wander on out. Years ago I did that, too, and it was a lovely experience. But this time I took my time, and went on one of the most popular hikes in the park, the **Lake Louise/Lake Agnes Trail**. It was four and a half hours of beauty, new friends and sweat.

The trail ascends unevenly for the whole 4 kilometres (2.5 miles) to Lake Agnes. It is forested most of the way, but there are frequent openings where you can get spectacular views of Lake Louise below you. The glacier-fed turquoise is astonishing. The forest is filled with the sound of birdsong or, in the case of the varied thrush, bird-ring. There were nuthatches beeping, and olive-sided flycatchers whistling from isolated trees at the edge of the mountain slopes. After 3 kilometres (2 miles), you come to **Mirror Lake**, a small tarn, which is so protected from wind that it reflects its surroundings perfectly. It is below a major landmark, the **Big Beehive Rock**. Above the lake is the goal of the hikers—**Lake Agnes** and its tea house.

Sitting on the porch of the teahouse, sipping cup after cup of tea (herbal only offered in this healthy environment), I learned something about hiking close to the alpine zone. I'd been extremely warm, since even the slightest ascent is a lot of work for me. Now, with a brisk breeze blowing, I was shivering within seconds. I had been sensible enough to carry a sweater and a windbreaker and, before long, I was fairly comfortable. But it was a lesson to be remembered through the rest of the mountain parks. Dress in layers, don't get overheated, and guard instantly against wind and cold.

For another spectacular Main Range setting, with another glacial lake, the **Moraine Lake/Valley of the Ten Peaks** area is a wonderful place to go. I went there to see the Moraine Lake facilities, which include a lodge, a picnic area, and interpretive exhibits. This is also the starting point for the trail to **Consolation Lakes**.

The area is reached by a marked road just off the Lake Louise access road on Highway 1A. The drive to Moraine Lake is 12.5 kilometres (7.5

miles) long. Once there, you are met by a view that is every bit as spectacular as that of Lake Louise. This glacial-green lake is surrounded by a series of mountain peaks, divided by avalanche chutes that send debris tumbling to the water's edge.

It is well worth strolling around the edges of Moraine Lake. There is a small stand of conifer forest, which has been fenced with rustic rails to preserve its extremely fragile soil. Immediately adjacent to the outlet of the lake there is a beautiful picnic area, which has kitchen shelters. There are toilets, as well. Also on the lakeshore is a lodge with restaurant, small gift shop, and several log bungalows tucked into another lightly wooded area. You can rent canoes from the lodge, and paddle out on the quiet lake.

Rising above the picnic area and lodge, at the near end of the lake, is a huge, imposing rock pillar called the **Tower of Babel**. There have been a number of rock falls from the tower and the adjacent slope of Mt. Babel. The resultant debris dammed the run-off from the surrounding mountains, and formed Moraine Lake. A very short trail leads to the top of this rock-debris hill. This trail has interpretive exhibits.

A number of trails start in the Moraine Lake area, but in mid-June only the ones with the least altitude gain were free of snow. I decided to take the trail to Consolation Lakes. When I went, the trail was very damp in places, but quite beautiful. Every once in a while, it was necessary to slog through patches of snow in the most shaded areas but, overall, the trail was easy. It took a relaxed hour to reach the wide valley that holds Lower Consolation Lake.

This short trail is heavily used later in the season, but you can then go farther away to Upper Consolation Lake, or you can take other trails in the area. For an autumn extravaganza, a trip to **Larch Valley** from Moraine Lake is supposed to be marvellous. The larch is the only conifer that turns colour and then loses its needles in the fall. The larch is, at any time, a beautiful tree, with its wispy, curving branches and graceful shape. A whole forest in autumnal gold must be spectacular.

Another spectacular trail, ending at a teahouse, is the **Plain of Glaciers**. Give yourself the day to do it.

The Back Country - Rocky Mountain High

With all the places to go in Banff, so many of them easily accessible by car or within an easy walk, it is sometimes hard to realize that most of the park's area is back country. Most of this is also high country—high river valleys, alpine meadows, and windswept icefields. The park has a video on back-country use, and brochures for back-country hikers. The backpacker can obtain topographic maps and the latest information on trail conditions, trail and campsite use, and bear encounters from the back-country desk in the Information Centre, where you can also see the video. The back country starts just some nine kilometres (four to five miles) in from the main roadways, so it is possible to make many different one-day, round-trip hikes. You can also camp in the primitive campsites that the park has established at reasonable intervals along many back-country trails.

For people interested in this kind of travel in Banff, the best thing to do is write to the Superintendent for back-country information. There are several excellent books on the hiking trails in the park, and these should be studied. Back-country-use permits are required; they are available free of charge at the Information Centre.

There is one other, very different way to get to alpine altitudes for good views and short walks in a limited area. This is by one of the several gondolas that run in summer for day-trippers, and in winter for skiers. The lifts are located at **Mount Norquay**, **Sulphur Mountain** and **Lake Louise**. **Sunshine Village** also runs a summer gondola ride to alpine meadows, and an extensive trail system at the top. Most have a gift shop and restaurant/snack bar at their destinations, and there is the opportunity to take short hikes. They are all commercially run. Advertisements, with schedules and (moderate) rates, are available at most shops and tourist facilities in the town of Banff or Lake Louise. Be sure to bring a windbreaker, even on a sunny day.

Park Services and Facilities

Interpretive Programme

Banff is a big, busy and varied park, and the interpretive programme reflects this. There are schedules available from both the Banff and Lake Louise Visitor Centres, campground kiosks and bulletin boards, and at many of the tourist facilities. Be sure to get one. The park publishes *The Mountain Guide*, which is an excellent source for all kinds of park activities, park history, facilities and services. There are theatres for slide shows in seven of the campgrounds. Not every campground has a programme every night, but you won't be far from one of the several that do. Rampart Creek Campground has campfire circles, where interpreters come to give talks and share some tea brewed over the fire. Evening programmes are also presented each night in the Information Centre, and on the main floor of the same building there is a photo gallery and mini-theatre with a video programme. Interpreters lead walks daily in the areas of the communities of Lake Louise and Banff. The interpreters can give you a good idea of each hike's difficulty and time. Finally, there are also special events, which

Trail to Consolation Lakes, free of snow by mid-June

vary with the season and the interests of the individual interpreter. For instance, there are guided walks to see spring flowers, to experience spring and fall bird migration on the Vermilion Lakes, to view the gold of Larch Valley in the fall, or to hear the bugling bull elk, also in the fall. In the winter, there are interpretive programmes at the Information Centre, and presentations that are given at local hotels on a rotating basis.

The interpretive programme also provides the really excellent signs at places like Bow Summit and Johnston Canyon, and the colourful informative pamphlets for the Icefields or Cave and Basin Hot Springs, etc. All publications are free of charge. There are some commercial publications, too, which are interesting and helpful. Check the shops.

The **Lake Louise Visitor Centre** is a very recent addition to the park, though it is part of a ten-year development programme at Lake Louise. From an architectural view alone, the Centre is worth a visit. The building is designed to repeat and reflect the slanted table-top look of the surrounding mountains. Inside, there are both information services and interpretive programming. There are twenty-four-hour computer-information terminals and, during regular working hours, you will find helpful staff, a video on back-country use, a trip-planner display, and just about any other information you could possibly want on how to have a wonderful visit to the park. There are also exhibit galleries, telling the natural and human history of the area, as well as a multi-media show that traces the geological history of the Rockies. The whole Lake Louise area is an important focal point for trails, accommodation, shopping, and all-round enjoyment of the northern part of the park, so do plan to spend some time there—starting at the Visitor Centre.*

*The Centre was just being completed during my most recent visit to Banff, so I am grateful to Donna Pletz, of visitor services, for providing the material from which this description is drawn.

Camping

Banff has 2,323 car-based camping sites, distributed among thirteen camp-grounds. The largest ones, and those that fill first, are near the town of Banff and Lake Louise; **Tunnel Mountain, Two Jack, Lake Louise.** There are no reservations for campsites, but you can call ahead to get an idea of how crowded the park is.

Note: The park provides fire grates at each tent/car site, and there is wood at depots, but the wood I saw was rounds about fifty centimetres (twenty inches) across. You'll need a wedge and maul to break them down. No hatchet will work.

Tunnel Mountain Campground is divided into three sections. **Tunnel Mountain Tent Trailer Camp** is 2.5 kilometres (1.5 miles) east of the town of Banff. It has 246 sites, kitchen shelters with stoves and fire-wood, flush toilets and showers. **Tunnel Mountain Village** 1 is 4 kilome-tres (2.5 miles) east of the town and has 622 sites, flush toilets and trailer sewage disposal. **Tunnel Mountain Trailer Camp** is adjoining the Village 1 and has 322 sites with three-way hook-ups. The campgrounds are wooded around their margins, but don't have much privacy. They are well located, if you want to be near town. There are several short trails near the camp-grounds, and a car pull-out for a view of the Bow Valley Hoodoos. This spot is also good for learning about the geology and railroad history of the area. The interpretive signs explain.

Two Jack Main is a densely-wooded conifer forest area, thirteen kilometres (eight miles) from Banff, on the road to Lake Minnewanka. It is not very scenic, but it does offer a sense of visual privacy. There are 381 sites, kitchen shelters, flush toilets, trailer-sewage disposal, and hot and cold water in washrooms. The small lakeshore area at **Two Jack Lakeside** fills up quickly. It has eighty sites, with the usual fire grates, picnic tables, kitchen shelters and flush toilets.

Johnston Canyon is set in a fairly mature forest that isn't as dense as at Two Jack Main. A number of sites lie along Johnston Creek. It is on Highway 1A, the Bow Valley Parkway, twenty-six kilometres (sixteen miles) west of Banff. There are 140 sites, kitchen shelters, flush toilets, showers and trailer-sewage disposal. Also on the Bow Valley Parkway, **Castle Mountain** is five kilometres (three miles) west of Johnston Canyon. Forty-four sites are available, with kitchen shelters and flush toilets. The campground at **Protection Mountain** is just over ten kilometres (six miles) further west of Castle Mountain on the Bow Valley Parkway. It has eighty-nine sites, kitchen shelters, flush toilets and trailer-sewage disposal.

The **Lake Louise Campground** is a lightly treed, quite open area near the main highway and the railway. It is bordered by the fast-flowing Bow River, which provides a nice contrast to the roads and rails. This campground is a ten-minute walk from the village of Lake Louise. There are 221 tent sites, 163 trailer sites, kitchen shelters, flush toilets, and trailer-sewage disposal. Regular interpretive events are held in the summer.

Campgrounds North of Lake Louise

Mosquito Creek is located at kilometre twenty-four (fifteen miles) of the Icefields Parkway. This is a self-registering campground. It has two sections; a big, gravelly field, and a wooded area with kitchen shelters, pit toilets and cold water from faucets every few sites. Picnic tables, fire grates and firewood are available, as usual. The **Waterfowl Lakes Campground** is at kilometre fifty-eight (thirty-seven miles) on the parkway. It is a lovely location by a stream and large lake, wooded, with a cleared area at lakeside. Mountains and glaciers are in full view—a good place for easy canoeing. There are kitchen shelters, flush and pit toilets and water from faucets every few sites. It's only fifteen kilometres (nine miles) from Saskatchewan Crossing, with its gasoline, restaurant, etc., and has eighty sites with trailer sewage. Waterfowl Campground has an interpretive theatre for evening programmes. **Rampart Creek** is at kilometre eighty-eight (fifty-four miles) of the parkway. It has the campfire circle for interpretive talks. There are fifty sites, kitchen shelters, and flush and dry toilets. **Cirrus Mountain** is situated at kilometre 102 (64 miles) on the parkway. There are sixteen sites, a kitchen shelter and pit toilets.

Primitive Camping

The back-country areas of Banff National Park have different user categories, in terms of what type of camping is allowed in each. This is necessary to avoid excessive wear and tear on the land and wildlife. There is a back-country guide available at both the Banff Information Centre on Banff Avenue and the Lake Louise Visitor Centre. In both places, you will be able to talk with staff about which routes are best suited to your interests and skills.

There are back-country campsites at about ten-kilometre (six-miles) intervals along the more popular trails in the back country. All have pit toilets, fire grates, wood and small picnic tables. Write to the Superintendent for detailed information, and check at the Information Centre upon arrival for updates on the trail conditions, and to get your free, required back-country permit.

Other Accommodation, Gas, Food and Supplies

There are six youth hostels in Banff National Park. A minimal fee covers beds and propane cooking. Some have electric light, some don't; most are wood-heated. For more information, write to Canadian Hostel Association, 203-1414 Kensingston Road S.W., Calgary, Alberta, T2N 3P9; Phone: (413) 283-5551. Most of the commercial accomodation in the park is concentrated at the town of Banff and at Lake Louise, but there is also accommodation at a number of outlying locations. The park has lists of them. Also, you can write to the Banff/Lake Louise Chamber of Commerce for a detailed booklet. The town of Canmore, just outside the east gate of the park, also has a good deal of commercial accommodation and related facilities. Gas, food and supplies are available in the town of Banff or in Canmore. Lake Louise has gasoline, restaurants and a mall, which includes a sporting-goods store, an organic food store, an excellent bookstore, and more. Saskatchewan Crossing has gasoline and a restaurant.

Recreation Services

Driving   Ask at the Information Centre for the pamphlets on drives in the Lake Louise and Banff areas, and on the Bow Valley and Icefields Parkways.

Hiking   The park has phased out its own brochures about park trails, but there are a number of commercial publications, which are filling this gap very well. They are to be found in many of the gift shops and book shops throughout the area, including the park gift shop at Cave and Basin. The park does have topographic maps at the Information Centre on Banff Avenue.

Boating and Canoeing   Power boats are allowed only on Lake Minnewanka, where there is a boat-launching area and boats may be rented. Canoes are allowed on any of the lakes and rivers. They may be rented at Lake Minnewanka, Lake Louise, Moraine Lake and at the town of Banff. There are commercial rafting tours. Write to the Chamber of Commerce, or ask at the Information Centre.

Fishing   Fishing is quite good in some waters. A National Park permit is required. A park brochure lists lakes, limits, etc. Stocking is limited to water bodies at low elevation. (e.g. Vermilion Lakes) and only native species are stocked.

Golf   There is an twenty-seven-hole course at the Banff Springs Hotel, with a driving range next to it. You can rent clubs and electric carts at the pro shop.

Swimming A dip in the Upper Hot Springs feels good after a day spent ski-ing or hiking. It is open year-round. The Cave and Basin pool is open in summer only. It is not hot enough for winter use!

Horseback Riding, Backpacking and Guided Back-Country Treks There are several commercially-operated enterprises, which offer a full range of these activities. The park has a list (write to the Superintendent), and so does the Chamber of Commerce.

Sightseeing Tours, Chair Lifts, Gondolas Various activities of this kind are provided by commercial operators. The best thing to do is write to the Chamber of Commerce, or ask at any hotel or travel agent in the town of Banff, Canmore or Calgary.

Winter Use Cross-country skiing and snowshoeing are very popular in the park. Write to the Superintendent for information, or inquire at the Information Centre in Banff. There is an excellent booklet on ski-tou-ring—how to prepare, twenty trails to use, what areas to avoid, etc. The park has three major downhill skiing areas—Sunshine Village, Mount Norquay and Lake Louise. These are all commercially-run and have the whole complement of tows, lodges, rentals, lessons, etc. Write to the Chamber of Commerce, or check with your local travel agent. There are three designated routes in the park on which snowmobiles may be used. Permits are required. Write for the park's informational booklet on this.

Further Reading

Banff National Park by George Brybyein and Dorothy Dickson (G.B. Publishing, 1985)
See titles listed in the chapter on Yoho National Park.

FOR MORE INFORMATION

The Superintendent
Banff National Park
Box 900
Banff, Alberta
T0L 0C0

PHONE: (403) 762-3324

Banff/Lake Louise Chamber of
 Commerce
Box 1298
Banff, Alberta
T0L 0C0

PHONE: (403) 762-4646/762-3777

JASPER

NATIONAL PARK

Jasper is the largest and northernmost of the five Rocky Mountain national parks. It lies directly north of Banff National Park and, like Banff, occupies a large part of the eastern slopes of the Rockies in Alberta.

Jasper covers an area of 10,800 square kilometres (4,170 square miles). It's made up of two of the three ranges of the Rockies—the Front Ranges to the east and the Main Ranges in the remainder of the park. These ranges run in a northwest-southeast direction, roughly parallel to each other. They are divided by deep valleys along major fault lines. The Front, Main and Western Ranges all originated at the bottom at a huge inland sea. The mountains were built by processes of sedimentation, compression and uplift. Mountain-building stopped in the foothills beyond Jasper about forty million years ago, and they have been losing ground steadily since that time, as a result of glaciation during the ice age, and ongoing erosion by wind, water and frost.

Because the mountains were eroding throughout the period during which they were being uplifted, the maximum height they reached remains open to debate. Today, many of the mountains are over 3,350 metres (11,000 feet). The townsite of Jasper is at an elevation of 1,058 metres (3,472 feet) above sea level. The largest icefield in the Rocky Mountains is here, and fifteen to twenty glaciers are visible from the parkway that runs from Lake Louise to the Jasper townsite. The mixed terrain and varied habitat of broad river valleys, wooded lower slopes, alpine tundra above the treeline, and the massive icefields make for a complex and fascinating environment.

How to See the Park

Jasper has the four ecological zones of the Rockies: the montane, with its dry Douglas fir forest and broad river valleys; the sub-alpine forest of

Engelmann spruce and alpine fir; the alpine tundra, with its rocky vastness and miniature plant life; and the awe-inspiring icefields and glaciers, which can be considered an extension of the alpine. Although each of the zones is extraordinarily accessible, Jasper is known particularly for offering the opportunity to get away from it all in one of the best and most extensive back-country trail systems in the national parks.

The hub of the park's activities is the townsite; the spokes are the highways. There are six main visitation areas: the Icefields Parkway, which highlights the Athabasca Glacier, 101 kilometres (63 miles) south of the townsite at the park's southern border; the 43-kilometre (27-mile) Maligne Lake Road, east of the townsite; the Miette Hot Springs, near the eastern entry to the park; Whistler's Mountain, just south of the townsite; Mount Edith Cavell, about 29 kilometres (18 miles) southeast of the townsite, off alternate Highway 93A; and the Pyramid/Patricia Lakes area, just west of the townsite.

Icefields and Glaciers

It is artificial to divide the Icefields Parkway into a Jasper stretch and a Banff stretch. But Jasper's section really does stand out, in that it boasts the **Athabasca Glacier**. This glacier is 6.5 kilometres (4 miles) long, from the rim of its source in the Columbia Icefield to its terminus, or toe. This toe extended past what is now the parkway, as recently as the turn of the century. It has melted back more than 1.5 kilometres (about a mile) since 1878, which is an extremely rapid retreat. The glacier is always in motion, always flowing downward and forward, but it has grown shorter because more ice melts each year than is added from the icefield source. It is about 15 metres (50 feet) thick near the toe, and about 300 metres (984 feet) thick at its deepest part, near the icefield rim. And you can drive to a parking lot and walk right up to it. (Walking on it is strongly discouraged, however.) There's nowhere else in the world where a glacier is this accessible. A quarter-million people a year go up to pat its toe. A private company offers guided walks on the glacier between June and September. Because space is limited and the walks are very popular, advance booking is recommended.

There's also a commercially-run giant snow-coach service, which takes you a few kilometres onto the main part of the glacier. It's a little time-consuming; you have to get tickets, you have to wait in the lower parking lot at the embarkation point, and then to be taken back, but the time spent on the glacier itself is very interesting.

The Icefields Centre, just across the parkway from the glacier toe interpretive area, has a continuous slide show, a relief model of the Icefield, and excellent art-work displays.

There's another area of the park to complement the Icefield/ Athabasca Glacier experience. This is the base of **Mount Edith Cavell.** From the parking lot at the end of the access road, there is a self-guiding trail called **Path of the Glacier.** It follows a lateral moraine, the ridge of debris that accumulates at the edge of a glacier. Interpretive signs explain the Little Ice Age of five hundred years ago, and how the area is changing as a result of the glaciers' retreat.

One difficulty in reaching this trail is that the road is usually not clear of snow and open to public travel until mid or late June.

Alpine flowers, mosses and lichen — low and spreading

Montane Zone

In Jasper, the **Athabasca** and **Miette River Valleys** represent the montane zone. The typical forest is dry and open. The rivers are wide, and their stream beds change now and then. Marshy areas in low-lying parts make excellent habitat for moose, beaver and waterfowl. The open slopes are ideal for grazing animals, such as mule deer, Rocky Mountain bighorn sheep and elk. Black bear frequent this zone, as do coyote. Mountain goats come down to the natural salt licks adjacent to the Athabasca River.

I found the best car-based view of this kind of environment, and the most beautiful drive in the park, to be the road north of Jasper on Highway 16, up to **Pocahantas** and the **Miette Hot Springs** turn-off.

For an even closer experience of the montane zone, the **Patricia Lake/Pyramid Lake** road and trails are excellent. I drove to the Pyramid Lake stables, where there is a parking area. The Patricia Lake Trail starts from the edge of the paddock area; the walk is only five kilometres (three miles) long, and it is very easy, although mosquito-ridden in the damp areas before Cottonwood Slough.

When you get back to the car, follow the road for a few minutes to Pyramid Lake. At the road's end, near the far end of the lake, there's a picnic ground on a little island, which you reach by bridge. The view is quite wonderful. Several short trails begin along the lakeshore, with places to launch boats, a small collection of bungalows, and a little tea house. You can rent fishing gear and boats.

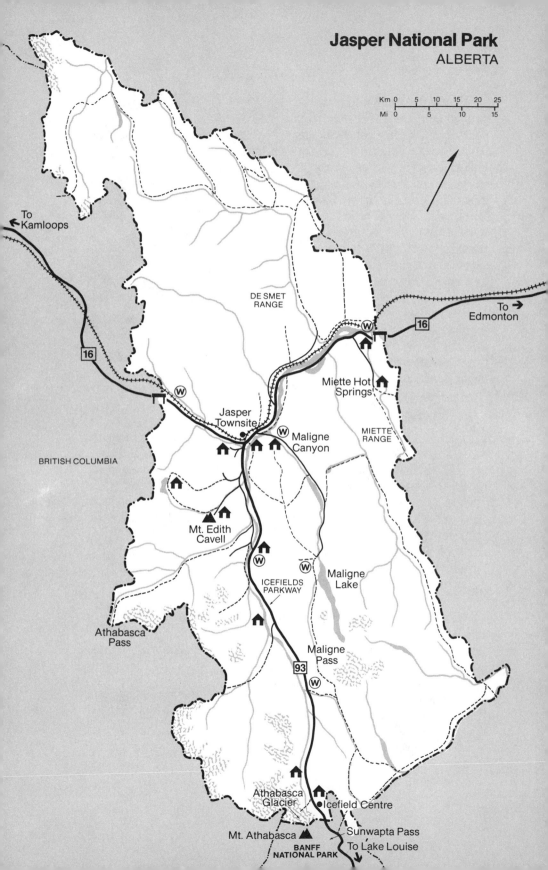

The Sub-Alpine Zone

Travelling the **Maligne Lake Road** is an excellent way to explore the sub-alpine world. **The Maligne Valley** is a hanging valley. It was carved into its U-shape by a glacier; at the same time, another, much larger, glacier carved its way at a right angle to the Maligne Valley, cutting the wider, deeper **Athabasca River Valley**. The floor of the Maligne Valley is 120 metres (393 feet) higher than the floor of the Athabasca Valley. Thus, the Maligne River, which flows on a very gradual slope for most of its journey, takes a sudden plunge where it joins the Athabasca Valley.

There are three major stops along the Maligne Valley road, and the site of this precipitous descent at **Maligne Canyon** is the first. The canyon is a spectacular example of the cutting power of moving water. You can see all the effects by walking along the trail that switches from side to side of the canyon, over four bridges. A well-placed interpretive exhibit and signs explain how water has carved and shaped layer after layer of rock.

When you've walked as far as you want, you can return to the visitor facilities, a restaurant, gift shop and washrooms located near the parking lot.

The second stop up the valley is **Medicine Lake**. It was a mystery lake for a long time: although it does not have a surface river as an outlet, each year it drains out until, in fall and winter, it is mostly exposed mud, with only a few channels and a pond in the middle. The Maligne River enters the lake at its southwest end, from higher in the valley, but doesn't appear to leave it. Yet the river resurfaces sixteen kilometres (ten miles) farther down the valley in and around Maligne Canyon.

The riddle of this sinking river has been solved only recently. Apparently, a network of caves extends in the valley floor under the lake, to Maligne Canyon. At least two horizontal levels are fed by numerous sink holes in the lake bottom. When the spring run-off is high in the upper Maligne Valley, the lake fills, and so do the caves. The amount of water that flows out of the lake into the caves greatly exceeds the amount that can drain out. As the run-off from snow and rain slows in late summer, the outflow below the surface exceeds the inflow and, by late fall, there is very little water left in the lake.

The final stop in the Maligne Valley is **Maligne Lake**, the largest glacier-fed lake in the Rockies. It Is 27.5 kilometres (17 miles) long. The lake is bordered by sub-alpine forest; the mountains rising around it show the grey/green shadings of alpine tundra, and then the ice and snow of mountain heights. A network of short trails starts near the boat-launch area. On the **Hummock and Hollow Trail** an interpretive sign describes glacial remains like kames and kettles. At the **Schäffer Viewpoint**, the signs tell of intrepid Mary Schäffer, the first white woman to explore the lake, and the mountain climbers, scientists and adventurous tourists who followed over the years.

For today's visitor there is a good road, several big parking lots, the nature trails, a restaurant and gift shop, a fishing-tackle and boat-rental dock, and two-hour tours to the end of the lake in large, weatherized tour boats. I thought the tour was excellent, but rather expensive, especially for a family. The boat tours go past **Spirit Island**, and stop on a point of land nearby.

Along with the short nature trails, the Maligne Lake area has a number of longer trails to the surrounding alpine areas, some of which take two or three days to complete.

Alpine Tundra

If you're a back-country hiker, you'll have no problems reaching this environment. Many of the trails go above the treeline, and wind along ridges and crests for many kilometres. But the majority of visitors will want another way to get there. Here are suggestions.

One is to hop into the reversible tramway to **The Whistlers**. The parking lot is at the end of a short, well-marked access road, just south of the townsite. This is a commercially-operated service, so there is a small gift shop at the bottom terminal and a cafe, restaurant and gift shop at the top. The tram operator gives a talk about the tram and the natural history of the area, on the way up. This is well-coordinated with the park's own interpretive messages, including an admonition not to pick flowers or feed the animals. The tram, shop/cafe, and mountaintop boardwalk are all wheelchair accessible.

The tram ride takes you from 1,300 metres (4,266 feet) to 2,286 metres (7,500 feet) elevation. A trail goes to the top of the mountain, and then winds along the ridge to other viewpoints. The beginning of the trail is all boardwalk. Several levels of platforms have interpretive signs. Then the trail begins its moderate ascent to the top. If you walk very slowly, it will not be too difficult, and it will take about thirty to forty minutes to reach the summit. The path is wide and smooth, but many people are not used to walking uphill, especially at higher elevations. When you get there, you will be at 2,465 metres (8,085 feet) elevation.

The other access to the alpine tundra is by the popular **Sulpher Skyline Trail**. Pack a lunch, and plan to spend the day. The trail winds its way up through the sub-alpine forest, past gnarled, stunted trees. Eventually, the ground cover becomes sparse, and you will find yourself on open, rocky ground, with small patches of plant life or the occasional brilliant flower emerging from a small rock crevice. At the top, the mountains stretch away on every side, in striking rock formations.

Athabasca Glacier from the Icefields Parkway

After your return hike, there is no better way to relax than to indulge in a visit to the **Miette Hot Springs**, located near the trailhead in the **Fiddle Valley**. There is a small fee. No long hike is complete without a visit to the hot springs. For that matter, neither is a visit to Jasper.

Park Services and Facilities

Interpretive Programme

Jasper has a very active interpretive programme. There are interpreter-led walks; evening slide shows in the outdoor theatre at Whistlers campground; other presentations at Wapiti campground; campfire talks at the less-developed campgrounds, Wilcox Creek, Wabasso, Honeymoon, and Pocahantas. The park also publishes a number of brochures, including an excellent series of four books on the Maligne Valley, Mount Edith Cavell, The Whistlers and the Columbia Icefield. These are available from the park's cooperating association, Parks and People. At special weekly events, interpreters present programmes keyed to their individual interests or skills, or tied in with particular seasonal happenings. I attended a marvellous talk on the human history of the park, focusing on the early explorers and backpackers. A warden brought a packhorse, packed and

Deer by the roadside, photographed from the car

unpacked it, and told us why horses could not be replaced by skimobiles in the huge back-country, with its heavy forests, steep trails and heavy snow. Ask at the Information Centre about the possibility of this type of programme being given when you're in the park.

Camping

There are ten campgrounds in the park, of varying degrees of development. At smaller sites, fees are collected by a mobile attendant.

Whistlers Campground is right by the townsite, in a lightly wooded area. It has 781 sites, 77 of which have three-way hook-ups for trailers. Forty-three sites have electricity only. There are kitchen shelters, and each car/tent site has a picnic table and fire grate. Flush toilets, and hot and cold water are provided in washrooms, with cold water on the exterior of the washrooms. There are showers. It fills quickly.

Wapiti is lightly treed, with 366 sites, 28 of them with electricity only. They are in a paved parking lot at the edge of the campground. There are kitchen shelters, flush toilets, hot and cold water in faucets, and new showers. Water is available from faucets at central locations. Most sites have picnic tables and fire grates, with firewood provided. This campground is less likely to be full than Whistler's.

At **Pocahantas Campground**, 140 sites are situated in lightly treed forest. Hot and cold running water, and taps at central locations are provided. There are flush toilets, picnic tables, fire grates and firewood.

Snaring River Campsite has 66 sites, 10 of them walk-in several hundred metres. Kitchen shelters, pit toilets, water from wells, picnic tables, fire grates and firewood are provided.

Wabasso, a beautiful, lightly wooded location, is accessible from alternate Highway 93A, near the junction of the Athabasca and Whirlpool Rivers, where fur traders used to meet. Highway 93A is a beautiful drive, past lakes and marshes and flowered woodland, so I would suggest this campground for people who have bicycles, or who enjoy easy roadside strolls. There are 238 sites, with flush toilets, cold water at the washrooms and in faucets around campsites. Two kitchen shelters, picnic tables, fire grates and firewood are provided.

Mount Kerkeslin, along the Athabasca River in a montane forest, offers good mountain views. There are 42 sites, with pit toilets. Water is taken from wells; picnic tables, fire grates and firewood are provided.

Honeymoon Lake Campground, by a small lake, is good for easy canoeing. There is a pump and well-water, or water from the lake, which has to be boiled. There are 35 sites, with pit toilets, kitchen shelters, picnic tables, fire grates and firewood.

Jonas Creek is in a wooded area, on a small hillside. The upper section is a short walk-in for 12 tents. The lower level has 13 sites, and is very near the highway. There are pit toilets, kitchen shelters with a water supply, picnic tables, fire grates and firewood.

Columbia Icefield Campground is just a few hundred metres south of the Athabasca Glacier, on the opposite side of the road. It is situated by a small creek on a hillside. There are 33 sites, with platforms for tents and a centralized water supply. Kitchen shelters, pit toilets, picnic tables, fire grates and firewood are provided.

Wilcox Creek, the southernmost of the Jasper campgrounds, just into the park, is lightly wooded and built on several levels. There are 46 sites, with kitchen shelters, pit toilets, faucet water, trailer-sewage disposal, picnic tables, fire grates and firewood.

Primitive Camping

There are a thousand kilometres (six hundred miles) of back-country trails in the park, and the longer ones have primitive campsites at intervals along the way. Hikers may stay overnight in these campsites only. A park use permit is required. Because of the popularity of back-country hiking in Jasper, the park allows reservations for up to thirty-five percent of a trail's capacity. The remaining sixty-five percent of the campsites are on a first-come, first-served basis. Write to the Superintendent for further information. When you get to the park, check at the Information Centre or (in summer only) the Icefields Centre, for the latest trail conditions and to pick up your park use permit.

Other Accommodation, Gas, Food and Supplies

Jasper is a townsite of about four thousand permanent residents and hundreds of thousands of visitors, winter and summer. Jasper has all types of indoor accommodation, a full range of restaurants, grocery stores, hardware and supply stores, curio and gift shops, filling stations, laundromats, etc. In the centre of town is the Jasper National Park Information Centre. There is also gas at a small cafe at Pocahantas, at the junction with the Miette Hot Springs road. There is a restaurant at Maligne Canyon and Maligne Lake. There are bungalows and a restaurant at the Miette Hot Springs area.

Recreational Services

Hiking   The park has several short, self-guiding trails, a number of them ranging from four to twelve kilometres (three to eight miles) one way, and many lengthy back-country trails. Ask at the Information Centre for information on day hikes. The snow does not clear, for the upper elevations, until late June or early July.

Fishing   Most of the glacial lakes are not good for fishing. However, Maligne Lake was stocked years ago, and the fish now maintain their numbers naturally. There is a boat-and-tackle rental there. A National Parks fishing licence is required. A brochure on regulations is available at the Information Centre.

Boating   Motor boats are allowed on Pyramid and Medicine Lakes. In most other lakes you can use canoes, rowboats or kayaks. Electric trolling motors are also allowed. Remember that the waters in Jasper are extremely cold, and accidents can be fatal. There are commercially operated rafting tours on the Athabasca and Maligne Rivers. Write to the Chamber of Commerce, for more information.

Swimming   Miette Hotsprings is for soaking, rather than swimming. The water is cooled from 54°C to 37°C (130°F to 100°F), for visitor use. There are suit and towel rentals at a moderate cost.

Tennis   There are six clay courts, maintained by the park, at the townsite recreational centre. No fee is charged. Jasper Park Lodge also has courts.

Golf   There is an eighteen-hole course at the Jasper Park Lodge; inquire there for information on use by non-guests.

Winter Use   Jasper is heavily used for downhill skiing at the commercially-run Marmot Basin, and for cross-country skiing throughout the park. Wapiti Campground parking lot, with electrical hook-ups, water and toilets, is kept open in winter as a self-registering campground. Write to the Superintendent for information on park-run winter use, and to the Chamber of Commerce about downhill skiing.

Further Reading

Jasper National Park by George Brybyein and Dorothy Dickson (G.B. Publishing, 1981)
See titles listed in the chapter Yoho National Park.

FOR MORE INFORMATION

The Superintendent
Jasper National Park
Box 10
Jasper, Alberta
T0E IE0

Phone: (403) 852-6161

Jasper Park Chamber of Commerce
Box 98
Jasper, Alberta
T0E 1E0

Phone: (403) 852-3858

ELK ISLAND

NATIONAL PARK

When I first went to Elk Island, I wondered where the island was. I drove past massive, muscular bison, went by beaver dams, saw people golfing and canoeing, set up my tent—but still no island. In fact, other than the impressive bison just a few feet from the car, things looked rather ordinary. But, after a few hours and, even more, after a few days, it became clear that Elk Island was a special place.

Staying in the park awhile, walking the trails and talking with the interpreters, I soon learned why Elk Island National Park is an island. First, it is an island in terms of its geological history and present-day topography. It is quite different from the nearly flat plains that spread out on every side. Secondly, it is an island of protection and preservation. A 2.5-metre (8-foot) fence surrounds the park; plants and animals can live almost undisturbed by human intervention.

Elk Island is oblong in shape, 195 square kilometres (75 square miles). It is situated just 45 kilometres (28 miles) east of Edmonton, in the Beaver Hills, where the terrain is that rather lumpy type called "knob and kettle." Alberta's plains are interrupted in several places by similar hilly land formations, which were formed because glaciers stagnated there. The glaciers would increase slightly in winter, melt a bit in summer, without much significant movement. At their tips, big chunks of ice would crumble off. When the glaciers retreated permanently, they left great amounts of debris around remaining chunks of ice. This debris formed knobs, and the melting ice chunks eventually formed kettle ponds.

When left to themselves, these hilly areas turn into very rich habitat for plants and animals. Year-round water supply and a good start on soil development make for luxuriant plant growth, on land and in the water. The surrounding plains are good for grazing animals to forage. The hilly terrain provides good shelter against winter blasts or baking sun. Buffalo, elk, moose, deer and small mammals can have their young here in relative safety, and then range out on the prairies at will. These mammals, in turn, provide food for predators like the lynx and coyote.

The kettles play a major role in the life cycle of waterbirds. These birds need lots of aquatic plants and ooze to feed on, and plenty of privacy, among cattails and reeds at the water's edge, in order to raise their young safely. Kettles are extremely rich in plant life, because they are shallow and, in summer, readily warmed by the sun. When plants die, their remains stay in the kettles, since there are few streams feeding or draining the ponds. Over time, large amounts of decayed organic material collect so, although kettles have a poor supply of oxygen, they contain rich supplies of nutrients for more plants to grow. These eutrophic ponds form a rather poor environment for fish. About the only fish that thrive are minnows and sticklebacks, both very small. They are good food for herons, kingfishers and grebes, however.

How to See the Park

Elk Island is a centralized park, with one main road leading from its southern to northern borders. About 14 kilometres (8.5 miles) north from Highway 16 is the **Astotin Recreation Area**, with picnicking, camping, canoeing, golfing, the Ukrainian Pioneer Home, the Astotin Interpretive Centre, and the start of several of the self-guiding trails. The other trails and picnic areas, and the buffalo paddock, are all just off the highway, north or south of Astotin.

For all trails in the park, I highly recommend waterproof footwear and mosquito repellent, especially during the rainy period in late June and July. The beaver are so industrious that even boardwalk sections of trails can be under several centimetres of water, and the mosquitoes abound in the very moist habitat.

Knobs, Kettles and Forests

Two trails are particularly good for getting close to the knob-and-kettle terrain, with its multitude of eutrophic lakes and ponds, its poplar groves or small stands of mixed-wood forest. For an easy trek, the best overall trail is **Amisk Wuché.*** The trail begins on the east side of the parkway, .5 kilometres north of the turnoff into the Astotin Recreation Area. Amisk Wuché winds around and over parts of a very irregularly shaped lake. This is a self-guiding trail, with boardwalks and signs describing the landscape features of the present-day park. In the sunny spots of open meadows, I saw a number of butterflies—mourning cloaks and anglewings, especially. And lots of dragonflies. Some of the time, the trail is in white spruce for-

*Pronounced, run on, uhMISKwushay. This is Cree for "Beaver Hills".

est, and at other times it is through the far more common aspen forest, with balsam poplar, white birch and trembling aspen. The latter forest makes the most rapid recovery from fire.

The lake is a wonderful habitat for animal life of many sorts—the ducks plow through the duck weed, and beaver flood the path in places. The thrill for me, though, was a mink that came up on the boardwalk ahead of me. It saw me, stopped, ran toward me a few feet, stood on its hind legs and peered intently, then scampered back into the cattails.

Red-necked grebe

To get a real overview of knob and kettle terrain, take the **Moss Lake Trail**. It is a much longer trail than Amisk Wuché, a blown-up version of that shorter, self-guiding trail. Moss Lake is thirteen kilometres (eight miles) long. The trail took me four hours, including many stops for photographing, a lunch break and a big detour around a basking bull bison. There are also a number of wet spots to avoid. The trail is a circle, and is very well marked. It goes up small hills, through small depressions, and past many ponds, meadows and marshy areas.

Within the knob-and-kettle environment, the water worlds deserve special attention. For one thing, there are over 250 lakes and ponds in the park, occupying twenty percent of its surface area. These ponds are mostly eutrophic. To get an impression of the life and processes of a pond, take the **Lakeshore Trail** north of Sandy Beach, the adjoining **Point of Good Hope Trail/Living Waters Boardwalk** just down the slope from the Astotin Interpretive Centre south of the beach, or the paved **Shoreline Trail** that starts just west of the end of the golf course parking lot. All offer superb chances to share the water world of Elk Island. Living Waters is the shortest, a small looping boardwalk around a marshy point. There are very well presented pictorial signs describing what lives beneath, on and above these teeming waters.

Two other trails are extremely good for bird and beaver watching. **Lakeview Trail** is warbler territory, but leads through several habitat types, thereby increasing the chances of seeing a diversity of birdlife. It also traverses an active beaver dam. This is a self-guiding trail, with a brochure describing wetlands development and succession, and the role beavers play in the process. If you go to the Shoreline Trail early in the morning, or about an hour or so before sunset, and walk quietly, I guaran-

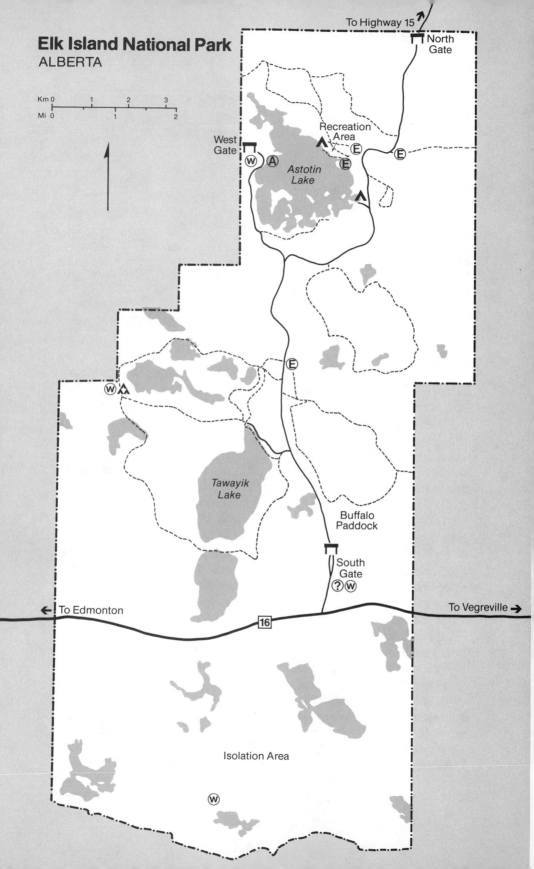

tee beaver. From the Shoreline Trail, an isthmus extends into the Beaver Bay picnic area; I watched beaver there for an hour. On the east side of the narrow band of ground, there are picnic tables, pump, and pit toilets. Just past this point, look out into the water, and see if there is a little reed island, perhaps thirty centimetres (one foot) across. If so, it's the nest of the park's "totem" bird, the red-necked grebe. I saw it there, gleaming gun-metal grey in the evening light, its rusty neck and white cheek craning now and then, to keep me in view. You can hear it, too, almost around the clock, making unearthly screaming and squealing noises, in what seems to be courtship and pair-maintenance behaviour.

Island of Protection and Preservation

The beaver and the large grazing animals, such as bison and elk, have a special history here. There are several places in the park devoted to enhancing the visitor's awareness of these animals. As far as beaver are concerned, any pond is likely to have its domed beaver lodge. There's one in the marshy area between the golf course parking lot and the campground access road, for instance. The **Beaver Hills Exhibit** and **Beaver Pond Trail**, just a short drive north of the Amisk Wuché, tells the story of the beaver in Elk Island. Be sure to wear waterproof footwear for this and the other trails.

As for bison and elk, the former are very visible and, in August and September at least, the latter are very audible. A few of the plains bison are maintained during the summer months, in an enclosure (Bison Paddock) at the south end of the park. Visitors can drive on a winding road, and are likely to see some of the bison, unless it's high noon and they're tucked in the poplar stands, avoiding the sun. In early August, however, there was absolutely no need to rely on the paddock to see bison. There seemed always to be some alongside the main parkway. Once, I found myself in the middle of a herd of fifty or so—bulls, cows and calves. Mid-July to late August is the rutting season, and the male bison can be quite aggressive. Occasionally, a car is butted and, if you're on a trail and meet a buffalo, it's best to give it a very wide berth.

The main parkway is a scenic drive, built lower, and for slower speeds, than other secondary highways. Its dips and curves give you a clear sense of the rolling landscape, dotted with lakes and ponds. The abundance of hoofed animals in the park requires drivers to exercise extra caution when using the parkway, day or night.

Elk are well established in the park but, in contrast to the bison, are quite secretive. I didn't see any, but I heard them every night. From mid-August to early October, they, too, are in rut and, late at night and in the very early morning hours, they bugle. The high notes are audible from far away, extraordinarily pure, like some ethereal human voice. As with so many experiences in Elk Island, you need to take time to wander away from the recreation area, or be by the lakeshore at very quiet times, to have a sense of the fullness of the natural world, in what is an oasis, even more than an island.

Park Services and Facilities

An attractive Information Centre is located near the south entrance. Visitors can examine displays on the park, ask the staff for suggestions, and pick up brochures, maps, etc.

Interpretive Programme
The Astotin Interpretive Centre, south of the beach, opened in June 1984. It has an information desk, a lobby display on various aspects of the park, the Friends of Elk Island bookstore, a theatre seating 150 people, where slide programmes, films, puppet shows and drama presentations are offered, and an exterior observation deck with telescope. Outdoor drama presentations are offered on special occasions, as well as special events geared to the seasons. Evening programmes run from mid-June until Labour Day, four nights a week.

Elk Island Radio broadcasts continuous, fifteen-minute, seasonal messages; topics include wildlife viewing, hiking, skiing, history and wildlife management. Dial 1540 AM (English), 1210 AM (French).

Camping
Sandy Beach Campground, located in the Astotin Recreation Area, has sixty-eight sites, plus forty-four sites in a walk-in tenting area, and an overflow site nearby. There are centrally located kitchen shelters and firewood, clean washrooms with hot and cold running water and showers, and picnic tables and fire boxes at each campsite (in the campground, but not available in the tenting and overflow areas). No hook-ups are available. The sanitary station is located behind the Snack Bar, south of the main parking lot, by the beach. Back-country camping in the summer and winter is available at the **Oster Lake Group Tenting Area** (a back-country user permit is required). Winter camping is also available in the Astotin Recreation Area, on boulevards surrounding the Boat Launch parking lot.

Group Tenting
Back-country camping in summer and winter is available for groups, individual hikers, and cross-country skiers at the Oster Lake Group Tenting

Plains bison

Area. Write to the Superintendent for information, or call (403) 992-6380. Reservations are required; tenting only is allowed.

Other Accommodation, Gas, Food and Supplies
Edmonton is a thirty-minute drive away, and it provides for all needs. Fort Saskatchewan is twenty-five kilometres (fifteen miles) west of the park, and Lamont is five kilometres (three miles) north. Both places can offer accommodation, gas and supplies.

Recreational Services
Hiking   There are fourteen established trails in the park, extending 103 kilometres. Check with staff for the condition of the larger ones. You can go completely around Tawayik Lake in the winter only; the narrows are too marshy and wet in the summer. The trails aren't rugged or steep, but they can be mushy. Dogs are not allowed on trails, because of potential conflicts with bison, and elsewhere they must be on leashes at all times.

Boating   No motorized boats are allowed in the park, but canoeing, windsurfing and sailing are allowed on Astotin Lake. During the nesting season, one arm of Astotin is off-limits to boats. It is signed accordingly, and there is still lots of room.

This sculptured mushroom is extremely poisonous

Swimming   You can sunbathe at Sandy Beach, but swimming is not recommended. The water is shallow and warm, and there is swimmer's itch at some times in the summer. This is caused by a microscopic, free-swimming larval worm, whose alternate hosts are usually snails, ducks, beaver or muskrats. It is harmless but irritating; it can be minimized by showering immediately after swimming and towelling vigorously and carefully. There is a changing area, with cold showers but no lockers. The beach area also has a take-out snack bar. Charcoal briquets, ice, and some other picnicking supplies can be purchased.

Golf   There is a nine-hole golf course near Sandy Beach. A small fee is required. There is a pro shop, rental of clubs and carts, and a licensed, cafeteria-style restaurant.

Winter Use   The summer hiking trails are used for cross-country skiing and snowshoeing (Amisk Wuché and Lakeview trails) in winter. Winter camping is permitted at the Boat Launch parking lot, in the Astotin Recreation Area (tenters can use the grassed borders of the parking lot),

Interpretive programme by the shores of the Astotin

and by reservation at the Oster Lake Group Tenting Area. There are chemical toilets at several of the trailheads, as well as at the Boat Launch parking lot. Picnic shelters, with firewood and stoves, are available for winter use at the Tawayik Lake picnic area, and in the Astotin Recreation Area.

Further Reading

Walk on the Wild Side - An All Season Trail Guide to Elk Island by Jean Burgess (Friends of Elk Island Society, 1986)
Finding Birds in Elk Island National Park by Judith Cornish (Friends of Elk Island Society, 1988)

FOR MORE INFORMATION
The Superintendent
Elk Island National Park
R. R. 1, Site 4
Fort Saskatchewan, Alberta
T8L 2N7
Phone: (403) 992-6380

KLUANE

NATIONAL PARK

There are two Kluanes* really, but only one, the greenbelt of lowland forests and broad valleys, is accessible to the general visitor. It is well worth turning off the Alaska Highway and taking a few hours, or even days, to explore this Kluane. The other Kluane, a land of glaciers and mountains, challenges the wilderness traveller, who may have prepared months in advance for an extended visit.

Kluane, a high mountain wilderness park, is in the Yukon, just two hours' drive west of Whitehorse. Two mountain ranges run parallel through the park in a south-easterly direction; the ice-bound St. Elias to the west, and the lower Kluane, or Front Range, Mountains near the eastern edge. The Front Range creates a 2,400-metre (8,000-foot)-high barrier along the Haines-Alaska Highway, almost always obscuring the towering St. Elias Mountains behind it.

The mountains of Kluane are the youngest and most active in North America, and the area is the most earthquake-prone in Canada. There are, on average, a thousand tremors a year there! Most are barely perceptible to human senses but, at the park's Visitor Reception Centre at Haines Junction, a working seismograph is on display. It picks up even slight tremors, and you have a good chance of seeing evidence of the shifts of the earth beneath you.

The shaping of the young, rugged landscape is the theme of the park's interpretive programme. It is fascinating to learn how contours, altitude and location have created Kluane's distinctive character. The ridges of the St. Elias Mountains are covered in snow, compacted over millenia, and linked to form the largest, most continuous icefields outside the north and south polar regions. Extending from these icefields are glaciers: Kluane has four thousand of them. Glaciers have a very active life, as they cut,

*Pronounced Kloo-ah-ney

113

grind and tear their way to lower levels. These rivers of ice usually travel very slowly. Occasionally, however, they flow at astonishing rates, becoming what is known as "surging glaciers." In the summer of 1967, Steeles glacier, on the northwest boundary of the park, began moving at a rate of twelve metres (forty feet) a day! In two years, it travelled more than eight kilometres (five miles) down its valley. Kluane has at least six surging glaciers but, unfortunately, none is accessible to the casual visitor.

Another type of glacier, easily seen from the main highway, is the rock glacier. Like an ice glacier, it is a flowing mass, but what moves are rocks that have collected in, and sheared from, high, narrow valleys. The rocks move over a skidding surface of ice that collects below.

But there is more than mountains, ice and snow in Kluane. The outer, eastern third of the park is lowland, called greenbelt. This is the environment most visitors will experience directly. The greenbelt area is phenomenally rich in plant and animal life, for several reasons. First, the greenbelt encompasses a variety of habitats, from broad river valleys with gravelly plains sloping upwards, to marshes, dense forest stands, alpine meadows, bare mountain slopes of the Front Range, and alpine tundra. Second, the greenbelt is relatively narrow, so that animals fill every suitable niche. Finally, as the animals are protected against hunters, they reach the maximum numbers that this rich environment can support.

Kluane is famous for having the largest known concentration of Dall sheep. Grizzly bears, too, are common here; there are perhaps 250 of them. This is one of the most densely concentrated populations in all of the national parks. Grizzlies are not often seen, though in summer they may roam anywhere in the greenbelt zone. There are also a number of black bears in the park. They stay fairly close to the patches of forest and are easily displaced by the more aggressive grizzlies, in those lowland areas where they overlap in summer. Campers are required to do their part to keep the bears wild, by putting all garbage in special containers in the campground, by putting food in bear-proof containers while in the back country, and by packing out all garbage from the back country when they leave.

Until the last century, there seems to have been no permanent human habitation in the Kluane area. Archeological records show that various aboriginal people did pass through, to take advantage of salmon runs or to hunt. As fur trading developed, trapping spread to the area and, eventually, a few Native people probably did live there year round.

Today, a small Indian village lies just outside the southern park boundary. It has been occupied for a century—the longest permanent habitation in the area. The village is situated on the Klukshu Creek, a salmon-spawning stream. Because of their aboriginal rights, the Indians are able to continue trapping fish for their own use. I was fascinated to see the weir system, the cleaning stands, and drying towers—not much has changed over all this time.

Surveyors and explorers came here, especially in the last half of the nineteenth century. But it was the search for gold in the streams, and for adventure in the mountains, that brought the major influx of people. The Klondike Gold Rush of 1897, the Kluane Gold Rush in 1904, and a subsequent rush in 1917, brought many prospectors.

Fire and time etch the tree, fireweed surrounds it

Kluane's position, between Alaska and the west coast, gave it great strategic importance during World War II. The Alaska Highway was built in a scant nine months, in 1941, to link north and south. Later improvements to the highway have made visiting the Yukon and Kluane National Park relatively easy.

The extreme ruggedness and great height of the mountains of Kluane attract mountaineers and scientists. The most famous climb, in the early mountaineering days, was the ascent, in 1897, of Mount St. Elias by the renowned Duke of Abruzzi. The ascent of Mount Logan, at 5,951 metres (19,525 feet) Kluane's highest peak, (the highest mountain in Canada, and the second highest in North America) was not achieved until 1925. Since then, it has been climbed over twenty times. Many of the other mountains of the St. Elias range have been climbed, as well.

How to See the Park

The first thing to do in the park is to go to the Visitor Centre at Haines Junction or the Visitor Centre at Sheep Mountain, at the northern edge of the park, on the Alaska Highway. Staff are on hand to tell you about the park, to give you the schedule of interpretive events, to help you plan hikes or side trips by car, and to register you for overnight back-country trips. Don't miss the award-winning slide show, *Kluane*, in the Haines Junction Visitor Centre, or any of the other audio-visual material that may be available.

The Back Country
The back country at Kluane requires the kind of experience and prepared-

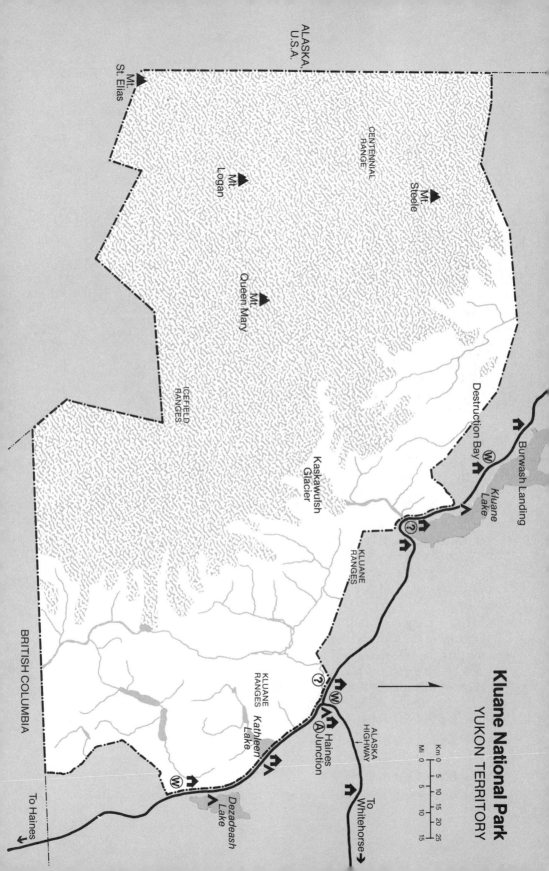

ness that most park visitors don't have. The back-country visitor must register with the wardens, or at the Visitor Reception Centre, and it's a good idea to write to the park beforehand, for hiking brochures, reports on trail conditions, etc., so that proper planning can be done.

It is possible to visit the back country with one of the local commercial tour-guiding outfits. This seems, to me, a good way to get out for a few days or weeks, when you don't have complete equipment, or are lacking back-country experience.

It is a disappointment to the car-based visitor not to be able to see, or visit, those massive mountains or great rivers of ice, which this park preserves for us all. The closest people can come, though relatively few do, is a twenty-seven-kilometre (seventeen-mile), two-day walk to the foot of the **Kaskawulsh Glacier**. A plane can provide a good overview, at least. A commercial, small-plane touring service operates out of Burwash Landing. You can select one of several routes, with varying flight durations (one to four hours). If there are four in the party, to share costs, the price is reasonable. Weather is very unpredictable in the area, so you cannot always be sure of actually being able to get a flight. The Visitor Centre and local stores, motels or restaurants have relevant information sheets.

Hiking in the Lowlands

The phenomenon of rock glaciers is easily seen from the road. A fifteen-minute drive south of **Kathleen Lake** takes you to the **Rock Glacier Trail**. It is about 1.5 kilometres (less than a mile) long, leading first over a stream, then through a long, damp, wooded area, full of monks' hoods and other flowers, and then up onto a rock glacier. Once you see this rock glacier, you realize that they occur every few kilometres, along much of the Front Range Mountains. They look like dark, blunt rivers of rock, running perpendicular to the direction of the highway.

The area east of the Front Range Mountains, running roughly parallel to the Haines-Alaska Highway, is the most-travelled part of the park. The campground is here, at Kathleen Lake. You can stop at a number of scenic car pull-outs with interpretive signs. There are many picnic or fishing spots, and Kathleen Lake itself is a major day-use area for motorboating, fishing, hiking and picnicking.

Most of the shorter hiking trails start at the highway. Several are excellent for exploring the greenbelt. You can get a descriptive brochure from the Visitor Centre. Here are some descriptions of several.*

*Because of uncertain weather, I was able to hike only the Auriol Range Trail, so I am indebted to Park Interpreter Allison Wood for these descriptions of trails to St. Elias Lake, Auriol Range and Sheep Mountain.

The **St. Elias Trail** is approximately 4 kilometres (2.5 miles) long. It is a steady climb to the lake, with a rise in elevation of about 150 metres (490 feet). The trail is an old mining road, blocked off to public vehicles. Watch for mountain goats around the lake, and for small mammals and birds. Hikers can use the primitive campsite at the lake. A food cache, a campfire circle and a pit toilet are provided.

The **Auriol Range Trail** is the most accessible hiking trail from Haines Junction. The trailhead is five kilometres (three miles) southeast of Haines Junction, on the Haines Highway. Watch for road signs. A parking area is provided. The loop is twenty-five kilometres (eleven miles) long. Allow six to eight hours to complete it. The trail covers easy terrain, but requires steady climbing. In winter, it's recommended for intermediate skiers. It provides a quick route to the alpine country of the St. Elias Mountains. You ascend through three distinct vegetation zones; the montane, the sub-alpine and the alpine. From various points along the trail, panoramic views of the frontal ranges and the broad **Shakwak Valley** can be enjoyed. Note the rock glaciers, the prominent landforms of the Auriol Range, and the faults of the Shakwak Valley. The trail actually follows an active fault line, the Denali.

The Auriol Trail offers a primitive campground, equipped with four tent sites, pit toilet and a cache to store food.

The **Sheep Mountain Trail** starts just beyond the Sheep Mountain Visitor Centre. From the centre, drive about two kilometres (one mile) down the access road to the gate. You can park there overnight, and a pit toilet is provided. On foot, follow the road 160 metres (176 yards) down, and turn right at the first fork. This mining road climbs Sheep Mountain gradually for eight kilometres (five miles). This path will not take you up to the top. You can find your own way up, but it is a long steep climb! This is the best place to see Dall sheep. In summer, they are usually in the higher alpine meadows; be prepared for a long, all-day hike to reach them. Water is not always available, so take a water bottle. Once you are up high, go across **Sheep Creek**—you'll see Sheep Bullion Plateau, known for its brilliant array of wild flowers, and numerous grizzlies.

The closest camping to the Sheep Mountain Trail is 9.5 kilometres (6 miles) north of the Information Centre, on the Alaska Highway at Cottonwood Park.

Human History

To appreciate the history of the Native peoples of the area, visit **Klukshu Village**, outside the southern border of the park. A small gift shop, furnished with antique tools and equipment, sells a modest selection of Native handicrafts. At the back of the village is the Klukshu Creek and, in

Kaskawulsh Glacier — 27 kilometres into the back country

late summer, you may see the bright-red spawning salmon, caught in the weirs laid across most of the stream.

To get a sense of the gold-mining days, you can visit the ghost town of **Silver City**, a few minutes' drive along the southern edge of Kluane Lake. This village had a North West Mounted Police station and barracks, a roadhouse and stables. Many of the buildings still stand, though their roofs are caved in and the floors are not in much better shape. It is a dramatic and eerie place to visit, though the multitude of completely spoiled arctic ground squirrels begging for food provides a winsome touch. The town is not protected in any way, so visitors must take responsibility for leaving everything intact.

The best place to see something of the mountaineering history is the Visitor Centre. It has an excellent display of photographs and artifacts of the Duke of Abruzzi's climb. Those big, sepia photographs and weathered equipment tell quite a tale.

Park Services and Facilities

Interpretive Programme
The summer interpretive programme provides the day visitor or car camper with the best introduction to the park. Ask for a schedule from the

At Silver City ghost town

centre, or check the bulletin board at the Kathleen Lake Campground or picnic area. I went to talks on the gold rush, on how to hike in the back country, on photographing nature, and on the geological history of the park.

During the summer, the members of staff, or contract guides, take a small group of people on day hikes to the back country. If you know when you'll be arriving, call ahead to find out when the next hike is planned, and if you can join up. I missed out on this opportunity, and really regret it. Unfortunately, financial cutbacks are threatening Kluane's interpretive programme. I hope it survives!

Camping

There is one park campground, at **Kathleen Lake**, about a twenty-minute drive south of Haines Junction. It has forty-one campsites in a lightly wooded area, with trembling aspen and a carpet of flowers between sites. It is open from mid-June to mid-September. There are flush toilets, but no washrooms. Water must be pumped; bring a container with a handle over the top. Picnic tables and fire grates stand at each site; firewood is provided. There is a small, outdoor campfire circle, where evening interpretive programmes are often held. The maximum length of stay is fourteen days.

Less than a kilometre from the campsite is the Kathleen Lake Day Use Area, and there is a trail from there, which goes very far around the west side of the lake.

Other Camping

The Yukon Territory has a very large network of campgrounds, and there are several sites all along the highway, but on the eastern side of the road, which is not park land. Most of these campgrounds are directly on the shore of a lake or stream, and fishing is a popular pastime. They provide water, pit toilets, and picnic tables. One lies just east of Haines Junction, three between there and the northern park boundary, and one at Dezadeash Lake, about fifteen-minutes' drive south of Kathleen Lake.

Other Accommodation, Gas, Food and Supplies

Haines Junction has a couple of modest hotels, and there is a motel/restaurant at Dezadeash Lake. Write to the park Visitors' Service for listings, or to Tourism Yukon.

Whitehorse is the largest centre for gas, food and camping supplies. There is a reasonable choice of stores. Prices do not seem to be inflated, considering transportation distances and short summers.

Parks Canada/L. Halverson

Grizzlies are at home in all the western mountain parks. This grizzly (photographed in Kootenany) is feeding on the remains of a black bear

At Haines Junction, there are several gas stations and small general stores. I was able to get everything I needed. Gas is available at Dezadeash, Kathleen Lake Lodge, Mackintosh and Bayshore.

There are several small café/restaurants at Haines Junction, and another near Kathleen Lake. There is a wilderness resort at Dezadeash Lake.

Outfitters and Guides

The park has a symbiotic relationship with local back-country outfitters and guides. For a number of visitors, particularly those from other countries, or those with limited time or experience, hiring an outfitter or guiding service can be very useful. A wide variety of services is offered; hiking, going by pack horse, going on day trips, or much longer ones. Write the park for listings, then contact the outfitters directly.

Recreational Services

Boating   Motor boats are allowed on Kathleen Lake. It is a big lake, which can get very rough, very quickly, so experience and caution are called for. Canoeing is not recommended.

Fishing   Fishing is especially good at Kathleen Lake, and reasonable in other lakes and streams. Ask for copies of National Park regulations, and buy the required permit at the Visitor Centre.

Climbing and Mountaineering   For overnight or trips of a few days in the back country of the greenbelt, you must register in and out with the park. For a trip into St. Elias and the Icefield Ranges, a permit must be obtained from the Warden Service of the park, at least three months in advance. The Warden Service must be informed as to the skill and experience level of the group, its provision for supplies, air and radio support, and there must be a physician's certificate of health for each party member.

Winter Use   There are seven cross-country and snowshoe trails in the park, a snowmobiling area at Kathleen Lake, and one area for dogsledding. The Visitor Centre is open weekdays during office hours and, occasionally, it holds evening programmes.

How to Get There

It is not particularly difficult to get to Kluane, but the trip can be time-consuming and expensive. You can take the Alaska Highway, or the Alaska or British Columbia auto-ferry system from Seattle or Vancouver. Alternatively, a number of commercial tour buses leave from Prince Rupert, sometimes in conjunction with the ferries. I flew to Whitehorse from Edmonton and rented a car, which I had booked with my plane ticket. The round-trip airfare was quite reasonable, but the five days' rental of the car ran to nearly twice the total of the airfare! I think the ideal way to travel would be to go with several others, sharing the cost of a camper or van, and taking two or three weeks for the whole trip from the south.

Further Reading

Kluane: Pinnacle of the Yukon edited by John Theberge (Doubleday Canada, 1980)

FOR MORE INFORMATION

The Superintendent
Kluane National Park
Haines Junction,
Yukon Territory
Y0B IL0

Tourism Yukon
Government of Yukon
Box 2703—YN
Whitehorse,
Yukon Territory

Phone: (403) 634-2251
Fax: (403) 634-2686

NORTHERN YUKON

NATIONAL PARK

Northern Yukon National Park is at the far northwest boundary of the Yukon Territory. It was established in 1984, and protects ten thousand square kilometres of some of the most productive wilderness in the Arctic. Native people continue to lead their lives in the park, as they follow the caribou, fish and hunt. The Porcupine caribou herd, at over 150,000 animals, makes this area its home, and is a key to the aboriginal lifestyle.

All three species of bear (grizzly, polar and black) are found here, with grizzlies being the most widely distributed type. Dall's sheep and Arctic fox are numerous.

The land itself is a gentle slope, rising from the Beaufort coastal plain. The British Mountains rise some 1,800 metres along the western edge of the park. Three main rivers wend their way to the Beaufort Sea. They are the Malcolm, the Firth and the Babbage.

There are no visitor facilities in the park, because it is exclusively a wilderness preserve. Most visitation occurs through organized tours. People backpack in, and whitewater rafting on the Firth is a favourite activity. There is also some recreational sport fishing. There are no roads into the park, with the nearest all-weather road ending in Inuvik, over two hundred kilometres from the eastern park boundary. Some people come in by charter plane, but the trip must be approved by the park beforehand, and aircraft access is restricted to only a few locations in the park.

It is important to come prepared, especially if you are unescorted, because this rugged land has potential natural hazards at any time. Weather is very unpredictable, and temperatures can plunge below zero in any month of the year. The waters are frigid year-round, and the biting insects are daunting. So be sure to write to the Superintendent for a list of outfitters, and for other information about visiting the park. You'll want to be able to get the most out of your trip, and preparedness is the key.

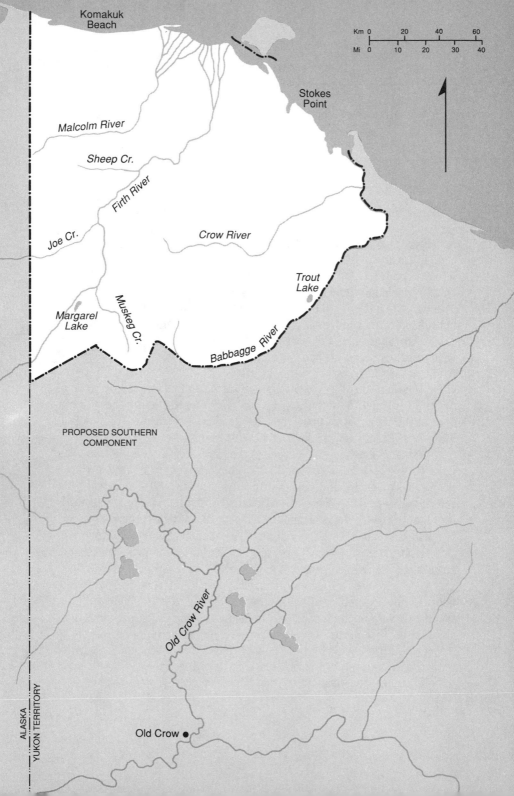

Northern Yukon National Park
YUKON

BEAUFORT SEA

Komakuk
Beach

Stokes
Point

Malcolm River

Sheep Cr.

Firth River

Joe Cr.

Crow River

Trout
Lake

Margarel
Lake

Muskeg Cr.

Babbagge River

PROPOSED SOUTHERN
COMPONENT

Old Crow River

ALASKA

YUKON TERRITORY

Old Crow

Km	0		20		40		60
Mi	0	10		20		30		40

FOR MORE INFORMATION

The Superintendent
Kluane/Northern Yukon National Park
Haines Junction, Yukon Territory
Y0B 1L0

Phone: (403) 634-2251

NAHANNI

NATIONAL PARK RESERVE

Rivers: raging or calm, flat and meandering or plunging through some of the deepest river canyons in the world—rivers and their mountain context are the basis of Nahanni National Park Reserve. The park is 4,784 square kilometres (1,840 square miles) large, encompassing over 320 kilometres (200 miles) of the 400-kilometre (250-mile)-long South Nahanni River. The long, thin shape of the park is distorted by a spur near its centre, which extends southwest for about 120 kilometres (72 miles), including about half of the Flat River. The setting for the park is the Mackenzie Mountains, in the southwest corner of the Northwest Territories.

The spectacular scenery, the distinctive geological history and landforms, the wealth of wildlife, and the unspoiled character of the South Nahanni/Flat River ecosystem have resulted in Nahanni being one of the first choices of UNESCO for a World Heritage Site, a site of such marvellous and unique qualities that it is to be drawn to the attention of the whole world, and protected for all people. It is also one of Canada's Heritage Rivers.

How to See the Park*

Glaciation has played a major and varied role in shaping this park, as it has in the shaping of most of Canada. Glaciers had much to do with the origins of the central feature of the park, **Virginia Falls**, one of the most impressive falls in Canada, if not the world. The falls are over 92 metres

---

*I was not able to visit Nahanni. For information on the park, I have relied on interviews with Lou Comin, chief warden of Nahanni for six years, and written material from Parks Canada, and from journals, etc. The writings of Derek Ford and George A. Brook were particularly useful. Sean Meggs provided information for this revised edition.

(300 feet) high. They are about 200 metres (656 feet) wide, and are broken in the middle by a huge chunk of rock, which seems like a small mountain in itself. The glacier tongue that gouged out the valley west of here, cut away a piece of the **Sunblood Mountain**, which stood in the way of its forward push. When the ice began to melt and recede at the glacier tip, a river was created by melt water. This river cut down into the soft sedimentary rock, undercutting the upper levels as it hit bottom, and pounded against the lowest levels. Just as at Niagara Falls, the top layers would break off, the river would begin cutting a new lower level, the new upper level would topple for lack of support, and the falls would move a few more metres up the river, leaving a deep gorge behind.

Above the Virginia Falls, the river course is slow and meandering, with only a slight gradient. Below the falls, it begins a steep descent. It crashes through hairpin turns and narrow chutes, and caroms through three canyons, with walls as high as 1,500 metres (4,920 feet). There is a contradiction here: how is it that such a fast river, running over soft limestone, has such a winding course? Why hasn't it carved out a much straighter path for itself, like the powerful rivers of Banff or Jasper? If the river alone doesn't have the power to cut, why haven't glaciers forged the straight, U-shaped river valleys of the west of the park?

There are two parts to the answer to the riddle of the Nahanni's winding plunge. First, this section of the park was not covered by glaciers during the last Ice Age, so no straight valleys were formed. The second part of the answer is a phenomenon called antecedance, that is, the river existed here *before* the three mountain ranges that intersect it. Long ago, this area, east of Virginia Falls, was fairly flat. Rivers did flow from higher land in the west, but the gradient was not great and, when they reached flat ground, they began to wander and twist. But then, enormous pressures from deep in the earth folded the earth's crust into individual mountain ranges, which now compose the three extraordinarily steep canyons. At about the same rate at which the mountains were uplifted, the river cut down through the soft rock, so its course was not greatly deflected.

Now and then, the river straightens itself a little, as the rushing water finds an even weaker spot in the rock, and leaps from one curve of a meander to its far side, taking a shortcut and stranding a loop of riverbed. You can see an example of this action at the extremely narrow section of the third canyon, called **The Gate**.

At the eastern edge of the park, glaciation once again played a role. Here, the glaciers filled the final mountain gateway for the South Nahanni, at what is now called **Twisted Mountain**, and blocked the flow of river water from the west. Over thousands of years, the water built up and flooded backwards, making lakes of whole valleys that once had only rivers at their lowest point. When the ice melted, the valleys could drain;

there was, once again, only a river at the valley bottom, collecting water from the run-off of rain or snow, and etching its way down through the soft sediment. Deep gorges have been formed at the centres of the valleys, and forests grow well on the debris of old lakes. This is the story of the **Flat River**. Its rapids at high elevations, and its calm flow and wildlife-rich floodplains, where it meets the South Nahanni, are magnificent additions to the amazing diversity of this park.

A shorebird feeds at Rabbitkettle Hotsprings

Parks Canada

Though the South Nahanni and Flat Rivers and their immediate environs make up the central elements of the park, there are two other places along the traveller's route, which contribute greatly to its fascination. One is **Rabbitkettle Hot Springs**, at the far western border of the park, and the other is the karstlands, which begin at the **First Canyon** and extend north for fifty kilometres (thirty-one miles) in a narrow band from the canyon's north bank.

The 21°C (70°F) water of Rabbitkettle Hot Springs wells up through highly mineralized rock, some of which dissolves and is carried to the surface of the earth. Here, the rapid cooling causes the minerals to separate from their watery medium and settle on the ground. This has resulted in a build-up of circular ponds, made up of *tufa*, a brightly-coloured calcium carbonate. There are two of these water-soaked mounds. The more distinctly formed **North Mound** rises over the surrounding area about twenty-seven metres (ninety feet). Its overall height is achieved by a stairstepping of small, semi-circular terraces, up to circular kettles at the top. Visitors can reach the kettles only when escorted by a warden, since this area is so fragile. There is a warden at the Rabbitkettle Lake warden station during the summer operating season, from July 1 through August 31. The warden has a number of functions, including providing information on this area and the park in general, giving interpretive tours to the Tufa Mounds, registering people for wilderness trips through the park, selling fishing licences, and serving as a contact in case of emergencies.

The karstlands of the First Canyon have also formed by interaction between water and limestone rock. Water dissolves limestone quite readily; for an area such as the eastern part of the park, with its hundreds of metres thickness of limestone and its plentiful water supply, the power

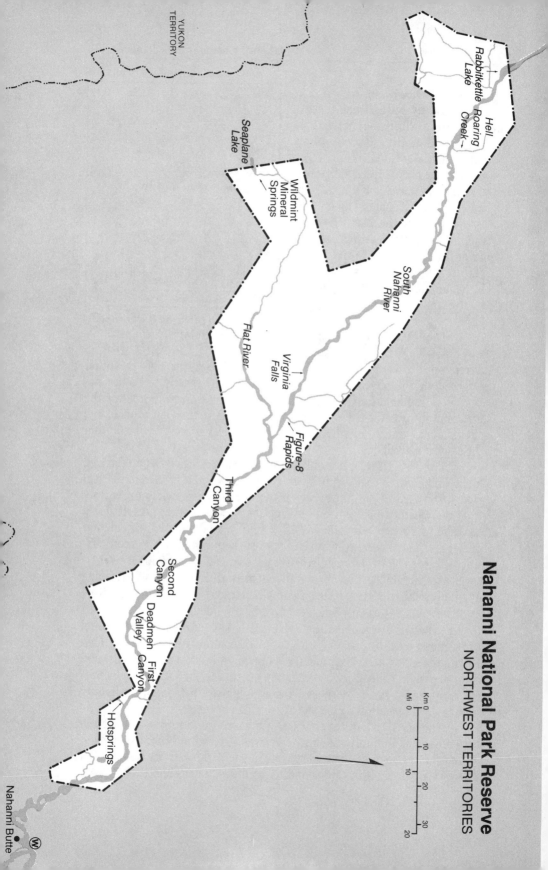

Nahanni National Park Reserve
NORTHWEST TERRITORIES

YUKON
TERRITORY

Hell Roaring
Creek

Rabbitkettle
Lake

Seaplane
Lake

Wildmint
Mineral
Springs

South
Nahanni
River

Flat River

Virginia
Falls

Figure-8
Rapids

Third
Canyon

Second
Canyon

Deadmen
Valley

First
Canyon

Hotsprings

Nahanni Butte

Km 0   10   20   30
Mi 0   10   20

Ⓦ

and range of erosive action is monumental. Underground streams create caves, sinkholes and lakes. The lakes often drain dry in late summer, or even for years at a time. Thus, heavy rains can fill them in hours, or raise their low levels many metres overnight. Then the water may slowly drain away again.

Above ground, the action of rain, and of the freezing and thawing of surface water, cuts deep into the earth's crust, forming great citylike mazes of cliffs, ravines, pillars, towers, corridors and occasional open spaces. All of these striking, bizarre landforms can be seen in a strip of land reaching north from the shore of the First Canyon. It's very difficult walking, and you have to climb the wall of First Canyon to get there, but it is possible to go far enough to get a sense of the karstlands' distinctive character. (Most of the karstlands in this area are actually outside the Reserve boundary.)

Visiting a Wilderness Park

The best time to go to the park is July and August. The weather is usually more predictable, and the likelihood of snow is least then. Nahanni is a wilderness river park. River canoeing and rafting are the best ways to traverse the park and to see the spectacular environment. Before you go, each party should write ahead to the Superintendent, and describe the group's size, wilderness experience and goals of the visit (for example, running the entire river by canoe, or a few days of easy paddling). The park can send you up-to-date information about the rivers themselves, about access, commercial outfitters, charter flights, equipment required, etc.

A number of people go down the South Nahanni with an outfitter, by canoe or raft. Rafting is particularly recommended for those with little boating experience, or who are limited in physical strength. All equipment, food and expertise is provided by tour operators.

Any trip in the park, with a guided group or a group on its own, will vary in the time it takes. The typical independent canoeing trip from Rabbitkettle Lake to Nahanni Butte will take a good ten days, but give yourself more time, if you can, for hiking and fishing. There are several established campsites along the way, and plenty of sandy beaches to make camp otherwise. The river above the falls is not particularly rough, but below them there are a number of spots with Class I white-water ratings, and they require real boating skill and experience.

No matter what kind of transportation is used, or what kind of group you go with, a trip down the South Nahanni and along at least the first few kilometres of the Flat River should give the visitor an opportunity to see some of the most spectacular scenery, fascinating geology, and rich plant and animal life to be found anywhere in our world. It takes planning, and it won't be cheap, but it should be worth just about any expenditure of time, energy and money.

Parks Canada/M. Beedell

Virginia Falls

Park Facilities and Services

Interpretive Programme
Because the park is a wilderness reserve, there is little formal interpretation. Wardens are happy to answer questions, and you can arrange tours to the Tufa Mounds with a warden at Rabbitkettle Lake. The park administrative building is in Fort Simpson, and there you can see movies and interpretive displays about the park, as well as get printed information.

Camping
There are a number of designated primitive campsites along the river, and parties that stop nearby must use them. Otherwise, any location is fine; dry sandy beaches are recommended.

Other Accommodation, Gas, Food and Supplies
Fort Simpson is now the headquarters for Nahanni National Park Reserve. There is one hotel, with twenty-eight rooms, and a dining room and coffee shop. There is a motel, with eight housekeeping and seven non-housekeeping units. In Fort Simpson, there are two grocery stores, two gas stations, a hardware store, a sporting-goods store and a laundromat. Air charter companies in Fort Simpson provide air transportation into the Reserve. Watson Lake has a grocery store, a general store and a gas station.

How to Get There
There is no direct car access to the park. The usual access is by air and water, unless you're one of the rare hardy adventurers who paddles in from other connecting rivers far to the west of the park. Most visitors take a regularly scheduled jet to Watson Lake, to the west of the park, or to Fort

Simpson, to the east. From either place, there are charter flights into the park. All visitors must register in and out of the park. There are several places to do so.

It is now possible to get to Fort Simpson by road, year-round (barring sudden storms). The Mackenzie Highway, going north from Edmonton, Alberta, and the Liard Highway, which starts in British Columbia, are the two access roads. Many visitors to the north take a circle route, joining the two, for a popular summer trek.

For canoeists, the park destination will be upriver, outside the park at Moose Ponds, at the headwaters of the South Nahanni, or at Seaplane Lake (for the Flat River), or inside the park at Rabbitkettle Lake for the South Nahanni River. Most visitors finish their trips at Blackstone Landing, a four- to five-hour paddle downstream of Nahanni Butte. Road access here allows pickup by prearranged transportation. Charter companies can carry canoes and all other equipment, but you must work this out with them ahead of time. No power boats of any kind are allowed in the park.

A number of visitors do canoe to the park, through the use of outfitter-guiding enterprises. For the names of current outfitters and operating charter flight companies, write to the Superintendent of the park, and the Travel Arctic section of the Northwest Territories Department of Information. The park also has a package of materials for pre-trip planning. It includes information on water conditions, canoe routes, access to the park, park regulations, weather, bears and insects.

Further Reading

The Nahanni Portfolio by Pat Keogh and Rosemary Keogh (Stoddart, 1988)
Birds of Nahanni National Park Northwest Territories by George W.
    Scotter (Saskatchewan Natural History Society, 1985)

FOR MORE INFORMATION

The Superintendent
Nahanni National Park Reserve
Bag 300
Fort Simpson,
Northwest Territories
X0E 0N0

Travel Arctic
Government of the Northwest
    Territories,
Yellowknife,
Northwest Territories
X1A 2L9

Phone: (403) 369-3151
Fax: (403) 695-2446

WOOD BUFFALO

NATIONAL PARK

Wood Buffalo is Canada's largest park, and the second-largest national park in the world, and is about the size of Switzerland. It is 283 kilometres (176 miles) long, north to south, straddling about 160 kilometres (100 miles) of the border between Alberta and the Northwest Territories.

Wood Buffalo was established as a national park in 1922, to protect the world's last remaining herd of wood buffalo. Since that time, it was discovered that Wood Buffalo encompasses the only natural nesting site of the whooping crane in the world. This magnificent and reclusive bird migrates yearly from its wintering grounds in the Texas wetlands, to lay its precious eggs in the interior of what is now not only a Canadian National Park, but a UNESCO World Heritage Site. The wood buffalo, which gives the park its name, is a subspecies of the large bison that inhabited the area north of the southern prairies, where the somewhat smaller plains bison lived. Though the park was created to preserve the bison, over the decades there has been a growing awareness of the importance of protecting the entire composition of the life forms in the park, because the park is an example of a massive tract of the northern boreal plains, which are threatened by logging, dam building, and activities associated with petroleum extraction and mining. Recently, there has been pressure from some agriculture interests in the federal, provincial and private sectors to eradicate the entire herd of wood buffalo in the park, because a number of them carry tuberculosis and brucellosis. There are those who fear that it will be transmitted to the cattle industry, many kilometres south of the park, in Alberta. The outcome of this struggle is not easy to predict, but my belief is that visitors will be seeing buffalo at the park for a long time to come.

How to See the Park*

Wood Buffalo's landscape can be divided into four major units; the Caribou and Birch Uplands, the Alberta Plateau, the Slave River Lowlands, and the Peace-Athabasca Delta.

The **Caribou and Birch Uplands** comprise a very small portion of the park, in the areas of the west-central and southern park boundaries, respectively. They are virtually inaccessible to visitors. Their plateau is about 420 metres (1,377 feet) above the plains that stretch out to the east and north in the park. The uplands are sedimentary rocks of the Cretaceous age, and they have yielded fossils including, in localized areas, great densities of fish scales, which are of great paleontological interest.

The **Alberta Plateau** covers most of the park. It is land with huge rivers, great swathes of muskeg, and countless bogs, swamps and meandering streams. One of its most distinctive features is the **karstlands**. This landscape results from the action of a vast underground water system on the gypsum bedrock. Gypsum is extremely susceptible to the dissolving action of water. Where pockets of gypsum are dissolved, caves and tunnels are created. When the surface collapses, karst valleys and sinkholes are formed. Most individual ponds are small and shallow, but some are as deep as 35 metres (115 feet), and twice that in diameter. If several are very close together, they may merge to form a lake. **Pine Lake**, the main recreation area in the park, was formed in this way, from six sinkholes. Wood Buffalo has the largest single area of karstland in the world.

The **Slave River Lowlands** occupy two narrow strips of the park, along its eastern border. The lowlands mark the end of the boreal plains, for they abut the granite-based hills of the Canadian Shield. The rivers of the interior plains contribute a great deal to the distinctive character of the lowlands. As well as the underground rivers that create karstland, there are others that seep out to the surface at the base of a low escarpment. The underground water passes through a layer of salt, deep beneath the surface and, when it reaches the surface, it deposits the salt, sometimes as a sheet, which glistens in the sun or, more frequently, in mounds almost two metres (six feet) high and six to nine metres (twenty to thirty feet) long. This action has created the **Salt Plains** area, with its distinctive landscape and plant life.

The rivers of the park are responsible for the formation of the fourth sub-area of the park, the **Peace-Athabasca Delta**. This is the southeast cor-

---

* I was not able to visit this park. I am indebted to former superintendent of Wood Buffalo, Bernie Lieff, for information on park visitation. He was there for five years, until the winter of 1981. Other material comes from Park publications and Parks Canada documents, and the revision was done with the help of Park Superintendent Mike Rosen.

ner of the park, where the **Peace,
Athabasca, Slave** and **Birch Rivers**
flow toward the **Great Slave Lake.**
The rivers carry enormous loads of
silt, which they drop in the Delta.
The land is low and flat, and the
rivers split, twist and meander,
making a vast network of streams,
interrupted by ponds and shallow
lakes of many sizes. The bulk of the
silt deposition occurs during the
yearly spring flooding of the Delta.
This annual renewal is very important for maintaining the richness of
the environment. The area is home
to a multitude of mammals, including the bison. In June and
September, waterfowl by the millions converge on the Delta, some
to nest, others on their way to and
from their nesting grounds. Bald
eagles and the endangered peregrine falcon are also found here.

*The endangered whooping crane
breeds here, far from visitor
access, though a few visitors
glimpse them away from their
nesting sites*

Parks Canada/R.D. Muir

All of this life depends on a delicate ecological balance. The construction, between 1968 and 1970, of the Bennett Dam, on the Peace River
in British Columbia, some one thousand kilometres (six hundred miles)
from the Delta, has dramatically altered the seasonal run-off that had set
the rhythms of plant and animal life. The area no longer has dramatic peri-
odic flooding, as it used to, and is slowly drying out. Much of the wildlife
is losing its habitat; the richness of life has definitely decreased.
Periodically, the Alberta government raises the possibility of building a
mega-dam on the Slave River, near Fort Smith, and considerable debate is
sparked. The impact on the Delta of such a project would be devastating:
much of the area would be drowned.*

Visiting a Wilderness Park

The main visitation of the park's special features is through back-country
hiking and canoeing. Because mosquitoes can be a trial, the best times to

---

* Readers who wish to be brought up-to-date on this, or other, protection issues
should contact one or more of the conservation societies listed in the chapter,
Conservation and Natural History Associations.

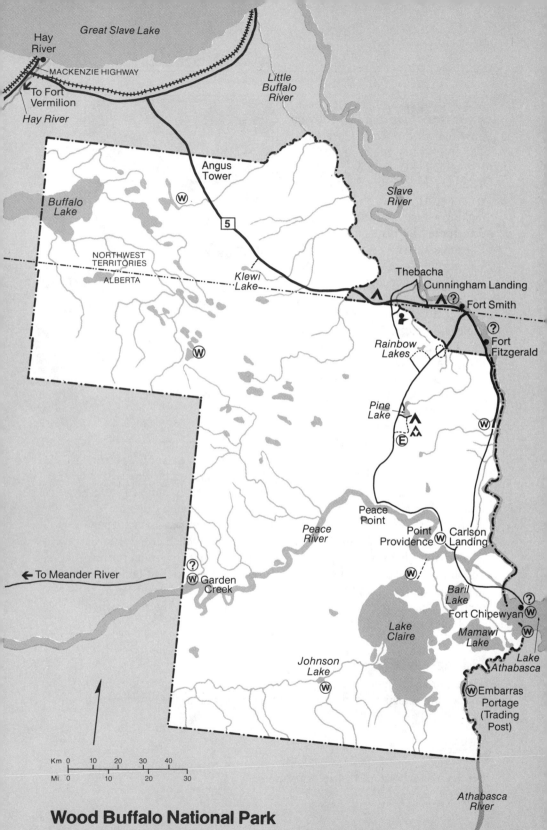

Wood Buffalo National Park
NORTHWEST TERRITORIES/ALBERTA

visit are May to June, and September to early October. Some people go on their own, but the interpreters conduct hikes and other events, varying from walks of a few hours' duration to special overnight trips to the Delta. A number of people visit the back country with outfitters based at Fort Smith or Fort Chipewyan. Write to the Superintendent for more information on their services.

The park has two Visitor/Information Centres, one at Fort Smith and the other at Fort Chipewyan ("Fort Chip").

Fort Smith

Fort Smith is on the Slave River, and is actually about twenty kilometres (twelve miles) outside the park. It is the park's administration centre, and offers the most direct access to **Pine Lake**, sixty-five kilometres (forty miles) away, where the park maintains a semi-serviced campground, an interpretive theatre, a warden station and a boat launch. Many of the interpretive events originate here. There are hikes, evening slide shows and informal gatherings with naturalists.

On arriving at Fort Smith, you should talk to the naturalists at the Administration Office about where to go, and inquire about road conditions. There is a wilderness drive that takes you near the Rainbow lakes, along the Parson's Lake Road. You can stop at the Salt Plains Overview, walk for just five minutes, and be right on the salt plains, to get a closer look. This part of the Salt Plains is one of the few places where you may see the whooping cranes, because they do feed here now and then, far from their breeding grounds in the far north of the park. Ask the interpreters or other staff if there have been recent sightings here. The chances of seeing buffalo and wolves are quite good on this drive, as well. This route is fifty-one kilometres long, taking you off the main road and back onto it. The Parson's Lake turnoff is marked. There is an interpretive display at the Salt Plains Overview.

There are several trails, of varying lengths, that can be taken from the roadways in the park. There is a group of four trails at the Salt River day-use area, just as you enter the park from Fort Smith. There are two that are short walks, and two longer hiking trails. The two short walks are **Karstland** (1 kilometre) and **Salt Meadow** (1.5 kilometres). They both can give a very good sense of this distinctive area, a typical karst topography, with sinkholes and crevasses etched in the limestone soil. The Karstland Trail has one of the most striking sights you could hope to see. It has a phbernaculum of the red-sided garter snake. Here, in May or June, out of a sinkhole come dozens of these snakes at a time. They form "mating balls," as they carry out this essential springtime rite, and then separate and go to the nearby marsh, to eat frogs all summer. In the autumn, they descend to their underground home and stay there safely all winter.

Parks Canada/R. Lewis

The Peace-Athabasca Delta. Will dams further erode the richness that remains?

The two hikes are two sections of the **Salt River Loop Trail** system. One section is nine kilometres long, and the other is seven. The terrain varies, with the trail winding in and around sinkholes (some of which have long ago filled with bush and trees), climbing the Salt River Escarpment, crossing salty streams and salt-pan lakebeds. This, too, is a good place to see buffalo.

Though hiking in the park can easily be done on your own, I recommend making full use of the interpretive services. You can participate in the guided drives and hikes, such as the "buffalo creeps," to get a close look at the imposing beasts, trips to the salt deposits, or canoe forays with interpreters deeper into the Delta. Canoes can be rented from outfitters in Fort Smith, or some tour companies offer canoe trips into the park.

Fort Chipewyan

The only way to visit the park from Fort Chip is with the park-licensed outfitting and guiding services. Their services include specialized boating and dog-team trips. Fort Chip is right on the Peace-Athabasca Delta, so is particularly suited for canoeing and camping, for those interested in water-based wildlife. The park has a special visitor site, called the **Sweet Grass Cabin**, which is reached by canoe, followed by a three- to four-mile hike in to the cabin itself. It is just south of a bend in the Peace River, right in the heart of the Peace-Athabasca delta. Tours go there in summer, but you can go on your own. In either case, you (or your tour guide) must register with the park before going. The bugs come in by the end of May but, any time during the summer, you are amply compensated by the strong possibility of waking up to some two hundred buffalo grazing away in front of the cabin.

Park Facilities and Services

Interpretive Programme

The park has a very personalized interpretive service. A maximum of two thousand visitors a year come to the park, so the staff can adapt their programmes to visitor interest. The only thing that interrupts programming, or curtails full use of the park in summer, is fire. As much as five percent of park area can burn in any given year, so staff may be preoccupied, and full use of roads or trails may be hampered.

Camping

There is a thirty-six-site campground at **Pine Lake**, with water, chemical toilets, fire grates and firewood. Back-country camping is allowed throughout the park, except in special protection zones. Free registration permits are required. Permits and information about rules and back-country conditions are available from the wardens. There is a wilderness campground at Rainbow Lakes. There is a pit privy, an anti-bear food cache, firegrates, and water from the lake. It is entirely a pack-in/pack-out situation.

Other Accommodation, Gas, Food and Supplies

Fort Smith offers the Queen Elizabeth campground, a forty-five-room motel and a small hotel. At Fort Chip there is some private accommodation.

Gas and other supplies are available at Fort Smith and, to a lesser degree, at Fort Chip. Prices are generally higher than in southern Canada, because of transportation costs. Camping equipment, cross-country skis, boating equipment and raingear can be rented in Fort Smith.

Recreational Services

Hiking There are two types of hiking in the park. One is day hiking on the park's short trails, to specific points of interest, such as Pine Lake to

Lane Lake. The alternative is to hire a guide to take you into the bush, travelling on bison trails for as long as the tour is planned.

Winter Use   The park is being used more and more by tour groups in the winter. (Few people would be sufficiently skilled and well-equipped to go into the park on their own.) There are "Northern Lights" tours, camping, visiting traditional users as they hunt and trap in the park. There is snow-shoeing, cross-country skiing and snowmobiling. Write to the park for a current list of licensed tour operators.

Dog Team Travel   There is increasing winter use by people who hire guides, to take them on dog-team trips to remote areas of the park.

Boating   Boating is a popular activity in the park. Canoes, for use in lakes and deeper streams, can be rented at Fort Smith and Fort Chip. Outfitters provide canoe tours, as well. Motor boats are allowed on the major rivers—the Slave, Peace and Athabasca. Write ahead for information on river use, navigation charts, safety precautions, required permits, etc. Rafting is increasingly popular with tour groups. There are five rapids along the Slave River, between Fort Smith and Fort Fitzgerald, though this area is not actually in the park. These rapids are not suitable for canoes. There have been fatal canoeing accidents here.

Fishing   Fishing is not particularly good in most park waters. Pine Lake is stocked with rainbow trout, but they are very difficult to catch; the other lakes and rivers yield pike, pickerel, whitefish and suckers. A park licence is required. It is available from park staff at Fort Chip or Fort Smith.

Flightseeing   Getting an overview of the park from a small airplane is increasingly popular. Flights are available in Fort Smith, winter and summer.

How to Get There

The easiest way to reach the Wood Buffalo area is by air. Flights leave Edmonton for Fort Smith six days a week, and for Fort Chipewyan twice a week in winter, and more often in summer. Check with your travel agent for details. You can rent a car in Fort Smith. Some summer visitors drive to Fort Smith; it takes two long days' driving, sometimes on packed dirt roads. The road to Fort Smith loops north of Peace River but, in winter, ice bridges and a winter road are constructed, so you can drive to Fort Chip. A few hardy people canoe in to Fort Chip, and even farther. It's also possible to hire a guide to take you by boat between Fort Smith and Fort Chip.

FOR MORE INFORMATION

Please note that, since this is a wilderness park, it is particularly important to write or phone ahead, to see if your interests and experience will be met at the park. Also, facilities and services, particularly commercial ones, are subject to sudden change, and planning ahead with park information at hand is essential to a fulfilling trip.

The Superintendent
Wood Buffalo National Park
Box 750
Fort Smith, Northwest Territories
X0E 0P0

Phone: (403) 872-2349
Fax: (403) 872-3910

PRINCE ALBERT

NATIONAL PARK

Endless plains, wind-blown snow, or grain waving in the blistering August sun—that's Saskatchewan's image. The map shows Prince Albert National Park located very near the geographical centre of the province, so that's what the visitor expects to see. On arrival, though, there's not a plain in sight.

The park is a preserve of 3,875 square kilometres (1,496 square miles) of parkland and southern boreal forest. In the parkland, segments of grassland are mixed with many stands of aspen forest. There are a few sections of fescue and other grasslands (where buffalo used to roam), but most of these small areas are inaccessible to the visitor. The boreal forest is damp, pocked by bogs and dominated by evergreen trees, particularly the moisture-loving black spruce and tamarack.

Underlying this varied topography there are, in places, up to 290 metres (900 feet) of till, the rocks, gravel and sand held by the glaciers that shaped and reshaped so much of Canada, and deposited as the ice melted.

Prince Albert National Park is a transition zone, from more southern aspen parkland to the edge of the boreal forest that covers so much of northern Canada. Transition zones are always rich in plant and animal life because, in one relatively limited area, the life forms of two different environments succeed side by side. Few of the life forms that so enrich Prince Albert National Park could exist now, in the heavily cultivated land surrounding it.

Prince Albert was established in 1927, as a public recreation area and to preserve its rich natural history. However, it has had a distinctive human history, as well. The park's most famous resident was Grey Owl, who lived here from 1931 until his death in 1938. He became a park naturalist, using Prince Albert as a home base for his vigorous campaigns to conserve animal life, particularly the beaver. His cabin still survives, and the many beaver throughout the park are a tribute to his work.

The park is a vertical oblong, looking rather like a miniature version of Saskatchewan itself. The transition from parkland to boreal forest takes place roughly along an east-west line, halfway up the length of the park, with Lake Waskesiu marking the change. Waskesiu townsite is the focal point for visitor services, including the car campgrounds, a number of recreational facilities, the interpretive centre and administrative headquarters of the park, and the shops, cabins and other services of a small townsite. As in most of the parks with townsites, you can walk for just a few minutes out of town, to find the quiet and solitude of the park's special natural features.

How to See the Park

The park offers a wide range of ways to see and appreciate its special natural and human history. There are slide shows at the campgrounds, guided walks, self-guiding walks, informative roadside stops, and hiking trails that can be travelled independently. There is also a special interpretive feature at Prince Albert, which has been designed to give the car-based visitor the most exposure, in the easiest manner, to the diversity of the park environment. This is the self-guiding auto tour.

The park has a newsletter called, appropriately, *Wolf Country*. A special issue guides the visitor by car from the townsite, along the south shore of **Lake Waskesiu**, to the **Narrows** Day-use Area. Ask for this brochure—its suggestions could make the two- to four-hour excursion the highlight of your visit. The tour starts at the townsite, and runs twenty-six kilometres (fifteen miles), to the end of the road on the south side of Lake Waskesiu, where there is a campground, picnic area and marina. There are a number of stopping points along the route, including at least four picnic sites, which are beautifully situated at beach areas along the lake, and interpretive sites, such as **Ice Push Ridge**. At this stop, you'll see several panels, right on the ridge, which explain when and how it was formed. This drive is excellent for seeing a variety of woodland, beach, and lake features. It ends at an area called the Narrows, where a peninsula reaches from the north side of the lake to within about twenty-seven metres (thirty yards) of the south shore.

The Land Forms

Prince Albert National Park owes its soil type, its myriad lakes and streams, and flatness to two factors. One is that the bedrock has never been pushed, squeezed or broken by the great internal pressure of the earth's crust that formed mountains near the edges of the continent. The

other, more recent, cause is glaciation. The entire area was under as
much as 1,600 metres (one mile) of
glacial ice during the three main
periods of ice advance, the last of
which retreated about ten thousand
years ago. Advancing glaciers dug
out the beds of some of the major
lakes, such as **Waskesiu, Crean** and
Kingsmere. As the glaciers melted,
the torrents of water often cut deeper into the lake beds, and formed
rivers flowing down to lower elevations. Eventually, they reached the
present-day Churchill River/
Hudson's Bay drainage system, or
the North Saskatchewan/Lake
Winnipeg drainage system. The two

Hispid moth

drainage systems are separated by an upland area, known as a height-of-
land.

If you drive along Highway 263, a little farther south than Shady
Lake, you come to the **Height-of-Land Lookout**. A three-part interpretive
sign describes what you see stretching before you. You can see several
lakes, and King Island, in Waskesiu Lake. The island is named for a former
Prime Minister, William Lyon MacKenzie King.

The cutting action of the glacial melt water is easy to see from the
Spruce River Lookout Trail, just north of the Spruce River, about twelve
kilometres (seven miles) north of the south entrance to the park. The trail
is a ten- or fifteen-minute walk on good gravel, and there are several places
along the way with benches and attractive interpretive signs. Keep to the
right of the fork at the beginning of the trail. The river meanders in what
was once a very wide channel, carved out by the glaciers. The lookout is
well-situated, and the view very attractive.

Land shaping did not stop with the end of the glacial periods, of
course. Ice continues to play a role, when it builds up in large lakes and
then begins to break up in the spring. Blocks of ice are pushed by strong
winds up onto land. The front edges of ice hit the shallow bottom of the
lake, close to shore, and actually push some of the lake bed up out of the
water, forming a low ridge. Plants often colonize the new surface and sta-
bilize it, making it much less vulnerable to wind and water. So, a small
new land form is created. The place to see this is the **Ice Push Ridge** display area, about halfway along the road to the Narrows Day-use Area.
Watch for the sign on the lake side, park, and take the minute or so to

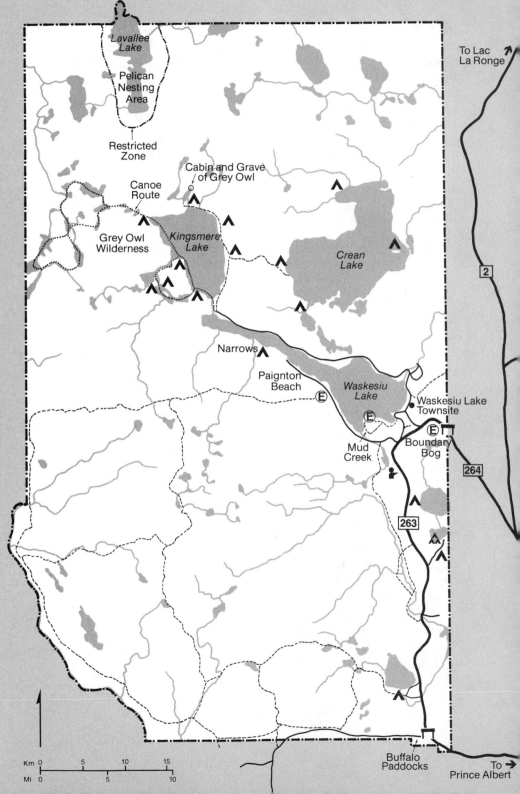

Prince Albert National Park
SASKATCHEWAN

Lavallee Lake

Pelican Nesting Area

Restricted Zone

To Lac La Ronge

Cabin and Grave of Grey Owl

Canoe Route

Grey Owl Wilderness

Kingsmere Lake

Crean Lake

2

Narrows

Paignton Beach

Waskesiu Lake

Waskesiu Lake Townsite

Mud Creek

Boundary Bog

264

263

Buffalo Paddocks

To Prince Albert

| Km | 0 | 5 | 10 | 15 |
| Mi | 0 | 5 | | 10 |

walk to the viewing platform, where the interpretive sign is. It's a great view of Lake Waskesiu, as well.

There are a number of other places to see the evidence of land formation, and the best way to see them is on the appropriate guided walks.

The Transition Zone: Aspen Parkland to Boreal Forest

If you can distinguish trembling aspen, with its straight, white trunk and twinkling, triangular leaves, from the Christmas-tree look of a conifer, the drive along Highway 263 from the southern entrance of the park, northwards forty-two kilometres (twenty-six miles) to Lake Waskesiu, affords an excellent overview of the change from the southern aspen parkland to the boreal forest. For an in-depth look at this transition, the park offers several guided walks to trails that are not too easy to find on your own. Look on the schedule, for walks to **Tea Pail**, **Treebeard** or **Shady Lake**.

If you wish to go at your own speed, two trails are particularly good for experiencing the transition. An attractive brochure maps the self-guiding trail to **Mud Creek**, and tells you about thirteen different points of interest along the way. The trailhead is on the road to the Narrows, and starts off to the right of the picnic area, at a lovely little beach, which is quite heavily used by boaters. The walk is extremely pleasant, moving from the aspen woodlands over to a damp area, where the creek flows into the lake. I was enchanted to see the black-and-white, harlequin-patterned Hispid moth, clinging to some fireweed. There are a lot of beautiful viewpoints of Lake Waskesiu, and of the areas where the beaver are busy. A number of stops along the way are well-keyed to the pamphlet, and point out beaver cuttings, fire remains, and the plant succession from alders to aspen to spruce.

The trail gains a little bit of height, just enough to give an overview of the melt-water valley in which Mud Creek meanders slowly toward the lake. This is an excellent trail, for its mixture of habitat, its openness and (perhaps because it was windy) its total lack of mosquitoes.

Kingfisher Trail, also along the south shore of Waskesiu, is the other trail to take for exploring on your own. It is about thirteen kilometres (eight miles) long, and will take about four and one-half hours at a fairly steady pace. There is no interpretive brochure; if you've already read some of the park information brochures, or have gone on a guided walk, you will probably be able to follow the transitions of the habitat from aspen forest, to the marshy home of the beavers, to boreal forest and back again, as you wind through several examples of each. It is not a difficult hike. The trail starts behind the Interpretive Centre, on a boardwalk, and stays fairly near the lakeshore. Bird-watching is very good from this trail.

There were about three species of "confusing fall" warblers, two species of sparrow, and some chickadees.

One area of particular interest on this walk is a clearing that opens out very near the shore. There is a natural animal lick, a large patch of open, grey, sticky mud, which you pass on the wooden boardwalk. When I was there, it was completely covered with the hoof-prints of animals, probably moose and elk.

The Boreal Forest

The boreal forest flourishes in Prince Albert National Park, because the park area has more rainfall than the surrounding prairies, and it has a lower average temperature, with less evaporation. The northern half of the park has particularly moist conditions, with many more lakes, ponds and streams than the southern part. Bogs form in any area that has poor drainage; but the most common place for them is the boreal forest, growing where glaciers scooped out millions of bowls, which collect water that cannot drain.

The park has a self-guiding trail, **Boundary Bog**, which takes you through the surrounding spruce forest, by a glacial kettle, past a wolf rendezvous site, to a bog where you'll learn a lot about the geological history, and plant and animal life here. The trail is just off Highway 264, about fifteen-minutes' drive east of the townsite. This is one of the best-designed self-guiding walks I have ever been on. It has its own brochure, which is keyed to thirteen numbered spots along the trail. You can see, and even hear, the transition from trembling aspen forest, through mixed trembling aspen and white spruce, to forest that is largely spruce. There are some beautiful sections, where the ground cover is almost entirely mosses and lichens of various sorts. In some places, sphagnum moss thrives and, in drier areas, feather moss mixes with caribou or reindeer lichen.

In the damper areas, orchids flourish—calypso, northern bog, hooded lady tresses, large round leaved, and others. As you approach the open water at the centre of the bog, you may see carnivorous pitcher plants.

Human History

Grey Owl's Cabin, on **Lake Ajawaan**, exists today, and the beaver lodge that once reached into its interior is still there. The car-based visitor cannot reach the cabin; it is a 19.5 kilometre (12 mile) hike, one way. The walk is an easy one, along the shore of **Kingsmere Lake**, and there are campsites along the way. The final campsite is at the north edge of Kingsmere, and then there is a three-kilometre (two mile) walk to Ajawaan, and the cabin itself. Of course, you can canoe or boat across Kingsmere, and walk in the last three kilometres to visit the cabin.

Visitors and residents can view each other on quiet evening walks

Special Preservation in the Park

The park preserves three very important types of life. Unfortunately, they are not readily accessible to the general visitor. One is the breeding colony of the rare white pelican, at the northwest edge of the park. The only people who visit are those involved in monitoring their status. But keep your eyes open, when you canoe or walk by any lake in the park, and you may see a flock dipping their bills in unison, as they herd fish and scoop them up.

The park also preserves an area of true prairie, the fescue grassland. There are small patches of it in the southwest corner of the park. Only intrepid hikers will pass through here. If you are particularly interested, and have the time and endurance for a looping hike of many kilometres, check with the wardens or other staff for detailed instructions as to the grassland location.

The third special preservation in the park is mammal life. This may seem fairly obvious, but it must be remembered that Prince Albert is one of the few undisturbed environments in this part of the province. Here, wolves, bear, moose, free-ranging buffalo, fox, otter, fisher, badgers, bald eagles and wolverine all thrive.

You can't expect to see many of these animals, they are so wild. The early morning and evenings are the best time to watch for them and, if you're quiet and walk slowly along trails by the lakes, there's a good chance of seeing beaver, moose or deer, with porcupine adding a little amusement, as they huff along.

Railroad portage to Kingsmere Lake

Park Services and Facilities

Interpretive Programme
The park has an active interpretive programme. In the summer, there are daily guided walks along short, but interesting, trails; slide shows are given nightly in the Beaver Glen Campground and, every Saturday night, at the Narrows Campground; and there are special events, such as wolf howls, elk bugling, canoe paddles or star gazing. Children's programmes are also offered. For any of these, check the bulletin boards at campgrounds or the Information or Interpretive Centre, or ask any staff person. The park newsletter, *Wolf Country*, has a schedule of events, plus interesting short articles on the natural or human history of the park.

Camping, Serviced and Semi-Serviced
There are three of these campgrounds. The largest and most developed are Beaver Glen and The Trailer Park. **Beaver Glen** is a couple of minutes' drive from the townsite, and about a ten-minute walk from the main beach. It has 213 sites, in a densely wooded area. The sites are all on the outside edge of each loop, leaving the inside area as intact forest. This greatly increases the sense of naturalness and privacy in the campground. It has kitchen shelters, with wood stoves and wood supplies. There are

washrooms, with showers, and also separate water faucets, though they both seemed, to me, to be very far apart and serving an unusually large number of sites per facility. There are fire grates and picnic tables at each site, and firewood is provided at several enclosures. There are no hook-ups for trailers, but there is a waste-disposal station for them. The Trailer Park is an all-trailer section of the campsite, right in town. It is on a lawn, with 153 spaces, and the trailers are simply slotted in. It seems to fill very quickly. For those who don't mind crowding, the attraction may be that it's across the road from the main beach, and very close to all townsite activities. It is fully serviced for trailers, although there are no grate fireplaces.

Narrows Campground is about a half-hour drive from the townsite, on the south shore of Lake Waskesiu. It is a much more natural setting than Beaver Glen. Some sites are very close to the shoreline. It is lightly wooded, with the campsites fairly close to each other. There are flush toilets, with cold running water there, and faucets around the campsites. Fire grates, picnic tables and firewood are available. The Narrows marina is nearby, with canoe and boat rentals, a small snack bar, a lawned picnic area and lots of shoreline fishing.

Group Camping

This is available near the **Trapper's Lake** camping area. Groups must reserve ahead, by writing to the Superintendent of the park.

Other Camping

Namekus is a car-accessible campsite, just to the east of Highway 263. There are twenty-one campsites along the lakeshore. Drinking water comes from the lake. There are pit toilets, fire grates, picnic tables and firewood. **Sandy Lake Campground**, situated on the west side of Highway 263, also has thirty-one sites, six of which are walk-in sites, about 150 to 300 metres from the parking area. All have picnic tables, fire grates and firewood, pit toilets and lake water.

Trapper's Lake Campground, east of Highway 263, just south of Namekus, offers five primitive sites, with firewood, fire grates, pit toilets and picnic tables. There are a number of primitive sites that are accessible only by hiking and/or canoeing. The most easily reached are at the south end of **Kingsmere Lake**, only a thirty-minute walk from the nearest parking lot. The other marked sites are along the back-country canoe and hiking routes. Most have pit toilets, firewood, fire grates and bear-resistant food-cache platforms. All are on lakeshores. Users must register with the wardens or other park staff, and pack out all garbage.

Other Accommodation, Gas, Food and Supplies

The townsite of Waskesiu has a full range of motel, hotel and cabin accommodation. For information, write to the Waskesiu Chamber of Commerce.

The townsite has just about anything the visitor might need. There are restaurants, a laundromat, gift shops, a drug store and a movie theatre. The city of Prince Albert is only a hundred kilometres (fifty-six miles) away, and caters to a full range of shopping needs.

Recreational Services

Facilities for the Handicapped Waskesiu River Trail is a short, scenic trail, beside the Waskesiu River, designed for wheelchair use. Ask the staff for exact directions. Also, the park has one "all-terrain wheelchair" for use on request. It looks like a wonderful innovation!

Hiking Along with the trails used for interpretation, or for walking along Lake Waskesiu, there are many kilometres of back-country hiking, particularly in the southwestern section of the park. Check with the staff for the conditions of the trails.

Canoeing This is a very good park for short or long canoe trips. Canoes can be rented at the Hanging Heart Lakes and Narrows marinas, and at the Main Marina, which is about ten minutes' drive from the townsite, on the road that goes along the northern shore of Lake Waskesiu.

There are canoe routes going from Kingsmere Lake to several loops through small lakes and over portages, and in Crean and Hanging Heart Lakes. Canoeing is allowed in Namekus, Trapper's, Shady and Sandy Lakes, as well.

Boating Motor boats, with a maximum of forty horsepower, are allowed on Kingsmere; there are no restrictions on Waskesiu, Hanging Heart Lakes or Crean Lake. At each of the three marinas, you can rent ten- and twenty-horsepower motor boats. Paddle-wheel boats are rented at the townsite beach, and you can take tours from there on a paddle-wheel launch.

Swimming There is swimming, in the summer months, at the main Waskesiu day-use area. Swimming is allowed in all lakes, except Lavallee.

Golf There is an eighteen-hole golf course in the townsite, with a pro shop, equipment rental and restaurant.

Bicycling Bicycles can be rented at a local service station. Watch for signs.

Horseback Riding Trail rides are offered at a local stable. Watch for signs.

Fishing A national parks licence is required to fish for pike, wall eye and lake trout. Inquire from the staff or townsite stores for information as to limits, open lakes, etc.

Winter Use The park has a very active winter season. Camping is possible in several sites, where winterized kitchen shelters and toilets are provided. There are snowshoe trails, and over 150 kilometres (90 miles) of cross-country skiing trails. Skiers must register in and out, on back-country overnight treks. Write to the Superintendent for the winter-use brochure, or call for the most up-to-date information, at (306) 663-5322. There are commercial accommodations and restaurants in the townsite, and a supply store. You can rent skis from operators of accommodation in the townsite.

FOR MORE INFORMATION

The Superintendent
Prince Albert National Park
Box 100
Waskesiu Lake, Saskatchewan
S0J 2Y0

Phone: (306) 633-5322

Waskesiu Chamber of Commerce
Waskesiu, Saskatchewan

Phone: (306) 922-3232 (winter)
/663-5410 (summer)

GRASSLANDS

NATIONAL PARK

Since the mid-nineteenth century, almost all of Canada's prairies have been drastically altered—human settlement and accompanying farming, cattle-raising and wholesale slaughter of large mammals, such as the bison and antelope, have permanently changed them.

However, a pocket of short-grass prairie in southwestern Saskatchewan has been left relatively undisturbed, and two small sections of land near Val Marie and Killdeer have been designated Grasslands National Park. Canada's twenty-ninth national park preserves a rich and complex ecosystem: badlands, with their stark outlines of buttes and ravines; sloughs, with their water supply and marshy edges that are the nesting grounds for an incredible array of waterfowl and shorebirds; broad sweeps of grassy plain that are the home of pronghorn antelope, sage grouse, burrowing owls, black-tailed prairie dogs and several species of snake.

Though the park was set aside in 1981, it will be years before final boundaries are set and visitor facilities and services, such as interpretive programmes or campgrounds, are established. However, there is an administrative office, open during normal business hours, at the Val Marie section. There are some displays and videos, which tell about the natural and human history of the park area, and there are several attractive brochures and maps available. The staff will be happy to answer any questions, and direct you to those roads that may be taken to enter the grasslands themselves. Check before wandering off on your own, as many of the roads are on private land, and sometimes they are not passable because of the weather.

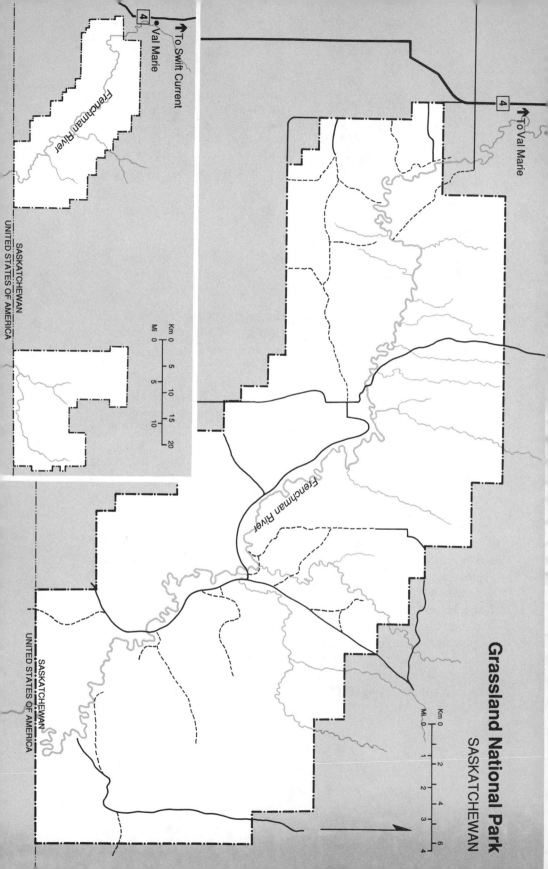

Grassland National Park
SASKATCHEWAN

To Val Marie

4

Frenchman River

SASKATCHEWAN
UNITED STATES OF AMERICA

Km 0
Mi 0
1
2
2
3
4
4
6

To Swift Current

Val Marie

4

Frenchman River

SASKATCHEWAN
UNITED STATES OF AMERICA

Km 0
Mi 0
5
5
10
10
15
20

The grasslands are the home of these burrow-dwelling prairie dogs

Parks Canada/W. Lynch

FOR MORE INFORMATION

District Superintendent
Saskatchewan South
Canadian Parks Service
Grasslands National Park
Box 150
Val Marie, Saskatchewan
S0N 2T0

Phone: (306) 298-2257

RIDING MOUNTAIN

NATIONAL PARK

Riding Mountain is a meeting place and a refuge. It's situated in south-central Manitoba, near the geographical centre of Canada, and covers 2,978 square kilometres (1,150 square miles). Plants and animals from three ecological zones are found in the park, and they all are protected here, safe from the radical changes that people have wrought upon the face of most of southern Manitoba.

Riding Mountain is located on the Manitoba Escarpment, a tilting shelf of siliceous shale, a form of sedimentary rock that is harder than the surrounding limestone. The escarpment extends into northern Saskatchewan, where it forms similar upland areas but, here in Manitoba, it has its own character and its own name—Riding Mountain. Relative to the plains that stretch away from it on all sides, it *is* a mountain. At its highest edge, on the north-eastern side, it is 756 metres (2,480 feet) high, the third-highest point in the province.

How to See the Park

The three ecological zones of the park are the eastern deciduous forest, with its Manitoba maples and bur oaks; the aspen parklands of mixed forest and grassland; and the boreal forest, with its white spruce and balsam fir. Each ecological zone is accessible by car. There are self-guiding trails, roadside signs at car pull-offs, and an interpretive centre in the community of **Wasagaming**.

An important thing to keep in mind is that the three ecological zones of Riding Mountain intermix. In an area that is a crossroads of different types of plant and animal life, it could hardly be otherwise. So, although each trail or location may be largely one type or another, you will see a range of habitat while visiting each.

The Boreal Zone

Areas that are mostly boreal forest can be reached by travelling north from Wasagaming on Highway 10, or east on Highway 19. If you take Highway 10, stop at **Moon Lake**. There is a small campground there, in case you want to stay awhile. This is the heart of the boreal forest zone, in the north of the park. An exhibit on the boreal forest, and a short, self-guiding trail, will help you explore it.

East of the townsite, two trails cut through boreal growth. Arrowhead and Brulé (Burntwood) Trails are located near the Lake Katherine Campground. **Arrowhead** is under three kilometres (two miles) long, and shows the progression of spruce superseding aspen. You can see evidence of the area's glacial history. There are exposed granite rocks, which could only have been carried here by glaciers from their place of origin on the Canadian Shield, at least 200 kilometres (125 miles) away. The ponds in the area are kettles, also known in prairie areas as potholes, formed by melting chunks of ice, which were left behind by retreating glaciers. It's beaver heaven here.

On **Brulé (Burntwood) Trail**, you can see how boreal forest recovers after fire. The trail passes though an area of spruce and jack pine that was burned over in 1929 and 1957, and burned in smaller areas in 1971. The trail route, and its self-guiding brochure, explain how fire and re-growth have been the dominant factors in shaping the forests and prairies of Riding Mountain. Some areas along the trail are dense, dark spruce forest. If you take the short side trip to **Kinosao Lake**, you will find more boreal forest, some of it charred. The lakeshore is quiet and beautiful. There is a small, rushy area with a boardwalk. Take care not to slip on the first part of it; it's still in the shade of the forest, and is moist, mossy and slippery. The last part of the trail is through a small section of fescue grassland. It's a lovely place to see typical prairie flowers.

The **Rolling River Trail** brings you even closer than the Brulé (Burntwood) Trail to the experience of fire. In 1980, there was a major burn, over 186 square kilometres (72 square miles), in the eastern segment of the park. It took weeks to bring it under control. On this short trail, you can study the pictures and texts that explain fire-fighting techniques, such as water bombing, starting backfires or digging barriers. The ground is covered with the earliest regenerative growth—fireweed and a particularly beautiful Indian paintbrush.

To get a really good idea of the terrain and habitat variation of the Manitoba Escarpment, which is the basis of the boreal zone, take one of the guided events to the **Wilson Creek** area. Check the interpretive schedule for these activities, and sign up early. There is a really good chance to see wildlife here. You'll leave your car and be taken off-trail, right into the bush. On a similar event, I saw nine moose in two hours!

Eastern Deciduous Forest

The best walk through this kind of forest is **the Burls and Bittersweet Self-guiding Trail**, at the eastern edge of the park, just off Highway 19. There are very few stands of eastern deciduous forest left in southern Manitoba, because most have been destroyed in clearing land for agriculture. But here you see a rich remnant of this complex ecological zone. The trail is oriented to **Dead Ox Creek**, a stream far more lovely than its name. In the

Prairie rose

surrounding forest, there is an understory of vines, berry bushes, mushrooms, fungi and flowers. The brochure will help you identify the poison ivy. The elm, bur oak, mountain maple and ash form a canopy overhead. A new, self-guiding brochure has turned this trail into a high point for family enjoyment. The brochure lets kids follow a Great Nature Detective and his assistant, as they discover the secrets of the changing land.

The **Oak Ridge Trail** and the **Beach Ridge Trail** have significant deciduous growth, as well. Beach Ridge Trail has interpretive signs along the way, which explain the habitat and land formations.

Aspen Parkland and Prairie Potholes

Open, rough fescue grasslands, with stands of aspen and mixed boreal forest, edge the eastern side of **Lake Audy**. There is a campsite in this area, and a plains-bison enclosure, where a small herd of about thirty bulls and cows are kept for breeding and display purposes.

There aren't established trails in this immediate area, but you can wander over the prairie area on your own. There are car caravans or interpreter-led walks there, at least once a week. I went on one of the walks, and was fascinated to learn about the adaptations plants and animals have to make in the prairie environment.

If you want an overview of what has happened to the expanse of prairie land that surrounds the park, visit the **Agassiz Tower**. It is about 6.5 kilometres (4 miles) in from the northern boundary of the park, on Highway 10. The tower stands on the edge of the Manitoba Escarpment

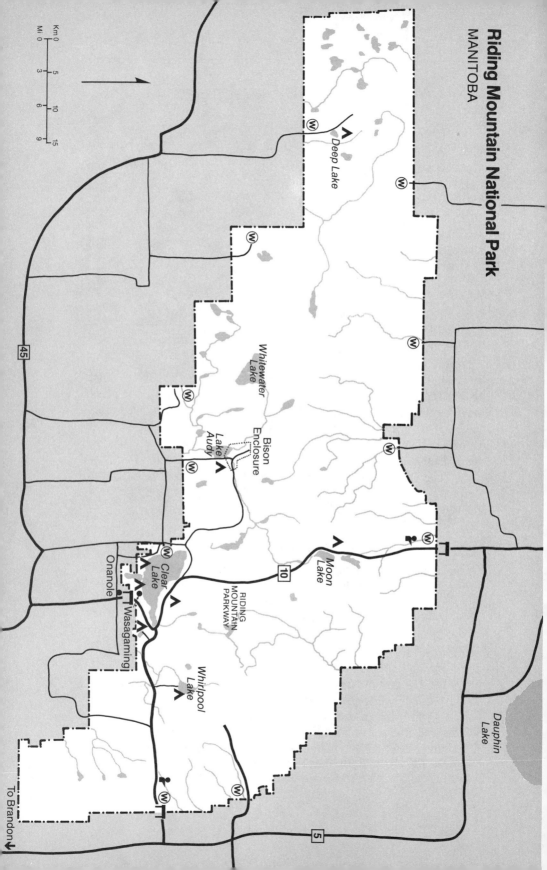

and, from it, you can look out over a massive quiltwork of agricultural land.

Manitoba is famous for thousands of prairie potholes, the lakes of all sizes that were left as glaciers retreated. These lakes are havens for waterfowl, fish, bird life and insects. There are dozens of potholes at Riding Mountain; the park is one of the few places in habitable parts of Manitoba where they have not been drained off and plowed under. The best place to see one is **Ominik Marsh**, at the edge of the community, off Wasagaming Drive, on the south side of Boat Cove Road. A small stream feeds and drains the marsh, and a boardwalk surrounds its edges in a rough circle. You can take guided walks here but, if you go alone in early morning or late evening, and listen and watch, you will appreciate the character of this beautiful environment. A floating boardwalk creates an unforgettable experience of the heart of a prairie marsh. Before you go out on it, sign out an Ominik Marsh Discovery Kit, available at the Interpretive Centre. It has a marsh dip-net, to temporarily ensnare some of the smaller inhabitants; magnifying cubes, to get a closer look; a book that tells you what you're seeing; and other useful equipment, for the curious of every age.

Park Services and Facilities

Interpretive Programme
At the core of the Riding Mountain summer interpretive programme, is a weekly slate of several different interpreter-led outings. These are off-trail walks to intriguing places, such as bear and coyote dens, or the remains of old lumber mills. There can be a little dust and a bit of uneven terrain, but visitors of all ages and levels of fitness enjoy them tremendously. Be sure to check the schedule at the Information Centre, and on all campground bulletin boards.

Riding Mountain has paid a lot of attention to facilities for the handicapped. There is Lakeshore Walk, which is suitable for wheelchair use. Send for the brochure, or ask at the entry kiosk or Visitor Centre, and watch for the numerous blue-and-white signs that mark handicapped-accessible sites and facilities.

The park has a varied and full schedule of interpretive events. Schedules are available at entry kiosks, the Information Centre, the Interpretive Centre, and on bulletin boards at campsites. The events occur at a number of different places in the park, so most visitor interests and schedules can be met. The Interpretive Centre is located in the centre of Wasagaming. The Centre has a movie theatre, where you can pick films from their listing and have them projected. I saw one on Grey Owl, who lived in the park for one season in 1931, and one on bears in the national parks.

Camping

There are five car-based campgrounds in the park. **Wasagaming** is the campground right downtown, and it has a full range of facilities. There are eighty-six sites with three-way hook-ups for trailers, and seventy-two sites with electricity only. There are 277 other sites that have picnic tables, fire grates, water from faucets, firewood, and washrooms with flush toilets and showers. There are kitchen shelters, as well.

    Lake Katherine Campground is five kilometres (three miles) east of Wasagaming, on Highway 19. There 108 sites in a mixed aspen and boreal forest, on a slightly hilly terrain. It is on Lake Katherine, which has its own picnic area, and which is a very good place for beginners to canoe. Several self-guiding trails—Arrowhead, Evergreen, Brulé (Burntwood)—start very near this campground, and other trails, such as Loon's Island, border the lake. The campground has washrooms, with hot and cold water and flush toilets, but no showers. Individual sites have fire grates and picnic tables, and there are depots for firewood. Water from faucets is available, every few campsites. At an outdoor theatre, evening programmes are presented.

    Whirlpool Walk-in Campground is also in the east of the park, on Highway 19. The parking area is only about 100 metres (325 feet) from the grassy camping area at the lake's edge. This seems to be a little-used, and very quiet, campground. There are just fifteen sites. There is a kitchen shelter, pit toilets, fire grates and firewood. You can use lake or well water.

    Moon Lake Campground is similar to Whirlpool Lake, but is car-based. It is near the northern boundary of the park, on Highway 10. There are twenty-nine sites, in a mixed-forest environment. This campground has cold-water faucets, flush and pit toilets, picnic tables, fire grates and firewood.

Primitive Camping

There are eleven back-country trails, with primitive campsites. Most have water, and are provided with fire grates and firewood. All have pit privies. Registration in and out is required, if you are planning to stay overnight. Check on trail conditions, fire-hazard levels, bear occurrences, etc., with wardens.

The edge of the fescue grassland — the transition from prairies to forest

Group Camping

There are two group campgrounds in the park, one for camping, and one with dormitories. Write to the Superintendent, to find out about the facilities in detail. It is necessary to reserve ahead of time.

Other Accommodation, Gas, Food and Supplies

Because Riding Mountain is a park with a townsite, there is a wide range of cottages, trailer sites, motels, hotels, restaurants, grocery stores, gas stations, shops, etc. The park can send you a complete listing of the facilities in Wasagaming.

Recreational Services

Hiking   The park has a wide range of hiking trails, from short, self-guiding trails to slightly longer walks around lakes, to lengthy, back-country treks. They have a very good trail guide, and an informative booklet especially for back-country travellers. Write ahead for them, or ask at the Information Centre or Interpretive Centre.

Swimming   Swimming is supervised at the main beach at Wasagaming during daylight hours, seven days a week. There are many places for

A large prairie pothole makes a rich marsh

unsupervised swimming at numerous lakes. Some lakes have the parasite that causes swimmer's itch; ask at the Information Centre for an update.

Boating Motor boats are allowed on Clear Lake, Lake Audy and Moon Lake. Clear Lake and Lake Audy have launching ramps. Moon Lake does not, so for practical reasons, smaller boats, which can be hand-carried, are used there. Water skiing is allowed on Clear Lake and Lake Audy. Boats can be rented at Clear Lake, behind the park administration office.

Canoeing Many of the lakes in the park are good for canoeing, but the rivers are often dammed by beavers, and are less suitable.

Fishing Fishing is allowed in all lakes, but the major ones are: Clear Lake, for pickerel, pike, whitefish, and a few lake trout; Lake Audy, for jackfish; Deep Lake and Lake Katherine, both stocked with rainbow trout. A National Park fishing licence is required. It may be purchased, for a nominal fee, at the Information Centre and park entrance kiosks, from park wardens, and in the hamlets of Rossburn and Lake Audy, just outside the park. The park has a brochure on fishing, which you can write for, or ask for once you are there.

Golf There is an eighteen-hole golf course in Wasgaming. There is a pro shop, and you can rent clubs and carts. There are washrooms and a licensed restaurant.

Tennis There are six hard-surface courts, and washrooms. A moderate fee is paid to an attendant, at an hourly, weekly or seasonal rate.

Horseback Riding There are two stables near Wasagaming, which rent horses and conduct trail rides. Watch for signs.

Winter Use The park is open for alpine skiing at Mount Agassiz ski hill. There is a lodge, cafeteria, equipment rental, chair lift, T-bar and rope tow, and snow-making. Hotel accommodation is available in the nearby towns of McCreary and Onanole. Write to the park for the list of concessionaires.

Cross-country skiing is a major winter use. There is extensive trail-grooming and, if you register, you can strike out into the back-country. There are a number of warming huts, each with stove, wood and axes. Write to the park, for its brochure on cross-country skiing, snowshoeing and snowmobiling.

Ice fishing for jackfish, pickerel, perch and whitefish, on Clear Lake, is a very popular activity.

There are winter campgrounds, with pit toilets and kitchen shelters, at Moon Lake, Whirlpool, and Lake Katherine day-use areas.

Further Reading

Riding Mountain Yesterday and Today by Eric Ringstrom (Prentice
   Publishing, 1981)

FOR MORE INFORMATION

The Superintendent
Riding Mountain National Park
Wasagaming, Manitoba
R0J 2H0

Phone: (204) 848-2811
Fax: (204) 848-2596

PUKASKWA

NATIONAL PARK

Pukaskwa* National Park covers 1,880 square kilometres (725 square miles), along the northern shore of Lake Superior. Most of its area is wooded wilderness and icy water; the park's theme is "Wild Shore of an Inland Sea." Canoe the wild rivers or the length of the coastline, or walk along the Coastal Hiking Trail, and Pukaskwa's special character will emerge clearly and impressively.

Pukaskwa has two main types of environment; the water of Lake Superior and of the rivers that flow into it, and the forests, which are boreal and mixed-wood deciduous. Underlying both environments is a complex geological history, with the granite rocks of the Canadian Shield dominating, and the extrusions of volcanic lava adding another dimension.

Lake Superior is the largest body of fresh water in the world. Its depth and its northern location make it extremely cold. A lake this size behaves as a small ocean would at this latitude, except that it has no tides. Its weather is highly erratic. Terrifying storms and fogs appear in minutes, seemingly out of nowhere, and calm returns just as suddenly. The cold water has enormous effects on the land: the lake chills the air above it, and moist air that seeps inland does much to determine the kinds of plant and animal life that can survive.

The boreal forest at Pukaskwa has been greatly affected by the cold lake. In July and August, average temperatures range from 7°C (45°F) to 15°C (60°F). There *are* hot, sunny periods, but the pervasive coolness, and thin soil on the Canadian Shield, have created the primary conditions for the dense, scrubby spruce forests of the boreal zone. There are places in the park that are so exposed to cold winds, and so lacking in soil, that species of arctic-alpine plants, usually found at least a thousand kilometres (six hundred miles) north, grow there.

* Pronounced Puck-a-saw

Not all is thin soil and blowing wind, however. Fault lines in the rock can result in surface depressions, where soil collects. This has happened around Hattie Cove, where patches of mixed coniferous and deciduous forest of balsam fir and white birch have taken hold.

There is little history of human use in the area, but it is thought that people living here five thousand to ten thousand years ago made the mysterious Pukaskwa Pits. These stone pits range from 1 to 2.5 metres (3 to 8 feet) in length, and have walls about 1.5 metres (4 to 5 feet) high. It seems that, since Lake Superior's level was higher at that time, the pits would have been at the water's edge. Were they observation posts, or shelters for fishing or hunting? No one really knows. There are over a hundred of them in the park, on the shoreline and on raised cobble beaches.

How to See the Park

Despite the wildness of this park, a non-hiker can learn a great deal about the lake, the wilderness, and how people travel it, by visiting the Interpretive Centre at Hattie Cove. There is also a campground, with nearby trail access to sandy beaches, the Southern Headland Walking Trail, the Halfway Lake Trail and a protected inlet for family canoeing. But, if you've come specifically for the wilderness, come with lots of previous canoeing or hiking experience, plenty of time, good equipment and a full share of mental and physical endurance.

The Hattie Cove Visitation Centre

Hattie Cove is just 20 kilometres (12.5 miles) from the town of **Marathon**, the administrative centre of the park. At Hattie Cove, there is a parking lot and a beautiful Interpretive Centre. The Centre's exhibits describe human use of the park, with displays of appropriate canoeing and hiking equipment. There are pictures and descriptions of the wildlife, too. Friends of Pukaskwa operates a small gift shop in the centre.

The **Southern Headland Trail** focuses on the fascinating geological history of the headland. Starting outside the Centre, it takes you through small stands of the mixed forests, and out to the shoreline. Farther along, the trail leads to a beach at **Horseshoe Bay**, and back through a strip of boreal forest. This walk takes perhaps half an hour. It's easy, varied and beautiful. I went with a naturalist, who explained points of interest. Most interesting were the small, fresh-water pools that collect in the protected parts of shoreline rock during storms. Here, you can see dragonflies, water striders and plant forms that live in the still water, warmed by summer sun. They could never survive in the cold, surging water of Lake Superior, only a few metres away. The **Halfway Lake Trail** is a short, two-kilometre walk along the shoreline of the small, boreal, rock-rimmed Halfway Lake (formerly known as Beaver Lake). Self-guiding interpretive signs have been placed along both trails.

The Coastal Hiking Trail

The Coastal Trail, as it now exists, runs fifty-seven kilometres (thirty-five miles), from the **Hattie Cove Nature Centre** and registration site to the **North Swallow River**. For a day-hike, you can walk the first leg of the trail, from the Hattie Cove Campground to the first primitive campsite, at the junction with

Plant life survives on soil caught in cracks in the rocks

White River. This takes three to four hours each way, and will give a good sense of the shoreline, the lake and the bordering forest. More intrepid visitors can get a full-fledged wilderness experience, by hiking the length of the trail—an average of seven days' travel one way. Most hikers set their goal by the length of time they have. This is not a loop trail, so they walk one way for half of the time and return by the same route.

The goal of the park is to equip the entire trail with footbridges over sizable streams or rivers, boardwalks over fragile, moist areas, and steps in a few places that traverse steep and dangerous rock. There will be numerous primitive campsites along the way. The trail is well marked and in good condition, as far as **Oiseau River**. From Oiseau to the **White Gravel River**, the trail is less clearly marked. From the White Gravel River to the **North Swallow River**, the trail-marking and surface improve greatly. No matter what time of year you visit, be sure to talk at length with staff about trail conditions. Write to the Superintendent for the trail guides, and for the lists of topographic maps and the kinds of equipment and experience required for a wilderness trip.

The Coastal Canoe Trip

The full trip covers 180 kilometres (112 miles), through **Lake Superior**, starting north of the park at **Marathon**, and ending at **Michipicoten Harbour**, just outside of **Wawa**. Many people choose to start at Hattie Cove, where they park and register for the trip. At Michipicoten Harbour, a short road leads from there to the Trans-Canada Highway. Some people hitchhike back to the park or, if the canoe party has two cars, one can be

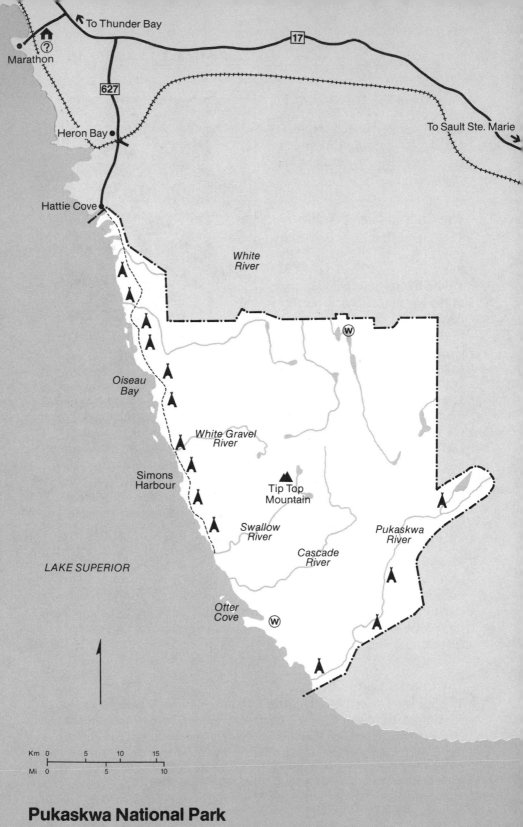

To Thunder Bay

17

To Sault Ste. Marie

Marathon

627

Heron Bay

Hattie Cove

White River

W

Oiseau Bay

White Gravel River

Simons Harbour

Tip Top Mountain

Swallow River

Cascade River

Pukaskwa River

LAKE SUPERIOR

Otter Cove

W

Km 0   5   10   15
Mi 0   5   10

Pukaskwa National Park
ONTARIO

left at each end of the route. Alternatively, the bus service between Wawa and Marathon can be used as a means of solving transportation logistics. The Coastal Canoe Trip is potentially risky; cold, fog and wind are always to be guarded against.

Because the shoreline is filigreed, there are many places to camp, or wait out the wind. In fact, canoeists are advised to expect to be grounded one day out of three, by wind. All the skills of the wilderness canoeist are required for this trip—orienteering, endurance, good planning and appropriate equipment. Visitors should write ahead to the Superintendent, for information, maps, transportation options, etc.

The White River Canoe Route

This is the way to experience the forests and rivers of Pukaskwa. The full route is 184 kilometres (114 miles) long, starting above White Lake. However, most paddlers choose to do the lower third, from **White Lake** to **Lake Superior**, near Hattie Cove. The White River was a route of voyageurs, and it passes through muskeg, past boreal forests, and through bare expanses of the Canadian Shield. There are many portages, as rapids, dams and falls impede progress. The trip takes, on average, five to seven days. The stretch on Lake Superior can be delayed by bad weather. Write to the Superintendent, for the brochure on this route, and for names of commercial outfitters and guides with whom you may want to make the trip.

Park Facilities and Services

Interpretive Programme

The interpretive programme includes guided hikes, slide and film shows, prop talks and special events, from late June through to Labour Day. During the fall, winter and spring, school and special-interest groups can request programmes that will accent their curriculum or areas of interest. Emphasis is on small-group interaction.

Camping

There is a sixty-seven-site campground at **Hattie Cove**. There are twenty-nine sites with electricity only. There are showers, flush toilets, and hot and cold water in washrooms. Unserviced sites have picnic tables, fire grates and wood, and a tent-pad area. It is densely wooded, with a good vegetation screen between sites. Expect a lot of biting insects.

Filigreed shoreline at Hattie Cove

Primitive Camping

There are frequent designated sites along the **Coastal Hiking Trail** and the **White River Canoe Route**. They have pit toilets, and fire rings may be set out. Use of your own camping gas stove is the most dependable source of heat, because wood may not be dry.

Other Accommodation, Gas, Food and Supplies

The small village of Heron Bay, five kilometres (three miles) north of the park, on Highway 627, has a general store and gas station. The town of Marathon, on Highway 627, north of Hattie Cove, has a variety of stores, hotels and motels, gas stations, restaurants, etc.

Recreational Services

Hiking   There are the short walks around the Hattie Cove area, and the lengthy Coastal Trail. Back-country and canoe trip/boating registration boxes are present, and registration is strongly encouraged, due to the rugged, and wilderness, aspects of the park.

Canoeing Although the major canoe routes are the Coastal Canoe route and the White River, some people also canoe the Pukaskwa River, to Otter Cove on Lake Superior. In Hattie Cove, the inexperienced canoeist can spend a safe, easy hour or two, paddling in sight of the centre and by the campground. For the long routes, canoeists are strongly encouraged to register.

Fishing Lake Superior and the rivers provide good fishing for trout, pike, pickerel, salmon and whitefish, depending on the season. A national park licence is required. It may be obtained at the Hattie Cove Centre, or at the administration building in Marathon.

How to Get There

You can reach Pukaskwa by private car from the Trans-Canada Highway, or by Greyhound Bus. The drop-off point for the bus is Marathon. There are commercial boat services to drop-off points for the Coastal Hiking Trail, although most people walk the round trip. With park permission only, canoeists who have taken the Pukaskwa River to Otter Cove can be picked up there. Write to the Superintendent for information on transportation operators.

FOR MORE INFORMATION

The Superintendent
Pukaskwa National Park
Hwy 627, Hattie Cove
Via: Heron Bay, Ontario
P0T 1R0

Friends of Pukaskwa
General Delivery
Heron Bay, Ontario
P0T 1R0

Phone: (807) 229-0801

BRUCE PENINSULA

NATIONAL PARK

Bruce Peninsula National Park is one of the newest parks in the national system, but it, like Fathom Five, has a previous history as an Ontario Provincial Park. It was called Cyprus Lake, the name of the largest of its lakes. The park is about 140 square kilometres in size, and it has a stunning array of natural features, all contained within quite a small area.

Several of the park's easily accessible trails wind along some of the most spectacular shorelines in Canada. There are gentle walks along lake shores, passing by stands of exotic ferns and orchids. The ground beneath you may have been scored and pitted by glaciers, and the boulders you skirt around may have been carried hundreds of kilometres from their northern points of origin. And not far from all this natural beauty is the multitude of activities and facilities provided for visitors to the area—the very popular tourism destinations of Bruce and Grey counties.

Bruce Peninsula National Park preserves a part of the West St. Lawrence Lowlands Natural Region. This is a limestone-based area, with a dramatically varying topography, and a rich natural and human history. The backbone of the park is the Niagara Escarpment, that finger of sedimentary rock bordering the western shore of Georgian Bay, which is the eastern segment of Lake Huron.

At one time, this area was covered by an inland sea, which was present during the Silurian Period of the Palaeozoic Era. The sequence of events that resulted in today's landbase is very complex but, in essence, the skeletons of the underwater corals and other sea creatures formed layer upon layer of calcium-based sediments, as they collected on the sea bottom. These layers were compressed at the lower levels by the weight of the layers above them. This pressure, and various chemical reactions, created a type of limestone rock, called dolomite, out of the sediments. This development took place about 415 million years ago.

When the inland sea retreated, the limestone bedrock was exposed to the eroding effects of wind, water, ice and the breakdown of organic materials. Over a period of some two to three hundred million years, the area was carved and shaped by these forces. Then, some one hundred million years ago, the first of the four major glacial episodes began. The last, the Wisconsin, ended about ten thousand years ago. The actions of the ice sheets can be traced today in the park, in the lakes left by the retreating glaciers, in the cobble shorelines, now many feet above water level, in the pitted and scarred surfaces of many rocks.

The fact that the bedrock of the Bruce Peninsula is dolomite also contributes greatly to the dramatic character of the area. Dolomite tends to break down in straight lines—vertical or horizontal. Water seeps down through vertical cracks, and then flows along horizontal spaces. When a rock is weakened by thousands of years of flowing water, or the pressures of that water freezing and then thawing and freezing again, the rock tends to break in straight lines. Where there is a thicker dolomite caprock, as is true for the whole of the Niagara Escarpment, the water action undermines the softer lower rock, and huge segments of rock may fall abruptly away along a fault line, making massive topographic features like the Escarpment itself. This process is seen on a smaller scale in the flowerpot, or pillar, formations that are found along the shoreline of the park (and of Fathom Five. For that matter, you can see the same kind of thing in several of the national parks in the Rocky Mountains, which also have a limestone base.)

The geology of the area is just one aspect of its distinctiveness and interest. The Peninsula may be very far from the ocean, but it has a maritime climate, because of the huge body of water that cradles it. The relative mildness of the climate, and the abundance of moisture, make a rich environment for plant and animal life. The soil quantity is very uneven but, for the visitor, the happy result is a wide variety of natural habitats to explore. There are bogs, marshes, swamps, deciduous forests characteristic of areas further south, and stands of boreal forest, which are characteristic of more northern areas.

How To See The Park

Bruce Peninsula National Park is a park in transition and, because of this, not all of the visitor sites are clearly defined or fully developed for use. There are a number of places, interspersed among park areas, that are private land holdings, the owners of which have been there for generations. As always in any national park, it is a good idea to start your visit at the Visitor Centre. Bruce Peninsula National Park and Fathom Five share the

Visitor Centre at Little Tub Harbour in Tobermory. Staff can help you match your interests with the best places to go in the park, and they can tell you exactly what facilities are available and whether you will be near private lands. In these cases, it is very important that you exercise a "good-neighbour policy," and be particularly careful not to disturb the area by careless parking, littering, or inconsiderate intrusion of any sort.

There are two main areas for visitors to the park. One is the Cyprus Lake section. The other main area is Singing Sands, a day-use area on the west side of the Peninsula, just opposite the Cyprus Lake area.

Cyprus Lake offers both a campground and a day-use area. On its eastern edge, along the shore of Georgian Bay, is one of the most spectacular walks in the whole national park system, to my mind. There is also a very interesting complex of lakes, forests and bogs in the Cyprus Lake area. The shoreline walk and the inland lakes and forest are all linked by a network of trails.

The Cyprus Lake visitor area is about seven kilometres south of Tobermory. The entrance is from Highway 6, and it is clearly marked. Since this is the only campground for the park, it is easy to combine a camping trip with easy hikes along the lakes or the shoreline. Of course, with all the campgrounds and other accommodation in the area, you should have no problem finding almost any kind of place to stay, and then visiting the trails from there.

The walk that you should not miss is a circle trail, starting out from the parking lot at the east end of Cyprus Lake. You can choose to follow the **Horse Lake**, **Marr Lake** or **Georgian Bay** trails, to start. You will be no more than an hour on the first part of the circuit, winding your way through the conifer forest, and passing along the shores of the inland lake. Then you will emerge along the shoreline of Georgian Bay. Here, you join the **Bruce Trail**, that famous trail that runs 730 kilometres along the Niagara Escarpment, from Niagara Falls right into Tobermory, at the tip of the Bruce Peninsula.

The story of this circle trail is very much the story of the geology of the limestone landscape that the park epitomizes. The park has an excellent map of the whole trail complex at Cyprus Lake, and it helps you identify and understand key points of interest. For example, there are shelves of limestone stretching out from shore. On these shelves are huge boulders, which have fallen from the cliff above. There are little coves etched out of the rocks, making small amphitheatres with shallow steps up to the sides of cliffs. Though parts of the shoreline are limestone slabs, there are parts where the action of the winds and waves has created cobble beaches. It is possible, in some places, to tell which cobbles have been there for a long time, and which have been thrown up by recent storms. Those that have been there for many years are darker, and have had a chance to accu-

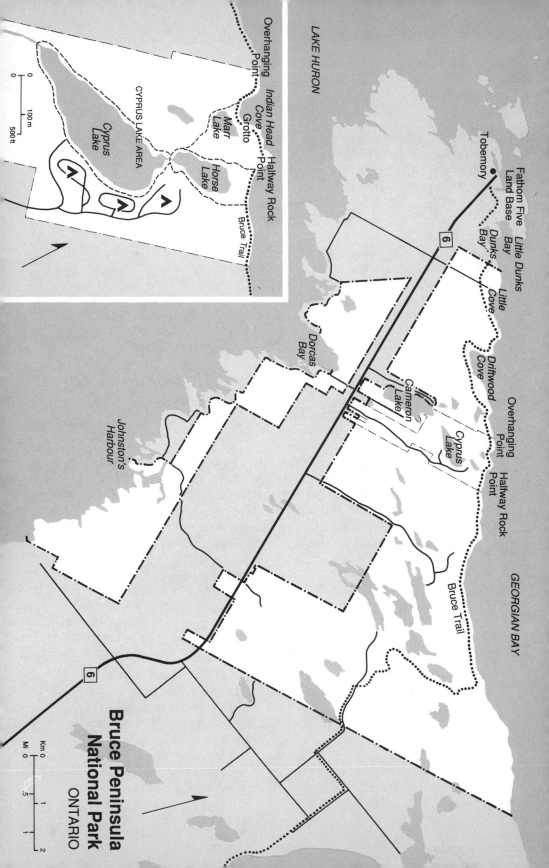

mulate lichen on their surfaces. The boulder beach that separates Marr Lake from Georgian Bay is a great place to see how active the interaction between water and land can be. The beach is constantly changing, as storms throw up rocks that have broken off from the cliffs and fallen into the water. Then the water itself, and the friction of rock against rock, smooths their edges and grinds their oblong shapes into rounded boulders and smaller cobblestones.

There are caves and grottoes along the trail. They have been formed in several ways. Some were formed as a result of the limestone being dissolved by the chemical action of water seeping along the faults in the bedrock. Other were formed by wave action. There are caves at ground level, which you can peek into from the trail, and there are others below the waterline that only divers can visit. Others are higher up the cliff face, and show where the water level used to be.

You can look up at the cliffs, and see very clearly the layer upon layer of sedimentary rock. The roots of windswept, gnarled white cedar show the outlines of the vertical cracks that they dig into for dear life. The roots may turn at right angles to follow the horizontal faulting, as well. Then, as the trail ascends to the top of the cliffs, you will be treated to vista after vista of brilliant blue water far below, green forest running to the edge of the cliffs, white shorelines and turquoise shallows. You think you've seen the most startling view and, a few metres along the trail, there is another one, more wonderful than the one before.

The trail does have a few places where you will cling to roots and rocks, too, to help you along. It's not too strenuous; you just have to watch your step and not be in a hurry. If you do have a time limit, it should be possible for most people to "do" the Horse Lake-Georgian Bay-Marr Lake Trail Circuit in about four hours. But pack a lunch and a warm sweater, even in the height of summer, and take your time.

Even though the lakes nestled in the network of trails aren't as immediately spectacular as the walk along Georgian Bay, they are well worth a leisurely stroll, especially if you take the time to look closely at the varied "micro-habitats." There are several places along the shores of Marr Lake and Horse Lake that have insectivorous plants. Bogs and fens are actually very poor in the nutrients that plants need, especially nitrogen. So a number of plants have devised ways to get nitrogen from animal matter, since it is not available in the watery mush of the bog.

Singing Sands

A visit to the Singing Sands is a dramatic contrast to the rugged cliffs, convoluted shoreline, and imposing forest of the Cyprus Lake area. It is on the western side of the Peninsula, just opposite the entrance to Cyprus Lake.

The surface of this side of the Niagara Escarpment is very flat. At first, it may not seem as interesting or as beautiful as the Georgian Bay side of the park. However, if you have an eye for sunsets on gently sloping beaches, or want to walk for hours with a toddler, along a shoreline that seems to have no dividing line between water and land, then Singing Sands is definitely the place to spend a few hours.

There are two distinct parts of the Singing Sands visitation area. One is the beach itself. It is a very firm, flat beach, which is perfect for wading. The water warms up considerably on sunny days, because it is so shallow, so far out. (You keep expecting the tide to come in, the expanses are so great, and the lake beyond stretches to the horizon like an ocean.) As you trace the shoreline to the morthwest, the flat rocks at the edge show pitted limestone. The indentations are caused when the rain and lake water splash onto the shore and are held in small depressions. The water evaporates, and leaves a concentration of acids behind. This happens over, and through, the centuries, and the indentations become more distinct pits.

As you move back from the shoreline, at the northern edge of the beach, there are several terraces of low rock perpendicular to the shore. There are low, parallel rock ripples, about five metres from crest to crest. The glaciers made these grooves over ten thousand years ago.

The other part of the Singing Sands area is the **Dorcas Bay Nature Reserve**. It was the first nature preserve purchased by the Federation of Ontario Naturalists. This was done in 1962. It is a part of the park area that is in transition, and it is not officially park land. However, it is an integral part of the park experience, and visitors can enter it freely from the parking lot at the inner limits of the beach. Visitors are asked to be especially respectful of this fragile area, parts of which should be avoided, because regeneration projects are underway. (These are noted at the site.)

The Dorcas Bay area is the wooded backdrop to the Singing Sands beach. It starts with the wet bog/fen areas that are the home of the orchids and insectivorous plants, including pitcher plants, sundew and butterworts. The pitcher plant is the one with the elongated red tubes, as much as six inches long, with an opening at the top, about an inch wide. The tube catches water, and insects are trapped in the water when they fall in, or come for a sip. In their waterlogged condition, they can only try to climb up the sides of the tube. But the fine "hairs," which line the tube, and slant downward, prevent the insects' escape. The insects then dissolve, aided by acids the plant releases into the water-filled cup. Then the plant "feeds" on the insect, by absorbing the nutritious elements of what is left of it. The pitcher plant has a single-stalked flower, often rising twenty or more centimetres above the fan of tubes at the plant's base. Even in the autumn, it is possible to pick out the pitcher plants from their surroundings, because the flowers seem to hold on, even if turning brown and dry, for a very long time. The sundew is equally fascinating, though a very tiny plant. It traps insects, by exuding a sticky substance that glues the prey to the plant leaves. The plant has chemicals that dissolve the insect, and the plant absorbs what it needs to survive.

Beyond the wet bog/fen area is the sandy forest, with stands of red and white pines. Streams meander down to the beach. There is a trail that leads away from the water, and into the woods to the east. There is dense cedar bush, with occasional clearings with low domes of rock, where soil has not been able to develop. These clearings are good places to see a number of kinds of lichen—which are able to take hold where little else can. There are also deep cracks cutting through the rock and, as you look down within them, there are ferns and mosses, which have been able to use the moisture and small amounts of soil that collect there.

The signs for Dorcas Bay were not fully in place when I visited, and it is very easy to get lost in this kind of terrain. So be sure you ask first, at the Visitor Centre, about the status of the trail and its signs, before you go very far away from the shore.

Park Services and Facilities

Because this park is so new to the system, and there are a number of issues that have to be resolved over the years to come, the park facilities and services are not as elaborate and well-established as they are in most of the other national parks. You will have a great visit in a wonderful setting, but the high-quality shelters, washrooms, picnic and parking areas that you find in other national parks will be in the process of completion over the next several years. As with a visit to any park, do start your visit at the Visitor Centre, at Little Tug Harbour in Tobermory.

Interpretive Programme

Most of the interpretive programming is provided out of the Cyprus Lake Campground, from June to September. There are signs posted on the bulletin boards that tell you the schedule and location of any events. There are park staff on duty who can answer any questions you have about the wildlife of the area. There are programmes at the outdoor amphitheatre, at the western edge of the campground complex, near Cyprus Lake itself. There are interpreter-led walks in the Cyprus Lake area, along the Georgian Bay trails, and at the Dorcas Bay Reserve location. The staff emphasize interpretive activities for children in their programming.

There are some interpretive walks that start in the Visitor Centre at Little Tub Harbour in Tobermory. These are explorations of the natural and human history of Fathom Five National Marine Park. The administration, and a number of visitor activities, for Fathom Five and Bruce Peninsula are combined, because of Tobermory, and because the two parks are so closely related, in location and in their natural and human histories.

Camping

There is one campground, with three sections, at the Cyprus Lake area. There are 242 sites, in all. **Birches**, with ninety-eight sites, is designed to have room for trailers to pull in. There are no services for trailers.

There is a pumping station for trailers, just before the campground office. The **Poplars** site, with sixty-three places, and the **Tamarack** sites, with eighty-one places, are tent-camping areas. Each site has a picnic table and a fire grate. There are toilets and water taps for every few campsites. There is no electricity. There is firewood available in the evenings, from a woodlot across from the Birches campground, for a fee. When the woodlot is closed, campers can obtain wood from businesses along Highway 6.

Other Accommodation, Gas, Food and Supplies

Because the whole Bruce Peninsula is such a well-developed tourism area, there is an abundance of services and facilities for visitors. There are at least twenty-five commercial campgrounds, some bed-and-breakfasts, and a number of motels along Highway 6. Places to eat, gas stations, and stores that carry any camping supplies or emergency items you may need, are readily accessible.

Many businesses have racks of brochures, with pamphlets on the local services and attractions. The regional tourist association has excellent publications. You'll be able to find out anything you need to know about visiting the surrounding area, from these sources. The Park Visitor Centre is an excellent source of information, as well.

Recreational Facilities

Swimming   There are two swimming areas at Cyprus Lake. The day-visitor beach is just to the left of the campground office. Campers may use it, also. The other beach is for campers, and it is in front of the Poplars site.

Boating   Non-powered boats are allowed on Cyprus Lake at any time. Motorboats are prohibited from June 15 to September 15. There is a great deal of powerboating and sailing around the Bruce Peninsula. The focus of this is Tobermory, where there is a marina. Call or write ahead to the park for information, or contact the regional tourism associations.

Fishing   Bass, perch, and yellow pickerel are found in Cyprus Lake. There are some trout in nearby streams, and there is good fishing in some of the coves in Georgian Bay. Fishing is allowed under provincial regulations. Ask at the Visitor Centre in Tobermory, for further information.

Winter Use   There is limited winter camping, snowmobiling on the Tobermory Ski and Snow Association Trail in the park, and cross-country skiing. Ask at the Visitor Centre, or call the park ahead of time, to see what the status is for any of these activities—snow conditions, trail quality, etc.

Further Reading

The Flora of the Tobermory Islands, Bruce Peninsula National Park by J.J Morton and Joan M. Venn, Department of Biology, University of Waterloo

---

FOR MORE INFORMATION

The Superintendent
Bruce Peninsula National Park
P.O. Box 189
Tobermory, Ontario
N0H 2R0

The Bruce Trail Association
P.O. Box 857
Hamilton, Ontario
L8N 3N9

Phone: (519) 596-2233

Bruce Peninsula Tourist Association
R.R. #2
Hepworth, Ontario
N0H 1P0

Phone: (519) 422-2114

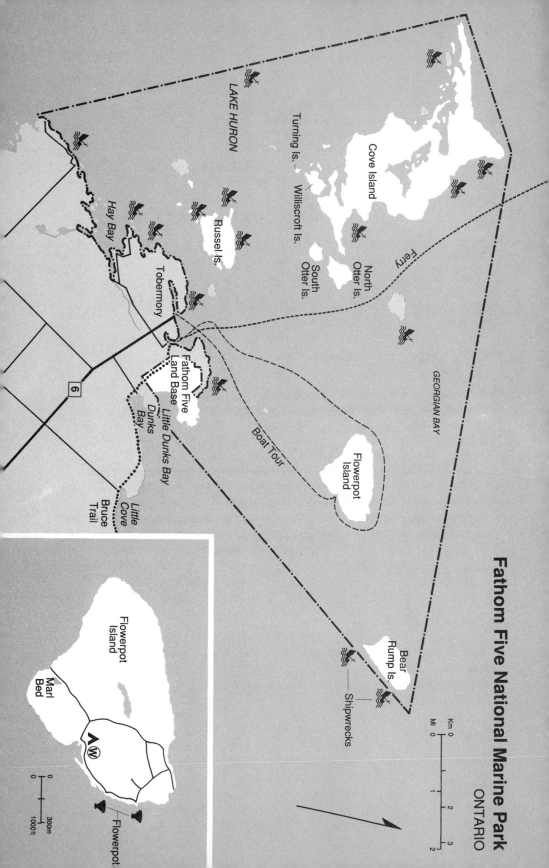

Fathom Five National Marine Park

ONTARIO

LAKE HURON

Turning Is.
Williscroft Is.

Cove Island

Hay Bay

Russel Is.

South
Otter Is.

North
Otter Is.

Ferry

Tobermory

GEORGIAN BAY

6

Fathom Five
Land Base

Dunks
Bay

Little Dunks Bay

Boat Tour

Flowerpot
Island

Little
Cove

Bruce
Trail

Bear
Rump Is.

Shipwrecks

Km   0   1   2   3
Mi   0   1   2

Inset Map

Flowerpot
Island

Marl
Bed

Flowerpot Island

0   300m
0   1000ft

Flowerpot

FATHOM FIVE

NATIONAL MARINE PARK

Many of Canada's national parks protect the shorelines along our oceans and gulfs. They offer the chance to camp by the sea, or hike for days along trails that follow "inland seas," like Lake Superior. But, in fact, the water is not included within the protective mantle of these parks (with the exception of Pacific Rim) because, until very recently, Canada had no marine parks. This omission was corrected in 1987, with the designation of Fathom Five as Canada's first national marine park. Fathom Five may be the first marine park under federal jurisdiction, but it made history as early as 1972, as Canada's first underwater park. In that year, it was set aside by Ontario as one of its provincial parks.

Fathom Five is at the tip of the Bruce Peninsula, which juts out into Lake Huron, separating Georgian Bay in the east and the larger portion of Lake Huron on the Peninsula's western side. The park also includes nine-teen islands that used to be part of Georgian Bay Islands National Park. These islands have been added to the mainland base of the "old" Fathom Five. Visitors come here to don their diving gear and explore the wrecks of ships, some only a few metres from shore. They come to visit islands that were once the floor of a giant inland sea. They peer at rare orchids, and wander around old lighthouses. All of this in one park, well within a half-day's drive of Toronto.

The Park preserves a beautiful example of the Georgian Bay Marine Natural Region, one of the five Great Lakes marine natural regions (and one of twenty-nine marine regions throughout Canada). The water surface area of the park is about 130 square kilometres. There are three main areas to visit—one is the water environment itself, another is the islands to the north and east of the tip of the Bruce Peninsula, and the third is a small segment of the rugged Georgian Bay coastline at the eastern landbase of the park. A visit to any of these three areas will likely start from Tobermory, the community that is the "base camp" for most visitors to the park.

The aquatic environment is a mixed one, because the park is located at the meeting place of the relatively warm water of Lake Huron and the colder, and less biologically diverse, waters of Georgian Bay, the eastern segment of Lake Huron. For the visitor, one of the most attractive features of the waters of the park is their clarity and brilliant colour. The hiker can peer down from cliffs into waters that are reminiscent of pictures of tropical islands, with shorelines of the palest grey bordering turquoise shallows and vibrant blue depths. For the diver, the water's clarity makes for some of the best diving in North America. The rugged underwater topography is fascinating but, for many, the greater appeal is the human history of the area, as evidenced by the remains of twenty-three shipwrecks, scattered over the lake bottom within the park boundaries.

Because of its strategic location in the Great Lakes shipping lanes, the waters of what is now Fathom Five have been a busy place for ships for a century and a half. The sudden squalls that characterize the area, and the cliffs and canyons of the lake bottom, which create irregular wave patterns, combine at times to create very hazardous conditions for boats. These storms have left a ghostly underwater heritage. Though divers can glide in among the skeletons of these wrecks, the location of some of them, in shallow water right in Tobermory's two coves, makes it possible for visitors to get a good look at several of them without every having to dive right in.

The landforms of the mainland part of Fathom Five are part of the famous Niagara Escarpment, a rocky ridge stretching from Niagara Falls, becoming the backbone of the Bruce Peninsula, and dipping underwater at the Peninsula tip. Then bits and pieces of the Escarpment appear as the many islands in this part of Lake Huron. They rise from the watery depths, like tips of earthen icebergs. The escarpment comes up for air again, so to speak, as Manitoulin Island, which stretches south to the Bruce, making a major part of the whole island chain that stairsteps down Lake Huron.

The bedrock underlying Fathom Five (and nearby Bruce Peninsula National Park) is limestone, sedimentary rock formed from warm inland seas that covered the area over four hundred million years ago. The seas retreated and the sea floor was uplifted, only to be scoured and eroded by the action of weather, of rivers and of repeated glaciation. The levels of Lake Huron have varied over time, and what were once shorelines now may be on high ground, or caves hollowed out by wave action may be deep under water, or far above the water's edge.

The human history of Fathom Five's land and waters is long and intriguing. Archaeological evidence shows that Native people have visited the area—trading, fishing, hunting, and camping—for at least three thousand years. The Cape Croker Indian Reserve is the home of Ojibway people and, though this is not a part of the park, the Native people of the Reserve offer camping and recreational facilities as a part of their ongoing life today.

From the mid-1850s to the 1920s, the area was an active crossroads for shipping between central and western Canada, and the three lighthouses in the Park Boundaries were built to aid in navigation. Commercial fishing also took place in the park area, though this has diminished considerably with the depletion of fish stocks. Recreational boats now far outnumber the commercial vessels to be seen, but nearby communities, such as Owen Sound, still benefit from commercial shipping.

How to See the Park

With all its distinctive aquatic and land features, and wonderful opportunities for enjoying them, its important to know that Fathom Five is an integral part of one of the most popular tourism areas in Eastern Canada. You'll want to visit the park, but you'll be glad if you make the visit part of a longer and larger visit to this appealing area.

Some 300,000 people pour through the tiny town of Tobermory each year, mostly in the months of June, July and August. The mode of choice for travel is the car ferries, *M.S. Chi-Cheemaun* and *M.S. Nindawyama*, which carry about 260,000 of these visitors between South Baymouth, on Manitoulin Island, and Tobermory. Often, ferry passengers make a circle of Georgian Bay, stopping to visit points of interest along the way. Fathom Five, and the two other national parks on Lake Huron— Georgian Bay Islands and Bruce Peninsula—also play a significant role in attracting people to the area. It is easy to fit in a rewarding visit to each national park within a week's vacation period, but it would be better to take more time, and see the other, non-park attractions. Each of the small communities has its own special character, there is a range of campground settings and levels of development, and the nearby Ontario provincial parks are good places to visit, as well. The main road access from the south is Highway 6. There is a marina in Tobermory, and many other boating centres in Georgian Bay.

The Land of Fathom Five

There is very little land base of Fathom Five on the mainland around Tobermory. These areas are in a transition period, with consultations going on between local residents and the park over possible changes; visitor facilities, the marina, local roads and parking, etc. So, by the time you get there, this information may be somewhat dated. However, the park publishes a map and newsletter, as well as other informational brochures that will bring you up to date. The local businesses usually have their own brochures, and there is a community newspaper that you should look for, as well, to get an overview of what's happening.

Tobermory has two harbours, around which most of the land-based visitor activities happen. They are **Little Tub** and **Big Tub Harbours**. There is a temporary park Visitor Centre at Little Tub, and a Diver Registration Centre, as well. On weekends, volunteers from the Ontario Underwater Council assist in the diver-safety programme. Also at the Visitor Centre, there are some items for sale from the Friends of Fathom Five, a volunteer association, which is very active in encouraging appropriate and safe park use. It is very enjoyable just to stroll in the town, and there is an excellent boardwalk now, along the southeast shore of Little Tub, which was built by the Friends.

At the northern side of the mouth of Big Tub Harbour, is the **Big Tub Lighthouse**, built in 1885. There is a small amount of parking there, and there is a brick walkway, built by the Friends of Fathom Five, which eases your way over the flat limestone rocks. This is a very small area, but it is always enjoyable to be so near a real lighhouse. You may be mingling with divers, too, because they come here for the easy access to the water, one of the popular shore-accessible dive sites.

The best-known part of Fathom Five's terrestrial area is an island, Flowerpot. It can be reached by private boat—there is an overnight mooring there—and by a range of water taxis, which can be boarded in Tobermory. Campers can be dropped off, but most people either circle the island and return to the mainland, or are dropped off for a few hours, for a wonderful hike.

Flowerpot Island

Flowerpot is a popular destination for visitors to Fathom Five. Flowerpot is an enchanting island, its geological history readily evident in its limestone cliffs, caves and "flowerpots." A 3-kilometre (1.75-mile) walk starts at the docking area at **Beachy Cove**, and a self-guiding brochure explains the natural history of the island. Take the trail in a counter-clockwise direction to follow the brochure and, if your time is limited, be sure to see the flowerpots, the tapered columns at the water's edge, for which the island is named. The trail has a few offshoots, one to a working lighthouse on the bluffs of the northeast corner of the island, and one leading from the southwest corner of the trail to a marl bed and the western shore of the island.

On the north side of the island, there are caves high in the cliffs above the trail. These caves must have been formed by the action of waves that once reached that level. Visitors must register with the park superintendent before entering any of the caves, except the main cave, which has a stairway and observation platform.

Further evidence of earlier high-water levels is the cobblestone corridor that you cross on the ten-minute walk from the main trail to the marl beds. The cobblestones, rounded by lapping waves, were the beach of a small bay, which once filled the indentation in the land. The marl bed itself has been formed by rain water running off the surrounding slopes, carrying with it fine particles of limestone, which have collected to form this dense, claylike bed. Since water drains so slowly through the clay base, the pond has formed.

The plants of Flowerpot Island are, of course, quite dependent upon the type of soil available—its chemical and organic composition, its depth and slope, its moisture content, etc. Because of glacial action, the soil on the island is deep in only a few places. Plants cannot put down deep roots, since they meet the underlying limestone in a few centimetres, or about a metre at most. The limestone base makes a very moist soil, because water cannot drain through it. These cool, moist, shallow soils create a boglike habitat that is ideal for plants such as orchids. When I was there, dozens of calypso orchids lined the trail, with striped coralroot at the edge of the lighthouse lawn, and northern twayblade and the rare Alaska orchid on the **Mountain Trail**.

With the richness of orchids, orchid photographers abound. I must say I was stunned by the disregard for the habitat and flowers evidenced by some photographers. All the orchids I saw were by the main trail—some of the flowers barely survived the photographers, but most were quite intact. Considering the variety of flowers that can be seen from the trail, it seems to me that a genuine love of rare flowers (not to speak of the park regulations) dictates leaving the less accessible areas untrampled, to carry on their life cycle undisturbed, no matter how much a photograph is desired.

The whole walk—loop trail, side trips to the lighthouse and marl bed—takes at most two and one-half hours. It is a must for getting a clear idea of the diversity of this park. And it is a simply beautiful experience.

The Water World of Fathom Five

To get more than a superficial view of the marine element of this national marine park, it is necessary either to take a boat or take a dive. There are docking and mooring facilities in Tobermory, and about two thousand boats a year make use of them. However, most people don't have boats of their own, and there are a number of boating options for these visitors. If you travel on the *Chi-Cheemaun*, you'll get a good overview of the expanse of water leading to the tip of the Bruce Peninsula. And there are tour boats to Flowerpot, charter boats for divers, for fishing, for nature lovers, and general sightseers. These boats range from inflatables to the fully covered, very comfortable motor launches. Any restaurant, store, gas station, or tourism centre is bound to have brochures on the boat services and, of course, the park's Visitor Centre at Little Tub Harbour can provide you with information, as well.

One really distinctive feature of the local boating services available to visitors is glass-bottom boats. They are not the glass-bottom boats that are found in the calm waters of Florida tourist attractions, because the waters of Lake Huron are too powerful for that. But they have windows along the hull, below the water, and you lean over and peer down through them to the shipwrecks or natural life of the underwater. I was told that water in the two Tobermory Harbours and nearby locations is so clear and shallow that, even if you are in another type of boat, you can get a very good view of some of the wrecks.

But it is scuba diving that is the big draw of the waters of Fathom Five, for over nine thousand people a year. They make an average of twenty-five thousand dives, in all—quite a lot for a summer! They come for the human history and the natural history of the underwater world of the park.

The human history is evidenced in the remains of twenty-one shipwrecks within the boundary of the park (though only nineteen have been identified). There are five sites right in the Tobermory harbour area. These are enjoyed by divers below, and boaters above. Most of these wrecks occurred between 1883 and 1907, and most were caused by the treacherous storms of autumn. The wrecks are quite varied, in how intact the boat remains are. Some, like the Sweepstakes, in Big Tub Harbour, are in very good condition, and others are just collections of lumber and other debris. There are schooners and steamers and tugs, barges, barques, and motor ships. Depths range from a few metres to the deepest, lying in forty-five metres.

The natural history of the marine element of Fathom Five is fascinating and readily accessible to divers, as well. Not all of the dive sites are actually within the park boundaries, and one is near the cliffs bordering Bruce Peninsula National Park's main campground. Diving in designated areas gives visitors a chance to get a stronger sense of the geological forces that shaped the Bruce Peninsula. It's easy to see the action of glaciers, including huge underwater boulders, the glacial "erratics" that have been carried by the sheets of ice far from their original locations, in the north. Pitting and scouring are evident, and there are underwater caves, as well.

Other Places of Interest

Because there are nineteen islands in Fathom Five, it is a good idea to ask at the Visitor Centre about other sites. For example, **Cove Island** has the oldest lighthouse in the Upper Great Lakes, built in 1856, one of six Imperial Towers built in that period. While it does not have visitor facilities, it is possible to tie up there and have a brief leg-stretch over the immaculate grounds around the lighthouse. Staff can make other suggestions, and the local residents, who operate boating services and other visitor amenities, no doubt can, also.

Also, bear in mind that the Bruce Peninsula is a very well-developed tourism destination. It is easy to get information on the points of natural or human history. These include limestone caves near Wiarton, the woodlands and waters of the Cape Croker Indian Reserve, five Ontario provincial parks along the Lake Huron shore, or a sawmill you can watch in action, and museums like the Bruce County Museum in Southampton. Many people trek the Bruce Trail, thus making Fathom Five and Bruce Peninsula National Parks part of their experience of the region. Write to the park, or any of the contacts listed at the end of the chapter, and you will receive an abundance of information for planning your trip.

Park Services and Facilities

Because Fathom Five has so little land base, and much of that is island and rather fragile, there is relatively little park development of the sort that land-based parks tend to have. There is a small, temporary Visitor Centre at Little Tub Harbour. It will not find its permanent home for some time, but as it is now, it is a good place to start your visit. There are very attractive displays on diving, maps of the area, staff to answer questions, and printed material on the park and how to visit it and the surrounding area. Parking can be frustrating in Tobermory, but there is no alternative but being patient—or coming in the early summer, or in September or October. Most of the services are still open, but there are fewer people.

Interpretive Programme

The interpretation of Fathom Five's natural and human history is done mostly through the Visitor Centre displays, an attractive newsletter, trail brochures for Flowerpot Island, and interpretive signs at Flowerpot itself. If you are staying at Bruce Peninsula National Park, the interpretation there often deals with some aspects of Fathom Five, and they have offered walks along the Tobermory harbour shoreline, as part of the FFNMP interpretive programming.

Camping

There are only six campsites in Fathom Five, and they are all on wooden decks, slightly above the shoreline on Flowerpot Island. They are offered on a first-come/first-served basis. Ask at the Visitor Centre, for news on how likely they are to be occupied. You must pack everything in and out. Camp sites have wood fireplaces and pit toilets. The nearest other camping in a national park is at Bruce Peninsula National Park. There are 242 sites there, in three campgrounds.

Other Accommodation, Gas, Food and Supplies

The whole Bruce Peninsula, and the areas to the south and east (Owen Sound, Grey County) bordering Lake Huron, are a wonderful combination of rural, nearly natural, and moderately urban life. There are at least twenty-five commercial campgrounds within an hour or two drive from Tobermory, and there is a 242-site campground at nearby Bruce Peninsula National Park. There are many motels in the area, restaurants to suit a range of budgets, and gas stations abound.

People with trailers will find a number of facilities welcoming them, and I saw one brochure for a mobile sewage-disposal service!

Recreational Services

The park itself does not provide recreational services, such as patrolled beaches. There is a ski route on the land base, and there are many recreational opportunities within the park boundaries, because of the commercial services available.

Boating As noted, there is a municipal marina with full services, in Tobermory. For boaters not familiar with the waters of Georgian Bay, it is essential that you familiarize yourself with local conditions. Wind and weather are extremely unpredictable, and the thousands of islands that are strewn throughout the area must be taken into account at all times. For visitors without their own boats, you are likely to find exactly the kind of commercial service you want—from taking the *Chi-Cheemaun* to going out for a few hours in an afternoon, or being dropped off at Flowerpot to camp, and being picked up on schedule a couple of days later. Prices vary, according to the service, and it's impossible to quote the range here. However, they did generally seem within most families' vacation budgets.

Diving There is a very wide range of diving opportunities in Fathom Five, and people with novice, to very advanced, skills will find something suited to their interests and experience. All divers must register at the Diver Registration Centre, at the waterfront of Little Tub Harbour. When divers register, they get the annual dive tags, which show that they have received the safety message. All the standard safety and courtesy requirements for divers must be observed, and the park urges divers to be particularly sensitive to the needs of local residents and boaters in the harbour areas. It can get rather crowded there. There are three dive shops with air in Tobermory.

Swimming With all the water of Fathom Five, there are no designated swimming areas, and few places along the shores with safe or easy access to swimming. Your best bet is to visit the Cyprus Lake Campground or Singing Sands of Bruce Peninsula National Park, for swimming at the beaches there.

Winter Use People visit Tobermory year-round, and the Park Administrative Office is open throughout the year, but boat services and diving run from late April to mid-October. This means no access to the islands, as well.

FOR MORE INFORMATION

The Superintendent
Fathom Five National Marine
  Park
P.O. Box 189
Tobermory, Ontario
N0H 2R0

Phone: (519) 596-2233

The Bruce Trail Association
P.O. Box 857
Hamilton, Ontario
L8N 3N9

Friends of Fathom Five National Park
P.O. Box 214
Tobermory, Ontario
N0H 2R0

Bruce Peninsula Tourist Association
R.R. #2
Hepworth, Ontario
N0H 1P0

Phone: (519) 422-2114

GEORGIAN BAY ISLANDS

NATIONAL PARK

The best publicists the Georgian Bay Islands have had were the Group of Seven artists. The windswept trees, the bare, pink rock of the ancient Canadian Shield, the trees with branches flagged out in the prevailing winds, the jagged coastlines and clear blue water—all are known to most Canadians from the paintings.

Three different geological factors have shaped the fifty-nine islands (or parts of islands) that make up the twenty-four square kilometres (nine square miles) of Georgian Bay Islands National Park. To understand how the islands came to have their exotic variety of shapes and sizes, it helps to imagine the park area as divided north to south. The islands that are on the east side of Georgian Bay are based on exposed Canadian Shield rock, which is composed of quartz, granite and gneiss. They are at least 600 million years old. But the northern and southern parts of this side of the bay were treated differently by glaciation, with distinct effects upon their life forms. The northern part was heavily glaciated, with the great masses of ice scraping down to the bedrock of the Canadian Shield, and leaving its now-gentle contours exposed. Here are stunted, windswept trees clinging to the edges of rocky inlets—the environment that entranced artists of yesterday and visitors of today. The southern part was the recipient of the debris of retreating glaciers, debris that formed the soil that supported the growth of the forests. Here Native peoples lived off the richness of the forest and the lakes, and archeological remains of these cultures show habitation as long ago as eleven thousand years.

How to See the Park

North/south differences are quite easily seen, by visiting several of the major camping or day-use areas of the park. Everything has to be reached by boat but, with the extensive water-taxi services, and some visitors using their own boats, it is quite possible to see key parts of these fascinating variations in a visit of only a day, though you'll be glad if you stay longer.

The park has one main access point; Honey Harbour. It has a marina, water taxis, and boat-launch facilities for private boats. If you want to visit Bruce Peninsula National Park or Fathom Five National Park, on the western side of Georgian Bay, it's best to trailer your boat from Honey Harbour to Tobermory, unless you're a very skilled sailor. The drive is about four hours.

Beausoleil Island: South and North

I started out at Honey Harbour, and was taken to the park's headquarters on Beausoleil Island, where you can see the finest example of the difference between the northern and southern variations of the Canadian Shield. The southern end is made up of glacial till, basically gravel deposits that form a glacial remnant, known as a *drumlin*. The debris left by the glacier forms a basis for soil development and, eventually, for full forest development, as is evident in the southern part of the island. In contrast, in the northern part of the island, the glaciers scoured the rocks, and did not leave sand or gravel to form the basis of soil. Soil appears only in crevices or ravines where, over the years, wind-borne debris, or bits of gravel or sand eroded from other areas, have collected.

Two drumlins make up **Southern Beausoleil Island**. They are the source of some fascinating Indian legends, about the founding and shaping of the area by an ancient giant. Three trails in the southern part of Beausoleil are very good for seeing the geological history of the area, and the life that has formed there. One trail is a circuit of the southern tip, and the other two are short loop trails, which show particular features of the area. Each begins from the Cedar Spring Campground area.

Bobbie's Trail starts just behind the camper-registration cabin, at Cedar Spring Campground. The entire walk takes thirty to forty leisurely minutes. It is a loop that is self-guiding; an interpretive booklet is available from staff, or in a box at the beginning of the trail. The walk begins with a short length of hardwood forest, up the slope of the drumlin.

Much of the rest of the walk traces the way through a cedar swamp. It's a very good area for flowers, and the yellow lady's slipper orchid is not uncommon in season. Along the walk, there are depressions that are water-filled, especially early in the spring, and the rich, moist environment is excellent for birds, particularly warblers. Unfortunately mosquitoes, too, abound.

The **Fire Tower Trail** begins five-minutes' walk from the Visitor Centre. It is approximately 1 kilometre (0.6 miles) long, and takes thirty to forty-five minutes at an easy pace. As you move into the woods, the trail ascends to the top of the drumlin ridge. There is a beautiful view down into the hardwood forest on the left, as the trail approaches the Fire Tower clearing, and then as the trail descends to lake level. At the bottom of the slope, look out for the glacial erratics, the large stones and boulders that were left here by glaciers, thousands of years ago, and which appear quite incongruous in the rich woodlands.

Lady's slipper orchid

The **Circuit of the Southern Tip** has a number of names that change as the trail progresses—the first section, leading out from behind the Visitor Centre, is called the **Christian Trail**. I took it in a counterclockwise direction. Along the circumference of this walk, about every thirty minutes, there are shelters and pit toilets, making it very convenient for a group to picnic and walk, or perhaps wade a little bit in the lake, at their leisure. The last leg of the trail, returning on the eastern edge of the island up to the Visitor Centre, provides the most intense experience of a hardwood forest that is available, I believe, in the eastern national park system. This short expanse is one of the few places to get some sense of the woods that once blanketed Southern Ontario and Quebec.

But, with all this richness of forest and water, Southern Beausoleil also has a long human history. Early Native people camped on the island from spring to fall, hunting and fishing for their livelihood. Archeological remains attest to this for the whole Georgian Bay area, though little archeological exploration has been done in the park itself. However, the Visitor Centre area is a good place to learn more about the more recent human history of this area, where a number of Native families farmed and fished from 1842 to about 1858. Then, as the difficulties of farming on land that was better suited to trees than to corn became almost insuperable, most of the families moved to the Christian Islands Reserve. But a few families continued to survive by farming, fishing, selling timber, and guiding tourists, until the park was established in 1929. However, one man came back and worked at the park for decades—as a warden, caretaker and labourer. The most obvious remnant of this settlement is the cemetery up the hill from the Visitor Centre. The cemetery is a small, quiet place, with a beautiful tree spreading its arms over much of it. Recently, the park invited the descendants of these last families back to the park to plant a

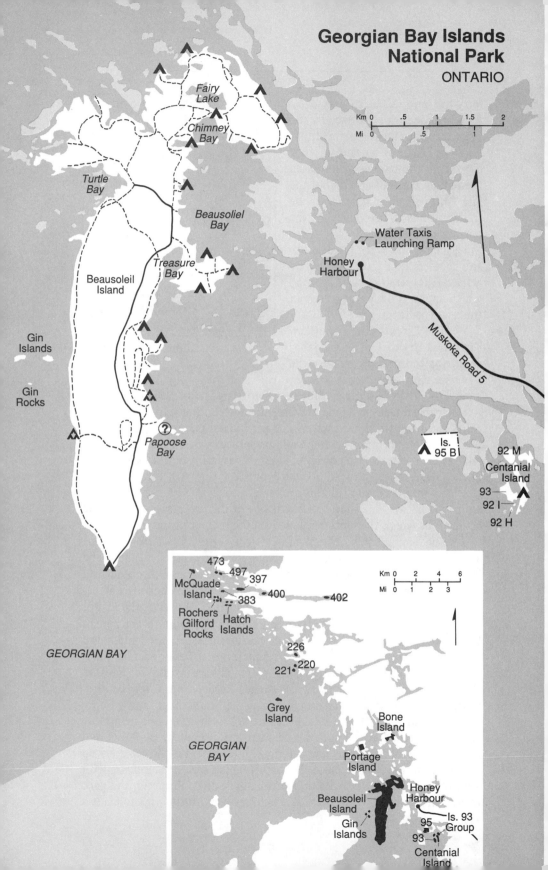

Georgian Bay Islands National Park

ONTARIO

Fairy Lake

Chimney Bay

Turtle Bay

Beausoleil Bay

Beausoleil Island

Treasure Bay

Gin Islands

Gin Rocks

Papoose Bay

Water Taxis
Launching Ramp

Honey Harbour

Muskoka Road 5

Km 0 .5 1 1.5 2
Mi 0 .5 1

Is. 95 B

92 M
Centanial Island

93
92 I
92 H

GEORGIAN BAY

473
497
397
McQuade Island
400
402
383
Rochers
Gilford Rocks
Hatch Islands

226
220
221

Grey Island

GEORGIAN BAY

Bone Island

Portage Island

Beausoleil Island

Gin Islands

Honey Harbour

Is. 93 Group

95

93

Centanial Island

Km 0 2 4 6
Mi 0 1 2 3

memorial grove, a stand of saplings near the Centre, each of which stands for a family that once made its home here.

Northern Beausoleil Island is the scoured, craggy land portrayed by the Group of Seven. Although this area is exposed Canadian Shield rock, like the very edges of southern Beausoleil, forest cannot grow luxuriantly, as it does in the south. Instead, in the north, there are domes and mounds and hillocks of the pink shield rock, with fingers of it jutting out into the lake. Vegetation takes hold here by sending roots into cracks in the rocks, or into crevices created by glaciers, or by wind, ice or water erosion. The largest plants are the white pines, gnarled and often reaching their branches out on their leeward side, like bizarre flags. The shoreline is very irregular, with many inlets, which make excellent mooring for the hundreds of boats that visit here on busy summer days. The area is only a fifteen-minute water-taxi ride from Honey Harbour, and people without boats should find it quite easy to visit here for an afternoon, or for days, if they bring camping equipment.

For a two- or three-hour walk, there is one main trail, with some offshoots that lead out from several of the campgrounds; Honeymoon Bay, Sandpiper Bay, and Chimney Bay. The primary trail is a circle around **Fairy Lake** and the smaller lake nearby, called **Goblin Lake**. The trail meanders over scoured rock, which shows signs of glacial movement. Faint scratch marks left by the glacier, and chatter marks—crescent-shaped grooves left when the glacier bounced large boulders across the resistant surface—mark the shield rock. You can also see dykes, quartz rock that, in a molten state, flowed into cracks in the granite. The trail is not easy to follow, particularly over the exposed rock areas; keep an eye out for the small cement pylons with the yellow-painted caps. It weaves into the occasional wooded area, where soil has collected in the indentations, good places to see the pink moccasin flower orchid. The visitor should do no more than observe. Even touching an orchid or other fragile plant can leave it susceptible to attack by bacteria, or small mammals who are attracted by the salt that is inevitably left in traces from human hands.

This trail can also be reached from the campsites much further south, along the eastern side of the island, all the way down to the Cedar Spring Campground. This would be a walk of perhaps four or five hours, round trip. It could make a good day excursion, if you are well-equipped with food. Take care to follow map and signs.

Other Places of Interest

Since Georgian Bay Islands National Park stretches over 150 kilometres (90 miles) of the Georgian Bay coastline, there are many places to visit, other than Beausoleil. Ask the staff for information on other areas suitable for visitor use.

Park Services and Facilities

Interpretive Programme
The park has an active interpretive programme, from mid-June through Labour Day. An attractive newsletter is available at the administration buildings at Honey Harbour, at the Interpretive Centre on Beausoleil, from any roving staff, and at many local restaurants, motels, stores, etc. This newsletter describes when and where the interpretive events occur. Often, there are guided walks, starting from the Cedar Spring Campground area, but the naturalists also travel to other camping areas and give talks, or just meet people informally to answer questions about the natural and human history of the park. Special events are held each year. Georgian Bay Day, with its activities, games and special programmes, is the most popular.

Camping
All camping in the park is tent only; visitors cannot drive onto any section of the park. The only access is by boat; privately owned or water taxi. There are many places to drop anchor, to tie up next to a dock, or to pull up on shore, and there are docking facilities for boats with self-contained accommodations. Information regarding fees for tenting and docking is available from the Superintendent.

Cedar Spring Campground is the largest campground, with eighty-seven semi-serviced sites along the eastern shoreline of southern Beausoleil Island. Fees are collected by self-registration here, and throughout the park. A commissionaire is on hand at Cedar Spring during the summer months. Access is from Honey Harbour, about twenty minutes away by boat. There are two docks, and the sites are just behind the narrow sandy beach. Large, wheeled carts are available for off-loading camping supplies from the boat, and rolling them to the campsites. There are fire grates at each site, picnic tables, flush toilets, hot showers, water from several faucets, and kitchen shelters, each with several large cookstoves and picnic tables. Firewood is provided in several places, on a cut-your-own basis. Saws are provided, to use on these four-foot lengths.

Many of the trails can be taken from the Cedar Spring area, and the Interpretive Centre is there, with its small museum and theatre for slide shows. There is a playground area for children, with swings and teeter-totters.

The Cedar Spring area is excellent for bird-watching. The variety of bird life in June is fantastic. Watch out for mosquitoes and poison ivy in your rambles, though. The poison ivy is prevalent in open, shrubby areas and at the edges of trails and woodland, and the mosquitoes are in the woods.

Primitive Camping

There are fourteen primitive campgrounds, which all have pit toilets. Water comes from the lake. There are fire grates with firewood, cleared tent-pad areas, picnic tables, and most areas have kitchen shelters. The largest area is **Tonch North, South** and **East**—three spots close to each other, and joined by paths—which has twenty-five sites, in all. All campgrounds, except two, are on Beausoleil Island. Each area has either docking or beach pull-up areas for boats. Fees are collected by self-registration.

Group Camping

There are two group-camping areas on Beausoleil Island. Occupation is by reservation only; write to the Superintendent. Access is by canoe, or hiking in from Cedar Spring—water taxis do not serve the Christian Beach area, because of the shallow waters. The Cedar Spring group campground has flush toilets and showers.

Other Accommodation, Gas, Food and Supplies

Honey Harbour and all of Georgian Bay is a major tourist and recreation area, so there are numerous motels and private campgrounds and some hotels. Gas, food and supplies are all available in Honey Harbour, and the other towns and villages in the area. There is a store and marina on Picnic Island (not within the park), just a short motorboat ride from the Cedar Spring docking area.

Water Taxis   You can be dropped off at any campsite or picnic area by water taxi, from Honey Harbour. It is not particularly expensive for a group of four, if you figure cost per person, depending on the distance you wish to go.

Recreational Services

Hiking   Special word of caution: this park has quite a complex *network* of trails, which pass through varying terrains, including wetlands, shield country and hardwood bush. Sturdy boots are recommended. Trails often cross over large, open expanses of rock outcrops, where paths are not easily delineated. Hikers must be ever watchful for the colour-coded stone cairns, for *it is easy in these areas to wander off the trail and become lost.* Although distances on the islands are not great, hikers should carry a compass. This is particularly true for Beausoleil Island. Pick up a *Trail Hiker's Guide* from park staff, and become familiar with the aerial-photography

The ruggedness of the Canadian Shield at Northern Beausoleil

maps, marking system and trail names, before heading out. Park staff can also recommend trails, if you wish to see specific features.

Mosquitoes can be a real trial, particularly in wooded areas in early summer (June). A visit in this season should be accompanied by an effective mosquito repellent.

The northern half of Beausoleil Island is also a refuge of the Eastern Massasauga Rattlesnake. These snakes are small and non-aggressive, but they are poisonous—a potential danger, which should be respected. If hikers encounter a rattlesnake along a trail, they should note the snake's location and give the reptile a wide berth. They should not attempt to pick up or disturb the snake in any way.

Boating Boaters are encouraged to use local nautical charts, available from marinas, or by writing to the Canadian Hydrographic Service, Department of Fisheries and Oceans, 1675 Russell Road, Ottawa. Caution is advised, because there are ninety thousand islands to dodge around, distances can be great, and the weather is extremely changeable and often hazardous.

However, this must be one of the most beautiful places to boat in North America. There are many local marinas and sailing or motorboating clubs in the area. Marine fuel, oil, boat repairs, and rental facilities are available in Honey Harbour, nearby Port Severn, Midland and Penetanguishene. In the park itself, there are many designated loading and unloading areas for camping or day use, and boaters should not obstruct these places. Camping or overnight docking is allowed only at designated areas, and the limit of stay for overnight docking is seventy-eight hours.

Bilge water mustn't be discharged anywhere in or near the park, since the lake is the source of drinking water for all areas.

Swimming   There is one area for toddlers at Cedar Spring, where some shallow water is roped off. There is no supervision, but the rope does keep the boats out. There are changing houses at Cedar Spring. Otherwise, unsupervised swimming is allowed anywhere in the park. There are many appealing coves and sandy beaches.

Winter Use   Beausoleil Island is used increasingly for winter recreation. There are cross-country skiing, groomed snowmobile trails, and snowshoeing (You can borrow snowshoes at the Visitor Centre on Beausoliel). The Visitor Centre is open weekend afternoons in winter, for information on trail conditions, and it's a good place to warm up in front of the fireplace. All primitive campgrounds are open for winter camping, with enclosed picnic shelters at Cedar Spring and Chimney Bay. Do contact the park before coming, to make sure that ice conditions will allow you to cross safely from the mainland for any of these activities. Usually, mid-January to early March is the good time to come.

FOR MORE INFORMATION

The Superintendent
Georgian Bay Islands National Park
Box 28
Honey Harbour, Ontario
POE 1E0
Phone: (705) 756-2415

POINT PELEE

NATIONAL PARK

Point Pelee National Park is a jewel of nature: small, rare, valuable. A thin triangle jutting into Lake Erie at the southernmost point of Canada, this spit of land stretches as far south as the border of northern California. Location, latitude and the surrounding water create a setting for plant and animal life unique in Canada. Point Pelee is one of the most-visited parks in Canada, and one of the most famous across the continent.

How to See the Park

Point Pelee is a tiny peninsula, stretching only ten kilometres (six miles) in length, and four kilometres (two and one-half miles) across. It is bordered on the east side by a marsh, which makes up most of the park area. The sheer concentration and complexity of life is staggering—careful examination is required, to appreciate its many facets.

The land base of Point Pelee is quite young in geological history—only about ten thousand years old. It has a sand and gravel base, with some topsoil to support woodlands, and some grasslands. Because of its exposure to the lakes, currents and fierce winds, the land is ceaselessly changing, especially at its fragile tip. The beaches that rim the park may be flat, wide and clear one day, but steep, narrow and awash with flotsam of many sorts, after a storm.

Access to all the park's habitats is by trails, boardwalks or picnic areas, with parking not far away.

Plant Life

Because of its variety of habitats, Pelee is a feast for the person interested in plant life. Over seven hundred species of flowering and non-flowering plants are evident, some found only here or in nearby southern areas of Canada.

In the dry forest area, the predominant tree is the hackberry. Hackberry requires a deep, dry soil, and grows in the drier and higher areas of the park, near the centre and towards the western side. The sycamore, black oak and black walnut are also found here. The low elevation and shallow, often soggy, soil of the swamp forest produce the right conditions for the silver maple. In the lower-lying areas, which are often soaked by rain and, occasionally, by flooding lake waters, silver maples abound. They like having their roots wet, and can survive by spreading them extensively a few inches beneath the ground surface. This kind of plant life is characteristic of the Carolinean zone, which once covered all of central and eastern North America. Traces of this zone still remain at Point Pelee, the most northern place for it to occur. A leisurely walk along the **Woodland Nature Trail** clearly demonstrates the relationship between the dry and swamp forests.

The flowers of the woodland are some of the earliest to be seen in spring in Canada, because of the temperature, the moderating effect of the lake, and the southern latitude of the point. The first spring beauties and Dutchman's breeches are a heartening sight.

The grassland and savannah areas are interesting, for being the habitat of the prickly pear. These are some of the few places in eastern Canada where this cactus is found. As the grasslands age, the red cedar, staghorn sumac and dogwood move in.

The marsh habitat shows the changes in plant life that occur at varying water levels. At the north end, visible from the park entrance and from the boardwalk, the most apparent plants are cat-tails. The winter waves of yellow-brown stalks are overtaken by green shoots in the spring, and they grow until they reach well over the heads of children walking on the boardwalk. In the open-water areas, waterlilies decorate the dark water with their glazed, round surfaces and brilliant, white flowers. The damp soil of the land that borders the southern end of the marsh supports water-loving plants and trees, such as the willow, cottonwood, dogwood and silver maple. The place to see these is along the trail to the **East Beach**.

The beaches dramatize the story of plant succession: the plants that are swept onto the beach, or whose seeds are dropped by wind or birds, begin to colonize the land above high-water marsh. The rotting, beached plant and animal matter enriches the sand. A few metres further from the water's edge, the enriched sand slowly becomes soil. Here, grasses, such as the lime grass, beard grass and witch grass, put down their lengthy and hearty roots, as they contribute to an increasing stability and growth of the soil. A big storm may wipe out months or years of growth at the interface between water and vegetation, but neither the plants nor the wind and water ever give up. Further inland, forests and dry fields become established.

Birds

The birds of Point Pelee are its glory, and its fame. There is no other place in North America that is so ideally located for the presence of great concentrations of such a wide variety of bird species. This is especially true in mid-May and, to a somewhat lesser degree, in the fall.

Parks Canada/A. Wormington

Saw-whet owl, common in migration in the fall

Birds migrate along fairly wide, and very long, "flyways." As the birds head for nesting grounds in the northern forests or the Arctic tundra, the central Mississippi and eastern Atlantic flyways overlap, in the vicinity of Point Pelee. Birds that have flown the long, foodless trip over the expanse of Lake Erie, virtually tumble onto the mainland; tiny, windswept Point Pelee.

About 350 species have been recorded at Point Pelee, since the turn of the century. Almost one hundred species nest there, and about fifty stay over winter. On a very active day in the spring, birdwatchers have reported seeing nearly two hundred species. An individual birdwatcher, or two or three observing together, can total as many as a hundred species sighted in a day. The number, *100*, is a magic one for birdwatchers—a "century day;" it means that, on one day, on one point of land, more than one species out of six, of all the kinds of birds in North America, have been seen.

In order to achieve a "century day," you need to make the effort. First, you have to catch the train to the point, from the Visitor Centre, at around 6:00 a.m. Then you work your way back up to the centre, perhaps follow the **Woodland Trail**, or those seasonal trails that are open only during spring migration. Then drive to the **Marsh Boardwalk**, maybe walk through the wooded paths, or picnic on the west side along the entry road, and *then*, as the day closes, watch the woodcock display, near the centre, in the fading evening light, and listen for the whippoorwill's repetitive call. It can be done fairly comfortably, if you bring a picnic, wear comfortable shoes, and layer your clothing, in order to shed or put on what you need during the temperature changes (or rain) of the day. Talking with birders, helping each other locate or identify puzzling or rare birds, seeing faces familiar from year-to-year visits all add up to a marvellous experience.

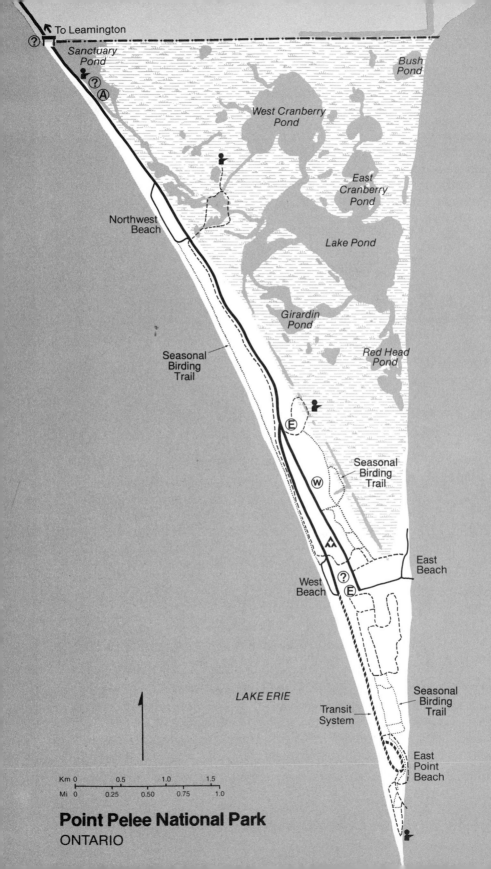

To Leamington

Sanctuary Pond

Bush Pond

West Cranberry Pond

East Cranberry Pond

Northwest Beach

Lake Pond

Seasonal Birding Trail

Girardin Pond

Red Head Pond

Ⓔ

Ⓦ

Seasonal Birding Trail

East Beach

West Beach

Ⓔ

LAKE ERIE

Transit System

Seasonal Birding Trail

East Point Beach

Km 0   0.5   1.0   1.5
Mi 0   0.25   0.50   0.75   1.0

Point Pelee National Park
ONTARIO

Mammals

Although mammals are not nearly as numerous as birds, careful observation can reveal an interesting array. For the casual observer, the mammal most likely to be seen is the grey squirrel. Deer are visible in the day, or at night, and they are always a pleasant surprise. Raccoons are also common. Weasels, mink, skunk and even coyote are there, though not often seen. There are five species of bats here. Although the bats can move in and out of the Point Pelee region, the other mammals are almost marooned. They are hemmed in by water on two sides, and by the built-up area of Leamington, a town of considerable size, on the northern boundary of the park.

Reptiles and Amphibians

The number of species at Point Pelee is quite large and varied. There are several uncommon, and even rare, species. In the marsh area, or in the swamp areas along the Woodland Trail, the sight or springtime sound of the bullfrog is occasionally heard. The somewhat-smaller green frog and the northern leopard frog are found there, too. Reptiles in the marsh area include six species of turtle; snapping, musk, spotted, map, painted and Blanding's. The painted is most common, and is beautiful to see, sunning itself, with its gleaming green back and gold-and-red-striped head and neck. The Blanding's turtle is common in the park, but rare elsewhere in Canada. Look carefully at any turtle with a plain back, to see if it has a bright yellow underside to its throat and neck. If so, it's a Blanding's, and a sight to be treasured.

Swampy areas are home for that tiny, vocal frog, the spring peeper, and the western chorus frog. It's much more likely that frogs will be heard than seen but, either way, they add a lot to the experience of woods or marsh.

Snakes inhabit the woods, as well as the marsh or swamp areas. The eastern garter snake is here, and there is a population at Pelee that is entirely dark, instead of having the familiar three light stripes on a dark body. The marsh area also provides a home for the northern water snake, which eats fish, frogs or even small mammals. The eastern fox snake—brownish-yellow, with dark spots—is often mistaken for a rattlesnake, but is harmless. There are no poisonous snakes in the park: the last sighting of a Timber rattlesnake was in 1895.

Insects

We often think of insects simply as creepy-crawly creatures to swat as we walk along a trail. That insects have a role as a central food resource for other animals is often overlooked. Unfortunately, the array of insects at

Point Pelee, the result of the rich, relatively warm and varied habitat, is often not seen by the casual observer. But there are exceptions. Dragonflies are one. You see them around the beaches, marshes, and in open fields. Their crystal-clear, veined wings and colourful bodies (green, purple, yellow and black, all in one species) are quite striking.

Underfoot in the fields, a wide variety of grasshoppers, crickets, katydids and walking sticks abound. Many more, such as the whining cicada, will be heard rather than seen, but try to get a close look.

The better-known insects are butterflies and moths. Point Pelee is famous for concentrations of monarch butterflies, which gather on certain trees near the tip of the land, from mid-September to early October. Once again, Point Pelee's shape and location favour this fascinating and beautiful occurrence. As the Monarchs emerge from the Northeast, to migrate south away from the cold, they follow the land as far as possible along the Great Lakes, before the perilous flight over the water. They are "funnelled" to the point, where they appear in great clusters, before they leave. This migration phenomenon is true for several other butterfly and wasp species.

Perhaps a word about mosquitoes is in order. They certainly exist at Point Pelee, but during the summer, in open areas of the trail, or in fields, or over the marsh when it's bright and hot, they aren't a problem. For wooded, shaded areas, or late in the day, repellent and a loose, long-sleeved shirt come in handy. Along the beaches, stable flies and horse flies can be annoying.

Fish

Even though Lake Erie has a wide variety, and a fair number, of fish (both changing and declining), almost the only kind park visitors catch is smelt. Since 1948, it has been possible to catch spawning smelt along the beaches of Point Pelee in April. Thousands of people come, to string out their nets, eat, drink (no alcohol permitted) and socialize for the nights of the smelt run. There is usually a peak week period, during the nine days when the park is open for smelting, where the catch can be really rewarding.

The other place where fish are an integral part of park life is in the marsh. The marsh is shallow and reed-clogged in most of its area. The water is warm, slow-moving and not terribly clear. Of the twenty-six kinds of fish recorded here, there are two "sport fish," the northern pike and largemouth bass, both of which are fairly common. Carp are so adaptable to these conditions that they flourish, as do yellow perch, bluegill and pumpkinseed. The supply of insects, crustaceans and vegetation is very beneficial to them.

Fishing is allowed in the seasons appropriate to the type of fish. A licence is required, to fish in the marsh. A chat with the person at the park entrance will bring you up to date. Of course, the fish can be watched, just like any of the plants and animals. The boardwalk is quite wide, and comfortable enough for pauses to lean over and watch the underwater life in the many reedless patches of the water.

Park Services and Facilities

Interpretive Programme

Walking is the key to seeing Point Pelee. Cars are allowed along the main road; you can pull off in the Marsh Boardwalk parking lot, at some of the picnic grounds, and at the main lot at the Visitor Centre. The brochures, available at the entry gate, will show these areas clearly.

The Visitor Centre is an excellent place to visit first. It has informative displays and daily showings of nature-oriented slide shows and films. There are several interesting free handouts, and the park's cooperative association operates a well-stocked store inside the Visitor Centre, for selling nature guidebooks and related materials. Special birding hikes are offered in the spring. There are clean restrooms and water fountains, as well.

The wonderful **Woodland Nature Trail** is right out the back door of the centre. If you have time for just an hour or two of walking, this is where to spend it. The main trail is three kilometres (one and one-half miles) of the most concentrated exposure to the wide variety of habitats in the park. Few signs mark the way, so it's best to bring any informative material you can get from the centre, plus your own bird or plant guides, your camera and binoculars. There is now a trail guide available from the bookstore. There are no picnic areas on the trails, but there are seven others in the park. You can settle down on the beaches, or on the few lawn areas near the centre or Marsh Boardwalk.

After the Woodland Trail, try the train ride to the point. The train will pick you up at the Visitor Centre, and drop you off at the new facilities, directly north of the **Tip Boardwalk Trail**. These facilities consist of a washroom/fountain building, and an open-concept building to house interpretive displays. The boardwalk trail goes very near the actual tip, which is a fascinating place in any season.

The Marsh Boardwalk is also fascinating. It now is over a kilometre in length, and forms a circle with a spoke off it at the farthest end. Daily, at the boardwalk, staff operate a live interpretive exhibit, known as the Marsh Cart, to introduce visitors to the life of the marsh. The times to see most activity in the marsh are early mornings and early evenings, when there are fewer people.

Marsh boardwalk, with its narrow forest border

The **DeLaurier Trail**, half-way between the Visitor Centre and the Marsh Boardwalk, is a delightful twenty- to thirty-minute walk through old fields, forests and old irrigation canals. The trail leads through **DeLaurier House**, the original, refurbished home of the first squatters on the Point. Parts of the house and barn are open to visitors, with displays and taped commentary.

Across the road from the Visitor Centre is the **Tilden Woods Trail**. This is a short version of the Woodland Trail, with a swamp/forest habitat, and is a favourite with birders.

Camping

No individual camping is allowed in the park. There are three group campgrounds, for which you must book ahead with the Superintendent.

Other Accommodation, Gas, Food and Supplies

There are several towns very near the park, Leamington being the closest. There are a number of modest, comfortable motels, and even quite a luxurious one, just a couple of minutes from the entry gate. If you plan to come in mid-May, and want to stay in Leamington or Kingsville, you usually have to book a motel by December. Windsor is about forty-minutes' drive away, and it is a city of over 200,000, so year-round accommodation shouldn't be a problem.

There is one fast-food concession in the park, at the Marsh Boardwalk. It is open on weekends in May, and on a daily basis in mid-June. You may find that you prefer to bring your own picnic lunch; if so, there are several small convenience stores on the way to the park, or in Leamington.

Gas is not available in the park, but there are a number of stations in the nearby towns. Many close at 7:00 p.m., though, so if you get in late, or want to be on the road very early, tank up during the day.

Recreational Services

A number of facilities are available in the park. Always check with the entry person or the centre staff for the most current information.

Canoeing A rental concession is based at the Marsh Boardwalk. You can bring your own canoe, and park there.

Bicycling The park has a bike concession, which is open in the summer. Some people prefer to bring their own bikes. The existing bike trail is in very good condition, and its use is encouraged. Bikes are allowed as far as the facilities at the Tip.

The Tram From April until Thanksgiving, there is transit service from the Visitor Centre to a point just north of the tip. At the height of the spring bird migration, it runs from 6:00 a.m. to 9:00 p.m..

Winter Use When there is enough snow, some trails are open for cross-country skiing. An area near the Marsh boardwalk is kept clear, and flooded for ice skating throughout January and February, or as long as the ice lasts.

FOR MORE INFORMATION

The Superintendent
Point Pelee National Park
R.R. I
Leamington, Ontario
N8H 3V4

Phone: (519) 322-2365
            322-2371 (recorded information line)

ST. LAWRENCE ISLANDS

NATIONAL PARK

Islands always have an aura of adventure. There's an excitement to spending a few hours "marooned" on an island, even if you can walk its length in ten minutes. The islands aren't the only feature of St. Lawrence Islands National Park, but they are what makes it distinctive.

This park, with under 3.5 square kilometres (1.5 square miles) of land area, is the smallest in the Canadian system. Nevertheless, the twenty-three islands and numerous tiny islets that make up the area stretch for eighty kilometres (fifty miles), north from Gananoque along the St. Lawrence River. There is only one small area on the mainland, at Mallorytown Landing. The park headquarters, a short woodland nature trail, campground, interpretive centre and displays, playground, services, swimming beach and marina are all there. The Thousand Islands Parkway runs the length of the park, offering a spectacular view of the myriad islands that dot the St. Lawrence.

Though the Mallorytown area is well worth seeing, a visit to an island leaves you with the strongest sense of this park's special qualities. All of the twenty-three islands have some part that is park area; seventeen of them have boat tie-ups, picnicking and/or camping facilities.

The Thousand Islands are actually the worn-away roots of an ancient mountain range, over which the St. Lawrence River flows. The mountains formed a bridge of rock that stretched between the southern edges of the Canadian Shield, which underlies much of Canada, and the area that is now the Adirondack Mountains of New York State. This bridge is called the Frontenac Axis. When the glaciers retreated from this area, and the St. Lawrence River became established, the high points of this rocky link remained evident as islands.

Broadleaved forests are the dominant landscape, with breaks for open fields, many of which have been cultivated over the years, and are now abandoned to their own regrowth. The islands are, characteristically, a meeting place for northern plants that find here the southernmost place where they can survive, and plants from the south that can exist no farther north. The latter include the pitch pine (which provided pitch for the seams of wooden boats long ago) and shag-bark hickory found on many park islands. Even from island to island, there is often quite a difference between those plants that thrive at either the northern or southern end of the land. Prevailing winds and protective locations, in relation to other islands, have a decided effect.

Animal life differs from mainland to island. Certain animals do not pass the water barrier to the islands. Animals that hibernate, such as chipmunks, never cross over the ice to the islands in winter, nor do they swim there in summer. But squirrels, some kinds of mice, and some shrews are active all winter and, thus, can be found living on both the mainland and many islands. Larger animals, such as the deer or porcupine, fox, and even coyote can also wander from island to island. Their numbers are limited by the size of individual islands. This is because size dictates the amount of food available—whether it's plants for browsing or mice to hunt. So the larger islands, such as Grenadier or Georgina, Camelot or Endymion (what wonderful names!), have deer in winter, but the smaller islands do not.

How to See the Park

St. Lawrence Islands National Park is both easy and difficult to visit. Mallorytown Landing area is easily reached by car from Highway 401, the Macdonald-Cartier Freeway, from Toronto to Kingston and Montreal. The turnoffs are well marked. But, to visit an island, it is necessary to take one of the privately-run charter water taxis that operate out of Gananoque, Rockport or Ivy Lea. The staff at the park have up-to-date information on where boat rides are given. For a longer stay, it is also possible to rent houseboats. The entire area is very well-developed for tourism, and many hotels, campgrounds and restaurants carry pamphlets from the Thousand Islands Chamber of Commerce, listing boats and other services that help in visiting islands.

Visiting the Islands

I went to the marina at Gananoque and asked, at a booth at the dock, about boats. The park naturalist had suggested a visit to **Aubrey Island**. The boatman was very cooperative, and we arranged to be dropped off for several hours. The trip was a slow, comfortable fifteen minutes, with accompanying commentary from the skipper. On the way back, he took a longer route, to point out special historic spots, good bird-watching areas, and to stop for photographing. This accommodation to our interests—like the price for the trip—is reputed to fluctuate with the season, time of day, and the skipper's mood!

Wild calla, in the Arum family

Aubrey Island has tent-camping facilities for a few, scattered sites, as do a number of other islands. Since the island is small (no more than a ten-minute walk down its length), more sites would result in crowding. There are cooking shelters, one at each end of the island, pit toilets at either end, and each site has its own picnic table and small, raised cooking grill. In season, there should be a supply of firewood at either of the two boat landings. There's a pump for water, but be prepared to work hard for it.

A stay on the island, however brief, is a lovely experience. One early spring visit meant an array of new flowers—Dutchman's breeches, trout lily, spring beauty, hepatica, white trillium. There were flickers starting their nesting, and brown creepers and white-breasted nuthatches combing the tree trunks for food, scouring oblong holes recently cut by a pileated woodpecker. Grey, black and red squirrels rustled and chattered everywhere.

For people with their own boats—even canoes—the park really comes into its own. Seventeen of the island locations have docking facilities, and another, **Thwartway**, has mooring and a beach only. Many have toilets and picnicking; some have weather shelters with cook stoves and firewood, small tent-camping areas, and drinking water. The islands range from **Mermaid**, less than two hectares (five acres), to the 155 hectares (385 acres) of **Grenadier**. Most islands are four to twelve hectares (ten to thirty acres) in area. They all have easy walks, amid varied and interesting plants and animals, and the water is close for swimming, fishing or boating. You can canoe among the islands, near the protection of the mainland shore. The park has its own maps, to give an overview of the islands and waterways, but Nautical Charts are essential for safe boating. They are numbered 1417, 1418, 1419, 1420 and 1421 (which is now 1439, metric), for the whole park area.

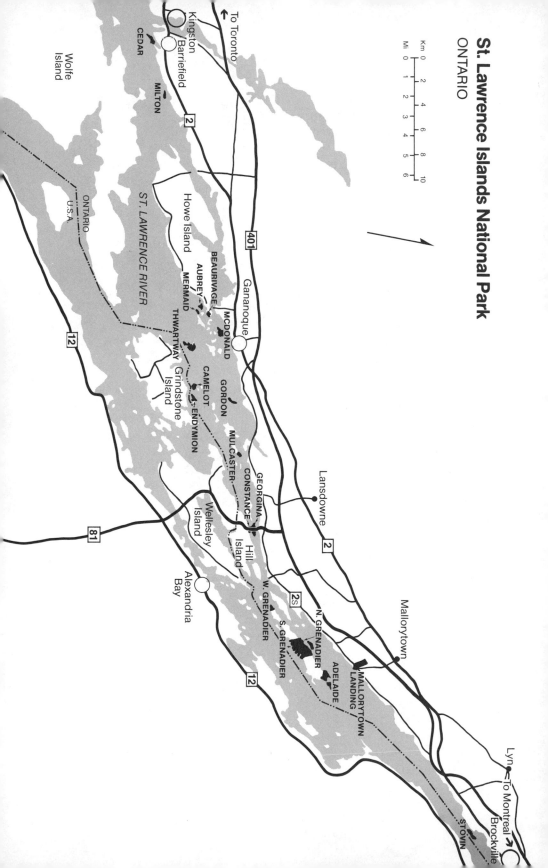

St. Lawrence Islands National Park
ONTARIO

Km 0   2   4   6   8   10
Mi 0   1   2   3   4   5   6

To Toronto

Kingston
Barriefield
CEDAR
MILTON

Wolfe Island

2

401

Gananoque

Howe Island

ONTARIO
U.S.A.

ST. LAWRENCE RIVER

BEAURIVAGE
AUBREY
MERMAID
THWARTWAY
MCDONALD
GORDON
CAMELOT
ENDYMION
MULCASTER
Grindstone Island

12

Lansdowne

GEORGINA
CONSTANCE
Hill Island

2

Wellesley Island

81

Alexandria Bay

W. GRENADIER

2s

N. GRENADIER
S. GRENADIER
ADELAIDE

Mallorytown

MALLORYTOWN LANDING

12

STOVIN

Lyn
To Montreal
Brockville

Exploring the Mainland

The short **Mainland Nature Trail** runs behind the park headquarters, starting at the north edge of the campground. It covers a wide variety of habitat, for an easy, half-hour walk. I was there in early May, on several clear, warming days, and it proved to be an intense experience of concentrated springtime. Skeins of geese were flying over, the rare rue anemone bloomed, along with the trillium, hepatica and May-apples. A ruffed grouse was steadily making its rapid *putt-putt* sound, as it notified other grouse of its presence. The first brown thrashers and yellow warblers of the year also sang constantly, nearby. The chipmunks and black squirrels were active everywhere and, in contrast, a big porcupine sat immobile on a fork of a tree above my head. I ran back to the car for my camera, and it hadn't moved when I got back, twenty minutes later! At the end of the walk, there was the most cottony-tailed cottontail rabbit I've ever seen.

Park Facilities and Services

Interpretive Programme

The interpretive programmes of the park are both stationary and mobile. At Mallorytown Landing, the Interpretive Centre is right at the shoreline, next to the swimming beach. A few metres away from it, there is the Browns Bay wreck display, a resurrected gunboat sunk in the last century. Since so many of the park's visitors are active boaters and do not stay in one place for long, there are roving interpreters who travel the waterways of the park in boats. They visit docks and campsites in their showboat, and are eager to enlarge upon visitors' knowledge of this beautiful area. The interpretive staff has prepared a large selection of booklets on many aspects of the park—its sports fish, geology, climate, birds, mammals, plants, reptiles, amphibians, and history; there is a newsletter, as well. All of these are free, from the Interpretive Centre or from roving staff, and they are a real help in understanding the park, in quiet moments of leisure.

Camping

There are over sixty sites at **Mallorytown Landing**, in a small field behind the Administrative Centre. Barbecues, firewood, toilets, and water are available, but there are no hook-ups. It's well located for walking the nature trail, and just across the road from the swimming beach, Interpretive Centre, Browns Bay wreck display, boat dock and launching ramp.

Parks Canada/E.M. Holroyd

Snapping turtle laying eggs

Primitive Camping

Fifteen of the islands have primitive campsites, with drinking water, pit toilets and flat areas for tents. There are cooking shelters and picnic tables, but no hook-ups. There is a docking area with a time limit of three consecutive nights docking per island. **Grenadier Island** has three camping locations. A self-registration system is in place, to collect docking, camping and firewood fees at Mallorytown Landing and on the islands. Park maps, available at the Interpretive Centre, have a very helpful chart outlining the facilities on each island.

Other Accommodation, Gas, Food and Supplies

The Thousand Islands area has many motels, a few hotels, and a number of very attractive private campgrounds, right along the Thousand Islands Parkway and in larger cities, such as Gananoque and Kingston. The park and many of the business establishments have informative brochures, supplied by the local travel and tourist associations. For more information, contact The Eastern Ontario Travel Association, 209 Ontario Street, Kingston, Ontario K7L 2Z1, (613) 549-3682.

Gasoline, food and supplies are easily obtained along the Thousand Islands Parkway. There are several marinas and marine-supply stores.

Recreational Services

Mallorytown Landing contains the main recreation complex, with its children's playground, supervised swimming beach, changing rooms, washrooms and boat ramp. The parking lot is large. The main season runs June through Labour Day.

Fishing About twenty species of fish are commonly caught in Thousand Island waters. They include Coho salmon, lake trout, northern pike, muskie, catfish, small and largemouth bass, sunfish, perch and walleye. Check in any fishing or sports store, for information on requirements for provincial fishing licences for certain fish. It is recommended that fishermen also consult the 1989 *Guide to Eating Ontario Sport Fish*, published by the Ontario Ministry of the Environment.

Boat Trips Rockport, Ivy Lea and Gananoque all have boat tours or boat rental businesses, in the summer months.

Further Reading

St. Lawrence Islands National Park: The Thousand Islands by Don Ross (Douglas & McIntyre, 1983)

FOR MORE INFORMATION

The Superintendent
St. Lawrence Islands
National Park
Box 469, R.R. 3
Mallorytown Landing,
Ontario KOE IRO

Phone: (613) 923-5261

Thousand Islands Chamber of
  Commerce
Box 36
Lansdowne, Ontario
KOE 1L0

LA MAURICIE

NATIONAL PARK

La Mauricie National Park is little known outside of the province of Québec and yet, year-round, it is one of the most accessible and well-serviced parks in the Canadian system. Located just 200 kilometres (124 miles) northeast of Montréal, La Mauricie encompasses 544 square kilometres (212 square miles) of the Québec Laurentians. The Laurentians here are knobbly, wooded mountains, incised by dozens of rivers and elongated lakes.

The Laurentians are nearly one billion years old, more than ten times older than the Rockies! The bedrock is gneiss, a metamorphic rock, which formed beneath layers of overlying sediment that were deposited in an ancient sea. About one billion years ago, all these rocks—the sediment and the rock beneath—were elevated above the sea, to form a mountain range as high as the Rockies. Millions of years of erosion eventually eliminated the layer of sediments, and left a plateau of hard gneiss rock. Beginning about one million years ago, and ending ten thousand years ago, four periods of glaciation filed and smoothed the rough edges of the Laurentians. Rivers, rain and wind continued to round them further, into the various gentle shapes of today.

Water collects as lakes in depressions in the mountains' surfaces, and is retained behind natural dams in long, narrow valleys. It runs from hillsides or other lakes, to form an intricate web of streams and cascades. Except for its southern boundary and half of its western edge, the park is bounded by two very large rivers, the Mattawin over half of the west and half of the north sides, and the St. Maurice on the northeast and east. There are about 150 lakes and ponds in the park, many of which—Wapizagonke, Anticagamac, Caribou, Edouard and Lac à la Pêche—are accessible, not only to the canoeist, but also to the car-based visitor.

In its present protected state, La Mauricie is densely covered with a jigsaw puzzle of forests. In rich, well-drained and deep soil, sugar maple is the dominant species, both in number and in size, with some yellow birch and beech mixed in. In damper soil, the fir may dominate, with yellow birch mixed in. On thin, rocky soil, or in very damp areas, such as bog edges or poorly drained depressions in the soil, at the higher elevations of the park, spruce forests are the most common. Although the entire park is near the northern limit of the deciduous forests that make up the St. Lawrence Lowlands forest area, the northern part of the park is not too far from the southern edge of the coniferous boreal forest that covers northern Canada. La Mauricie is, then, a transition zone, where southern forests mix with trees typical of the north.

People have played a considerable role in the history of the park. For more than eight thousand years, the forests were home to a sub-group of the native Algonquin people, called Attikameks. These nomadic people travelled the rivers and forests, as they hunted game or foraged for berries, roots and other plant materials. In the summer, they gathered at what is now Trois-Rivières, to socialize and to barter furs with the Iroquois, for the clay pots and agricultural products that these more-sedentary southern neighbours had to offer. In the winter, the Attikameks would break up into family groups for hunting and trapping.

The respect that the indigenous people had for the environment was not shared by the first European trappers, traders, loggers and farmers and, until 1970, when the park was established, not by our contemporaries, either. The area has been logged extensively, and fires have ravaged large sections of it. Now the major threat is from acid rain. The bedrock and soil of La Mauricie cannot neutralize the rain, as it percolates through. Alkaline limestone bedrock can alleviate problems caused by acid rain, but La Mauricie isn't limestone-based. So one form of destruction ends, but another, far more threatening, danger is present.

How to See the Park*

To appreciate the geological history, the story of the lakes, rivers, forests and human history of the park, it's best to combine participation in the interpretive programme with hiking and driving on your own. From June through September, there are up to three guided activities a day, and a slide talk in each of the three amphitheatres every night of the week.

In the fall, on weekends, there are slide shows at the Visitor Reception Centre at Saint-Jean-des-Piles, and occasionally an interpretive

*Julie Cartier visited this park for me in August, to round out my spring and fall visits. She was able to participate in the (all-French-language) interpretive events, and generally experience the park at its busiest season. I am indebted to her for much of this chapter's material.

event. The interpretive activities for all the seasons include guided walks, canoe tours, car tours and various special events. For the canoe tours, the park has two huge, yellow freighter canoes, the *Rabaskas* and, if they are filled, people can rent regular canoes, or bring their own, to follow along. The canoe tours are a great way to learn more about lakes. The car tours are especially good for understanding the geological history. You follow the highway from Le Passage Viewpoint, and stop many times along the way, to have geological features explained.

Decaying stumps support new forms of life

All the talks are in French, but since the interpretation is unique, and the walks, canoe paddles and drives are through wonderful scenery, a lot of the language barrier is overcome. Also, I found that, when I told the naturalist that my French was shaky, she gave me quick English summaries. Organized groups can phone ahead, to make appointments for an informal session with a bilingual naturalist.

To explore on your own, drive from end to end of the park, to get an excellent idea of the shapes created by the cracking and eroding of the land. There are a number of viewpoints where you can pull out and read the bilingual panels, which explain in detail what you are seeing. The most spectacular one, **Le Passage**, is near the northern end of **Lake Wapizagonke**.

To see how a forest grows and changes, there is the beautiful trail, **Les Cascades**. It starts from the major day-use area at the Shewenegan picnic area. Cross the big wooden bridge, and follow the interpretive signs. You travel through many types of forest. From this trail you can take a side trip to the **Les Falaises Trail**, which brings you close to one of the looming rock outcroppings that are exposed here and there in the park.

Another very easy trail is the one to **Lac Gabet**. It is a 1.5 kilometre walk, through maple, yellow birch and beech forests. The trail winds slightly uphill, and then ends at a small lake. The lake is slightly boggy on one edge, with some sphagnum moss and heathlike plants, such as Labrador tea. A small blind has recently been installed, to make observing waterfowl and wildlife easier.

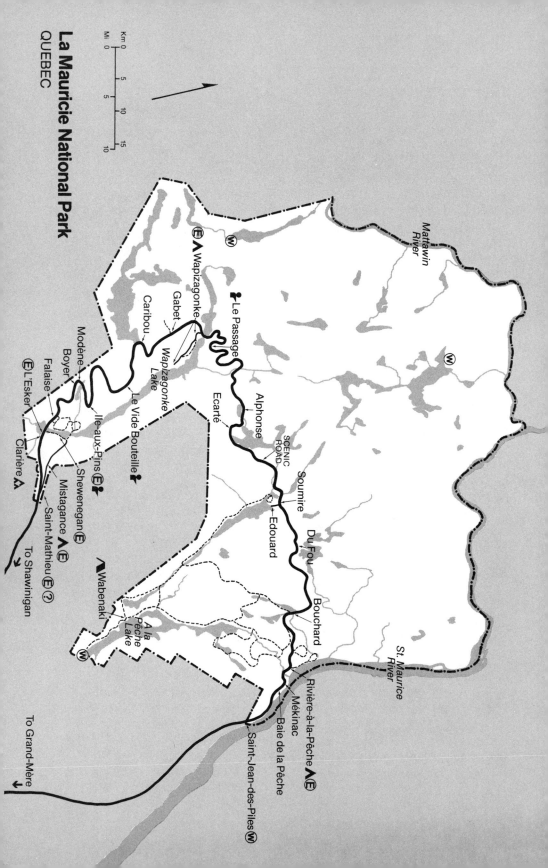

If it's winter, and you're cross-country skiing along the seventy kilometres (forty-three miles) of trails, look at the shelters for the interpretive panels that explain the winter inhabitants.

For a very special visit, there is a short interpretive trail at the bog area, off the main road at the south end of the park, just before the first bridge over Lake Wapizagonke. Take the L'Esker turnoff and park there, or follow the **Vallerand Trail** from the Shewenegan area. It is about 1.5 kilometres (1 mile) to the bog trail. This **Tourbière Trail** is very short. It is mostly a boardwalk, which takes you out on the sphagnum moss mat at the edge of the small lake, and then back through the spruce forest that has taken hold where there is solid ground. In mid-June, pitcher plants and sundew were in abundance. Wild orchids bloom here in the first two weeks of July.

For the human history of the park, you must rely upon the interpretive programmes and the exhibition room in the Saint-Jean-des-Piles Visitor Centre. Once you have heard the stories, the park takes on another dimension; rivers become canoe routes, moving masses of logs; forests become sources of food and shelter; history surrounds you.

Park Services and Facilities

This is a year-round park, with very heavy use from late June through mid-August, extensive cross-country use in winter, and moderate camping, hiking, and day-visiting use in late spring and well into autumn. In my opinion, there are great advantages to visiting a park in the quieter, "shoulder" seasons of spring and fall.

Interpretive Programme

The park has an invaluable interpretive programme and a number of self-guided, bilingual walks. There are schedules, posters and bulletin-board notices at the entrances to campgrounds and picnic areas. A few bilingual brochures and booklets on the park's natural and human history are available; most are free or moderately priced, and well worth the cost. All publications are available at the Visitor Centres at either of the main entrances to the park.

The Saint-Mathieu Centre provides maps, and a desk run by the local park cooperative association, Info-Nature Mauricie, sells books. Park staff can help you decide where to go, and give you park brochures or appropriate maps of trails and campgrounds.

At the Saint-Jean-des-Piles side, the centre has all this, and much more. It is a much larger building, with a theatre and extraordinarily attractive graphic displays, indoors and out, of the natural and human history themes of the park. It also has a very helpful series of displays about camping, canoeing, cross-country skiing and other activities in the park.

Camping

Three large campgrounds, accessible by car, are open in summer: **Mistagance**, nearest the Saint-Mathieu entrance; **Wapizagonke**, about thirty-minutes' drive north of it, just off the park's main road; and **Rivière à la Pêche**, a few minutes from the Saint-Jean-des-Piles entrance. The last is the slowest to fill, but all can be very busy in summer. Try to come in mid-week, if possible. You can stay up to two weeks. All campgrounds are wooded. Mistagance is the nearest to the boat concession and swimming beaches at south Lake Wapizagonke. Wapizagonke is actually situated at a beach. They all have hot showers, washrooms, flush toilets, picnic tables, fire grates, firewood depots and (except Mistagance) kitchen shelters. Rivière à la Pêche has facilities for people in wheelchairs. It is also at the trailhead of the entire system of hiking and cross-country-skiing trails that cover the southeast segment of the park. Each campground has an amphitheatre for the nightly slide talks. In the spring and fall, the Wapizagonke Campground isn't open, but there is plenty of room at the others. There are no trailer hook-ups, but there are waste-disposal stations. Information on campsite availability is broadcast on local radio stations: AM frequencies 550, 1140, 1220, and FM 102, daily between 10:30 a.m. and 11:30 a.m.

Primitive Camping

Since there is such an extensive network of canoe routes in the back country, there are many primitive campsites along the way. You must register at the Visitor Centres and indicate which sites you intend to use, to avoid overcrowding. Some sites have firewood and fire grates; some don't, and require portable campstoves. In times of high fire hazard, only campstoves may be used. Open fires are never allowed, except in the fireplace at La Clairière Group Campground. All sites have tent pallets and pit toilets.

Group Camping

Write to the Superintendent for information and reservations.

Other Accommodation, Gas, Food and Supplies

There are a number of commercial campgrounds outside the park; a list is available from the park. In the park itself, in summer, there are snack bars at the Shewenegan day-use area, the Lac Edouard day-use area, and at the the Wapizagonke picnic area, a few minutes' drive from the campground. There is a small grocery/supply store at the Wapizagonke day-use area. There is no gasoline in the park. In the villages just outside both entrances to the park, there are small grocery and supply stores and gasoline. Just

The start of the canoe route up Wapizagonke

before the entrance on the Saint-Mathieu side, there is a grocery store and snack bar, open in summer only.

Recreational Services

Note for Senior Citizens Lakes Boyer, Modène and Alphonse are reserved for the use of senior citizens, for fishing only.

Facilities for the Handicapped Organized groups of handicapped persons are invited to inquire (c/o the Superintendent) about the availability of interpretive and other services that can be arranged for their group. Both Visitor Centres, the major day-use areas, the interpretive centre, and all viewpoints are wheelchair-accessible. Lake Boyer has special facilities, too.

Canoeing Most of the lakes are accessible for canoeing. A number of lakes touch upon, or are within a short walk of, the main highway. Canoe and row-boat rentals are available every day of the week, from mid-June to Labour Day, at the Shewenegan day-use area, at Wapizagonke North and at Lake Edouard, and on weekends only, from Labour Day to Thanksgiving, at Shewenegan. You can rent paddle boats at Shewenegan. For canoeing for a few hours or so, the lakes most often used are Wapizagonke, Edouard and Caribou. You can park near the launching

Learning about the history of Wapizagonke

areas. The many kilometres of back-country canoe routes are connected by portage trails. Ask for the brochure on canoe routes in the park. You must register in and out for overnight trips, and also pack out all garbage. There is self-registration during spring and fall, at the Visitor Reception Centre.

Hiking   Trails are generally short and easily accessible; some are interpreted. To help decide where to go, use the map from the main park brochure to pick the area you want to visit, then ask for the map the park has for its central (Wapizagonke) and eastern (Rivière à la Pêche) sides and Shewenegan. It lists the trail names, lengths, approximate times, and where the trails start.

Swimming   There are unsupervised swimming beaches at the day-use areas of Shewenegan, L'Esker and Wapizagonke, and supervised swimming at Lac Edouard. In addition, many sandy lakeshores offer canoeists the possibility of a quick dip.

Fishing   Fishing is allowed in thirty-nine lakes. You must purchase an inexpensive permit, available at Visitor Centres, at campground kiosks, or from convenience stores in Saint-Gerard-des-Laurentides, Saint-Mathieu or Saint-Jean-des-Piles. At the same time, you can find out which lakes are open to fishing and what early limits are. Fishing season is from the last Saturday of May to Labour Day.

Scuba Diving   Scuba diving is permitted on Lakes Caribou, Wapizagonke, and Edouard, every day from the last Saturday of May through Labour Day, and on weekends after that, through Thanksgiving. Divers must register and obtain a permit at either Visitor Centre. Certificates of competence must be shown.

Winter Use   The park has an extremely well-developed winter-use programme, centred on the Saint-Jean-des-Piles side, at the eastern entrance. Ask for the brochure that has a map of the numerous trails, and describes the equipment and skills necessary for enjoyable and safe cross-country skiing, snowshoeing, and winter camping.

There are seventy kilometres (forty-three miles) of skiing trails of varying degrees of difficulty, and there is a four-kilometre (two-and-one-half-mile) snowshoeing trail that begins at the waxing room of the Rivière à la Pêche Campground area. You can camp at this site in winter. There is also a waxing room, toilets, a rest area, and first-aid facilities. Every five kilometres (three miles) along the trail system, there are warming huts, which have firewood, stoves and pit toilets. It is possible to camp in primitive campsites, if you are equipped with tents, etc., but there is no overnight use of the shelters. Near the south end of Lac à la Pêche, there is a Wabenaki lodge, which sleeps thirty people. An additional sixteen people are accommodated in another building. There is a common area, with fireplace, a fully-equipped kitchen area, water and washrooms. Users must bring their own sleeping bag, food and toiletries. You must reserve at Info-Nature Mauricie, (819) 537-4555, from the third Monday of November, to assure a place. It is accessible only on skis, and a modest nightly fee is charged.

You can rent ski equipment in the small villages near the park entrances, or in Shawinigan and Grand-Mère.

FOR MORE INFORMATION

The Superintendent
La Mauricie National Park
C.P. 758
465 - 5th Street
Shawinigan, Québec
G9N 6V9

Phone: (819) 536-2638

Info-Nature Mauricie
C.P. 174
Shawinigan, Québec
G9N 6T9

Phone: (819) 537-4555

MINGAN ARCHIPELAGO

NATIONAL PARK RESERVE

Even though the Mingan Archipelago is the only readily accessible park in the system that I have yet to visit, it is one of my favourites, already. The archipelago has always been well known in Québec for its exotic shorelines and wealth of wildlife, but it was added to the national park system only in 1984. Before that, the islands were often visited by nature lovers, so the park facilities and services have been established on a firm groundwork of local services to visitors. Key to these services is a number of water-taxi and boat-tour services, so the islands are easy to get to, yet retain so much of their natural character.

The reserve protects some forty islands and many islets, which are a part of the Eastern St. Lawrence Lowlands natural region. The archipelago is located along the north shore of the St. Lawrence River, with the islands paralleling the mainland shore at an average distance of about 3.5 kilometres. The whole reserve stretches some 150 kilometres, starting across from the town of Longue-Pointe. About halfway along the length of the park, on the mainland, is the town of Havre-Saint-Pierre. This community is the end of the road for auto traffic along the north shore of the St. Lawrence. In other words, visiting the Mingan Archipelago means you are well on your way to getting away from it all.

What makes the Mingan Archipelago so distinctive, aside from the fact that is is off the beaten track, and camping out on islands is pretty special in itself?

A major feature of the islands is their dramatic topography. The islands are limestone-based, unlike the exposed Canadian Shield of the mainland. The limestone bedrock here was uplifted millions of years ago, with periods of submersion, at least at the end of the last glaciation. Over time, the chemical and mechanical erosion of the sea has carved the landscape into the most intriguing and varied shapes. This is the place to see raised beaches, now high and dry, to wander among sea stacks that punctuate island beaches, and to explore the largest concentration of shoreline arches and grottoes in Canada. You can trace the layers of sediment deposited on what was once the bottom of the sea. Fossil remains of over one hundred marine organisms are evident in the rocks of the reserve. Hiking, camping, beachcombing, or kayaking, it's all very easy to get close to these characteristic features of the archipelago.

But the influence of the sea goes much beyond the impact of waves or chemical processes. The archipelago is at a meeting place of a relatively mild boreal maritime climate and much more harsh semi-Arctic conditions. On the one hand, most of the land mass of each island enjoys a boreal maritime climate, which means that, because of the moderating influence of the sea, the average yearly temperature is over one degree Celsius. There is a great deal of precipitation, including considerable fog, at any time of year. This relatively mild climate is in strong contrast to climatic conditions further inland.

On the other hand, the very cold Labrador current passes by the islands, and the east-facing shorelines of the islands in particular, which bear the brunt of the very cold prevailing winds, have tundra-like vegetation, usually found much further north. Those shores that slope gently to the sea are known as moorlands, and they are very diverse in their appearance and vegetation. Here you can find the miniaturization of plants that occurs in the Arctic, and there are areas where only moss and lichen can survive.

The cliffs of the islands, and there are about forty-five kilometres of them, in all, rising to a maximum of fifteen metres, also have much more in common with the Arctic, than with the boreal forest that makes up the gently sloping interior of most of the islands.

In all, there are about five hundred species of vascular plant in this quite-small area. Close to forty of them are rare in Québec, or are plants that are usually found as far as four thousand kilometres further north. There are 150 kinds of moss and 190 kinds of lichen living here, as well.

The richness of the plant life is mirrored by the diversity and accessibility of the animal life. The waters of the area are visted by nine members of the whale family, some of which—like the minke whale—can be seen from the islands. Unfortunately, the whale population in the area is declining, and sightings are becoming increasingly uncommon. On very rare occasions, humpback whales can be seen much further out to sea, and you will need to take one of the boat tours to get out to them. Grey seals, harbour and harp seals can generally be seen from as early as May. The harbour seals breed locally.

The bird life of the islands is extremely varied, because of the diverse habitat, the distance from major human disturbance, and the location of major migratory routes. At least 160 species of bird have been recorded in the islands. Many of the shorelines, moors, and cliffs are breeding grounds for gulls, terns and kittiwakes. Double-crested cormorants, razorbills, the black guillemot, and that most attractive of Atlantic seabirds, the puffin, nest on some of the islands, as well. In fact, the puffin is so popular that it has been designated the "totem" bird of the Mingan Archipelago Park Reserve. Of course, the forests are the breeding grounds for many songbirds.

Puffin

Parks Canada/M. Boulianne

The islands are an important resting and feeding area for migrating shorebirds, and considerable numbers gather there in spring and fall. The archipelago is also an important wintering area for ducks. There is a population of seventy-five thousand common eiders that spends the winter months locally, and there are small numbers of oldsquaws, common and Barrow's goldeneyes, and red-breasted mergansers. There are some eider ducks that nest locally, as do black ducks.

How to See the Park

Getting to the Mingan Archipelago is quite easy, with the main access route being Québec Highway 138, which follows the north shore of the St. Lawrence to Havre-Saint-Pierre. There is also ferry access from Rimouski on the south shore, and by air from Québec City and Montréal. Both ferry and air travel go to Havre-Saint-Pierre. Once in the park area, there are tour boats operating out of the villages of Mingan and Havre-Saint-Pierre. Water taxis, which will drop you off and pick you up from the islands according to arrangements you make with them, originate in Havre-Saint-Pierre and Mingan.

Even though camping on the islands can be an important part of a visit to the area, it is possible to camp on the mainland, or to stay in local

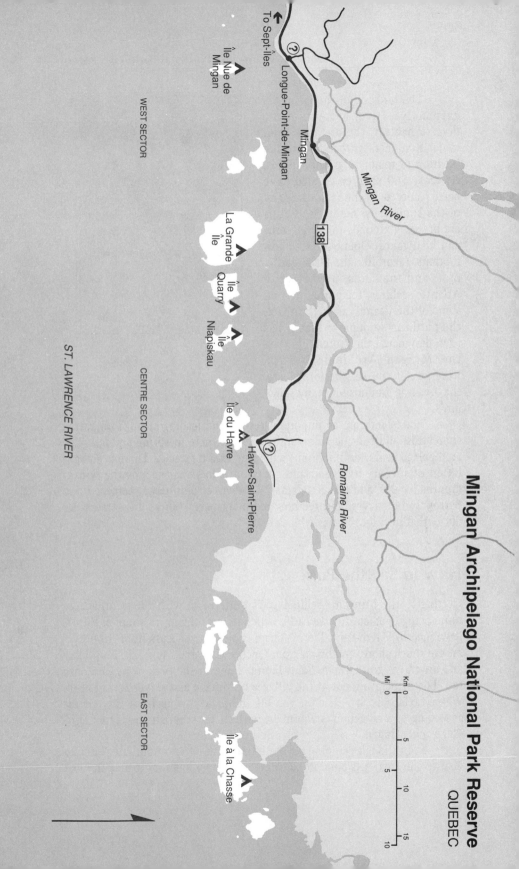

Mingan Archipelago National Park Reserve
QUEBEC

ST. LAWRENCE RIVER

WEST SECTOR

CENTRE SECTOR

EAST SECTOR

To Sept-Îles

Longue-Point-de-Mingan

Mingan

138

Île Nue de Mingan

La Grande Île

Île Quarry

Île Niapiskau

Île du Havre

Havre-Saint-Pierre

Île à la Chasse

Mingan River

Romaine River

Km
0   5   10   15
Mi
0   5   10

hotels or motels, and take day trips on cruise boats, or by water taxi, to the islands. You can hike, picnic, and beachcomb for an afternoon or a day at a time. (Just remember to make your beachcombing "no-impact," because every rock and blade of grass is protected in a national park, and they may not be disturbed, much less removed.)

Some islands are especially good for bird-watching, or for good views of the seals, or for exploring exotic plant life. The interpretive staff can suggest the best way to use your time, given your interests and energy level. Whatever you do, be prepared for erratic weather, even on an afternoon or day trip. You may be basking in the sun one minute, and enveloped in fog the next. So always bring along raingear, sturdy shoes, a hat and an extra sweater.

Park Services and Facilities

The major mainland facilities are the visitor reception and interpretation centres at Longue-Pointe-de-Mingan, at the western entrance to the park, along Highway 138, and at Havre-Saint-Pierre, at the end of the road. They are both open daily, from mid-June through Labour Day. Since you are very likely to want to know about boat transportation, and may well want to camp for several days, it is especially important to inquire at these centres about schedules, local weather conditions, facilities on the islands and available space.

Any overnight use of the park requires free registration beforehand, at one of the centres. This is very much a safety issue, because of the potential hazards of pleasure boating, kayaking and wilderness camping in rather rugged conditions. So do register in and out, and be prepared for cold, wet, and surprises. One essential element of that preparation is including at least two days extra food if you are camping, because it is quite common to be held down, when the weather gets bad and kayaking or water-taxi transport becomes impossible.

Interpretive Programme
The park has a varied interpretive programme, and some of the most informative and attractive publications in the park system, to my mind. They are additionally distinguished by being in three languages— French and English, of course, but also in Montagnais, the language of the local Native people. At the two visitor centres, you can see fixed displays about the natural and human history of the islands, and about how to plan your visit. There is also a movie on the archipelago. There is a regular schedule of evening slide-show talks at the centres,

and the interpreters visit Quarry and Niapiskau islands, on a rotating schedule, to give guided walks to visitors. Interpreters also accompany some of the commercial boat tours. The schedules are posted in the visitor centres.

Camping

There are primitive campgrounds on six islands, and a group campground at one of them (Île du Havre). Primitive or wilderness sites have tent pads, pit toilets, picnic tables, wood-burning cookstoves, and sheltered firewood. The group campground has ten pads, two of the stoves, four tables, and two firewood shelters. A camping permit is required, and is available from the two visitor centres. It is important to return your permit to a centre when you leave the reserve. The islands and number of sites are: Grande Île (four sites at Havre à Petit-Henri and four at Barachois à Montpetit), Île à la Chasse (six sites), Île du Havre (four sites), Île Niapiskau (four sites), and Île Quarry (four sites).

It is possible to camp in the off-season, for those who can get there on their own, when water taxis are no longer operating. The permit, at this time, is available from the park office in Havre-Saint-Pierre.

You can reserve individual sites up to seven days in advance, and the group site can be reserved up to six months in advance.

There is a maximum stay of six nights in the park reserve. Camping is free, but the water-taxi services are commmercially run, and their prices vary according to your destination and the size of the group.

You must pack in and pack out everything, including cigarette butts. The park supplies garbage bags.

Other Accommodation, Gas, Food and Supplies

The park has an excellent booklet, which includes information on local private accommodation and services. Write ahead for it. It lists a municipal campground of fifty-four sites in Havre-Saint-Pierre, a bed-and-breakfast phone number, an eighty-four room hotel in Havre-Saint-Pierre, a hotel in Mingan and Longue-Pointe-de-Mingan, and two motels in the latter village. Bus, ferry, and water-taxi information are listed, as well as a central number for information on restaurants in the area.

Because Highway 138 is a primary provincial road, you will be able to find gas and other auto services along your route.

It is possible to top up your food and camping supplies in local stores, but it is probably best to bring your essentials along with you from home.

Recreational Facilities

Boating   Pleasure boating is a major activity in the area. However, it is important that you be very familiar with the nautical charts and weather and water conditions of the area, and that your boat and equipment meet all Canadian Coast Guard standards for safety. The charts you will need are numbers 4432, Mingan Islands, and 4456, Piashti Bay. You cannot find these in the Islands, so obtain them before you leave home, from the Hydrographic Service, at Fisheries and Oceans Canada in Ottawa, or at your local marine-supply outlet.

Ocean Kayaking   From what I have seen in researching this park, it looks like kayaking is an ideal way to explore the area—*if* you are fully prepared to kayak in very cold conditions, with erratic weather and unpredictable seas. Of course, the standards for pleasure-boating apply to kayaking as well, but there are additional factors to take into account when kayaking in this wonderfully scenic area. One is that you are in an ocean, not a river, and the other is that you are in near-Arctic conditions. You must have a wet suit at the very least, but a dry suit is preferable. You should take at least two extra days of food with you. You will find that the early morning or late afternoon are the best times for travelling any distance in these waters.

Scuba diving   This is an increasingly popular sport in the area, but it too, requires your being prepared to dive in semi-Arctic conditions. You must obtain a diving permit from the park office. A dry suit is essential, and the usual safety precautions, such as never diving alone, using a dive flag, and having a lookout at the surface at all times, are particularly important here.

FOR MORE INFORMATION

The Chief, Visitor Services
Mingan Archipelago National Park Reserve
P.O. Box 1180
1303 Digue Street
Havre-Saint-Pierre, Québec
G0G 1P0

Phone: (418) 538-3331
Fax: (418) 538-3595

AUYUITTUQ

NATIONAL PARK RESERVE

Auyuittuq* means "the land that never melts." A great part of this arctic park is glacier, which does melt at its edges in the summer, but is brought back into line in winter. However, much of the ground is in the zone of permafrost, where the earth's moisture, not far below the soil's surface, is forever in an icy form. For summer hikers, it may seem that the tussocks and gravel and mud below their boots are completely liquified. Knowing that there is frozen earth a few centimetres below is no comfort, and no foothold, whatsoever. But raise your eyes to the glaciers pouring down between the high valley walls, or come close to the glacially-carved peaks of Odin and Thor, and you're not likely to regret the hardship of a true arctic wilderness experience.

This is Canada's second most northern park. Its 21,470 square kilometres (8,290 square miles) protect a pristine part of the eastern Arctic, on Baffin Island. The coasts of Baffin are very rugged. They were deeply etched by glacial action, which has come in several waves, some extending farther than others, some areas being carved more than once. The glaciers formed the U-shaped valleys and the multitude of fiords that radiate from the heights of the main island and the ridges of its peninsulas.

Glacial action is still having an impact on the topography of the park. Approximately one-third of the park's surface is covered by the Penny Ice Cap, the central part of the mountainous Penny Highlands. A number of the mountains of the highlands are over two thousand metres (seven thousand feet) high, but the ice cap dominates them. Glaciers, some as long as twenty-five kilometres (fifteen miles), swoop down to the sea at the Davis Strait, on the northern boundary of the park, and emerge before visitors' eyes along the main travel route of the park, the Pangnirtung Pass, which crosses the peninsula from north to south.

*Pronounced, approximately, Eye-you-eé-tuk.

Parks Canada

It would be a mistake to envision Auyuittuq as a place of only ice and jagged mountains. In fact, unless the visitor has come to the park specifically to climb mountains, most of the visit will be spent in the ice-free valley of Pangnirtung Pass, which is only 400 metres (1,400 feet), at its highest point.

The arctic ecosystem is shaped by the interrelation of soil conditions, climate, water supply, and length of days and seasons. In general, the soils in the park range from rock or gravel outwash from glaciers, which can support little vegetation aside from mosses or lichen, to tundra communities, based on deposits of wind-blown sand supporting dwarf shrubs or some grasses. These grasses often grow in large tussocks, almost a metre tall, in a pillowy growth called a *thufor*.

Tidal-flat plant communities have developed on the edges of fiords, where the walls are not too steep, and along the coastline of the Davis Strait. Finally, there are patches of snow (not ice), which persist throughout the year and, in summer, a few kinds of flowering plants can grow there. All the soil, whatever type, is frozen, all year round, just a few centimetres below the surface. The maximum ice-free depth is fifty centimetres (twenty inches), but often it is far less than this.

Soil poor in nutrients, soil that is very thin, weather that is very cold, and summers that are very short—these factors severely limit the kinds of plants that can exist here. The one compensation is that Auyuittuq, almost all above the Arctic Circle, enjoys twenty-four hours of daylight in the summer. Plants depend upon sunlight for photosynthesis, and for the conversion of mineral nutrients to energy and plant tissue.

The sparse vegetation growth, and its limited diversity, mean that the number of species of animals is small. You can expect to see only lemmings, the large arctic hare (up to five kilograms!), ermine and arctic fox.

The most apparent wildlife in the park for the summer visitor, from June to August, is the bird life. Although there are just thirty-two species of birds, the population of each kind is fairly large. There are fifteen species of water-based birds, such as loons, eiders, murres and kittiwakes; there are snowy owls, rock ptarmigan, shorebirds, such as Baird's and purple sandpiper, ringed plover, ruddy turnstone and seedeaters, such as the Lapland longspur and snow bunting. All of these land-based birds nest directly on the tundra. The rare gyrfalcons and peregrine falcons nest in crevices of rock in valley walls, or on cliff edges and rock shelves on mountain sides.

How to See the Park

Auyuittuq is a rugged wilderness park. Having a safe visit depends on being in good physical condition, having considerable outdoors experience, making detailed plans for the timing of the visit, choosing the proper equipment, and taking plenty of supplies. However, visitors should not take more than they can carry on their backs, because they must be totally self-sufficient and ready to meet any emergency. Once out on the trail, help may be several days away. Airborne rescue is available on occasion, weather permitting, and mountain rescue is limited.*

Parks Canada/R. Marois

Arctic plants crouch low to survive high winds

The Pangnirtung Pass Route

Though there is one main route through the park for hikers, there are several ways to go about it. The pass is, overall, ninety-seven kilometres (sixty miles) long. It follows the **Weasel River**, from the south at **Pangnirtung Fiord** to **Summit Lake**, about one-third of the way along the total route, and then along the **Owl River** to **North Pangnirtung Fiord**. Travelling the whole route thus takes the hiker right across the Cumberland Peninsula.

The first decision prospective visitors must make is whether they wish to go the entire route and, if so, in what direction. If your goal is hiking the entire route, remember that the southern segment of the trail is nearer to the stations at **Overlord**, and that this segment does have four shelters, and somewhat more visitation. The incline to the adjoining **Summit** and **Glacier Lakes** is steeper in this northern direction than from the lakes on the northern end of the route. So, if you want to do the more isolated section of the hike when you are fresh, if you want to avoid slogging the steeper segments of the trail while wearing a nearly-full pack, and if you want to be closer to "civilization" on the last two to four days of the trip, then consider doing the whole route from **Broughton Island** south to Overlord. Allow nine to twelve days.

It is not essential to travel the entire route, however, to get a strong sense of the arctic environment. Many visitors start out at the twelve-tent campground at Overlord, in the south, and then make a round-trip trek to Summit Lake, or on past it to Glacier Lake, and then back to Overlord via

---

* I did not visit this park. I am basing this chapter on printed material from Parks Canada, and especially from the book, *The Land that Never Melts*. For the visitor-use section, I am relying on interviews with Roberto Cavalcanti, who hiked the entire length of Pangnirtung Pass. Jack Ricou helped with revisions.

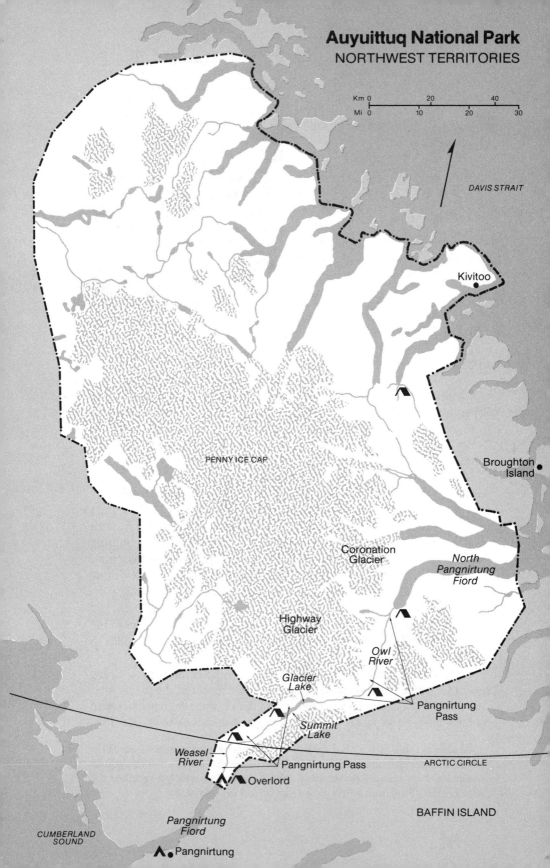

the other bank of the Weasel River. There is the full range of spectacular glacial scenery, of arctic plant life, of rushing glacial-melt streams to ford, and maddening thufor tussocks to circumnavigate. This round trip takes at least a week.

For any kind of hiking, always plan to go more much slowly than you expected, and to eat much more than you believed possible. The Weasel Valley has designated trails, but in the Owl Valley this is not so, and a lot of time is spent in localized route-finding. Getting lost is not a problem, because the pass walls define the limits of travel. However, north of Glacier Lake there are no designated trails, because frequent use of one route on permafrost-based soil is quickly destructive. Also, established routes would often be obscured by changing stream direction, spring avalanches, etc. So, within the broad valley walls, hikers are on their own. The terrain is rarely dry or solid; the higher areas at the foot of the valley walls are often littered with unstable talus, or obstructed by the previous winter's avalanche remains. Hikers must have patience, stamina, and plenty of energy-giving snacks and hot drinks. Fresh water is plentiful, but you must carry your own stove and fuel supply.

Also, hikers must be extremely cautious when crossing the numerous streams that flow into the pass. Try to cross very early in the day, before the mid-day heat increases the melting and, thus, the stream volume. Rope up, if there are three or more people. Use a stout pole if you're not roped and, above all, *unfasten your pack's hip belt*. People have drowned, even in shallow water, when they slipped and could not release their heavy packs.

The weather is very capricious on Baffin Island, and the Pangnirtung Pass may have snowfall any month of the year. On average, one day out of three or four will have frost, throughout the summer. Rain is frequent, and wind is constant. Days are long and may be bright, with temperatures up to 20°C (68°F) in high summer, but you have to be prepared for the most severe conditions possible.

By spending a few days at either of the Inuit settlements of Pangnirtung or Broughton Island, and by hiking for a number of days in the pass, Auyuittuq should give the visitor an unforgettable introduction to Canada's eastern Arctic, the life of its people, and its very special natural history.

Park Facilities and Services

Interpretive Programme

A wilderness park does not offer the interpretive programmes and visitor services found in the southern parks. Wardens at Pangnirtung or Broughton Island do patrol the trails and maintain the few emergency shelters, toilets and garbage depots. The shelters are for emergency use only and, for most of the trail, human waste must be disposed of by shallow burial, and garbage must be packed out. Hikers are expected to register in and out with the wardens, who can advise about trail conditions, freight-canoe availability and reservation, etc. The wardens can operate a limited rescue service, but climbers cannot expect rescue unless they have been able to return to the valley floor.

Camping
There are three primitive campsites, at **Overlord**, **Windy Lake** and **Summit Lake**. Overlord has twelve tent sites, pit toilets, fire grates, and water from streams. There is no fee. All other camping in the park is according to visitors' choice. There are seven main shelters along the whole trail, which people may use in case of extreme weather or a physical emergency. Every shelter area has flat places for tents, and does have primitive toilets. Dryer, gravelly areas are recommended.

Other Camping
In **Pangnirtung**, there is an eight-site campground, run by the territorial government. It has toilets, kitchen shelters and drinking water.

Other Accommodation, Food and Supplies
There is a lodge in Pangnirtung that sleeps thirty-three, in seventeen rooms. In Broughton Island there is a hotel, which costs about $100 a night. There are Hudson's Bay stores in Broughton Island and Pangnirtung. They are small and expensive, and supplies are often limited. There are supply boats in August and September. Since most visitors come in July and August, supplies will be at their lowest. Plan to carry all supplies from home, but it is just possible the store will have that one item you forgot.

Recreational Services
Mountain-Climbing This is a definite draw for visitors. There are a number of very rugged peaks about 2,000 metres (6,560 feet) high. The desire to make a first ascent of a remote mountain, or to scale clean, granite rock faces that no one else has touched, has brought increasing numbers of climbers to the park in summer, for well over a decade. Check back issues of the *Canadian Alpine Journal* (Numbers 37, 47, 49, 55, 56 and 57), for descriptions of some of these climbs. Write to the park, at least a year

Emergency shelter and warming hut, Summit Lake area

ahead, for information on routes, other climbers' experiences, equipment required, etc. A favourite trip for climbers is skimobiling in from Pangnirtung in mid-June, climbing for days or weeks in cold, but possibly clear, weather. This is the time with the minimum amount of snow, and the maximum twenty-four hours of daylight. By the end of August, there will be snow falls regularly at six hundred metres (two thousand feet) and up.

Fishing   Fishing for arctic char in the fiords of Davis Strait is very good, but is usually not the main goal of a visit to the park.

Other Services   There are commercial outfitters, near the park and from other areas of Canada, who take groups into the park. Also, outdoor clubs, such as Canadian Youth Hostels, sponsor a yearly trip to the park. Write to the park for information, or to Travel Arctic, a service of the territorial government, for names and addresses. Several of the nature/conservation magazines carry advertisements for these services.

How to Get There

There are regular jet flights from Montreal and Ottawa to Iqaluit (Frobisher Bay), on southern Baffin Island. From there, flights go to the village of Pangnirtung, on the southern edge of the Cumberland Peninsula, or

Pangnirtung Pass from Overlord

Parks Canada/M. Beedell

to the Broughton Island settlement, on the Davis Strait. From either settlement, it is necessary to go by freighter canoe to the trailheads, at the north or south end of Pangnirtung Pass. The Inuit run this service after the sea ice breaks up, usually in late June or early July at Pangnirtung, and early August at Broughton Island. The ride from Pangnirtung to the southern trailhead at Overlord takes about one and one-half hours. In 1989, it cost $150, one-way, for three people and their supplies. The ride from Broughton Island to the northern trailhead, at the mouth of the Owl River, takes four and one-half to five hours. In 1989, this trip cost $150 per person, one-way. Prices tend to go up annually.

Visitors must write ahead to the park to find out what kinds of service may be expected—times, cost, capacity, etc. This is especially so for the Broughton Island service, because it is much less used. Once at either settlement, checking with the wardens and local tourism officers is essential to ensure transportation at the end of the trip. It is also possible to be skimobiled from either end of the entry to the pass in June, before the ice breaks up. The pass will be snow-free, and the weather quite stable. The thin edge of ice along the rivers makes hiking easier, too.

Further Reading

The Land that Never Melts, Auyuittuq National Park, edited by Roger
    Wilson (Peter Martin Associates, 1976)

FOR MORE INFORMATION

The Superintendent
Auyuittuq National Park Reserve
Pangnirtung, Northwest Territories
X0A 0R0

Phone: (819) 473-8828
(7 days a week, summer)

FORILLON

NATIONAL PARK

Forillon stretches its full length into the sea. The relationship between land, sea and people gives it a special character. Explore this park by driving, bicycling or walking along its paths and shorelines.

Forillon lies at the tip of the northernmost continental reaches of the Appalachian Mountain chain, which extends southwards as far as the state of Georgia. The steep, grey-white cliffs, gleaming over the ocean, are formed from limestone. Over time, the elements have broken this limestone down in places into pebbles, creating the beautiful, crescent-shaped beaches that dot the perimeter of the Gaspé Peninsula. At one time, these beaches provided the basis of a distinctive way of life. Expeditions from Europe, primarily France and Spain, came to fish in the cold, rich waters off the Continental Shelf. The long journey back to Europe made it necessary to preserve the catch first, by drying it on the pebble beaches of the Gaspé. This process required long periods of dry weather, for which the months from April to November were ideal. The rapid drying of the fish flakes meant less salt was required to ensure proper preservation. Thus, Gaspé cure was particularly mild, and became the most sought-after of all the dried cod that was sent to the markets of the world.

It was too far to return to Europe between seasons, so people began to settle in the New World. They planted gardens on the cliff-tops, and felled wood from the forests for building houses and boats, and for winter heating.

Forillon has more than a spectacular and historic coastline to offer the visitor. The mountainous interior, with its wooded hills and valleys, stretches back into the inner peninsula and out to the steep edges of the sea. The woods are mixed boreal (fir and white spruce) and Acadian (maple and birch). On the periphery of the forest, in places such as the exposed cliff faces and talus slopes, where other plants cannot survive, about thirty species of rare arctic-alpine plants grow.

The Penouille beach area, at the southwestern edge of the park, is a low peninsula about two kilometres (one mile) long. Long, smooth beaches and low dunes grace its open side, and a rich salt marsh lies on its inland edge. In the centre, vegetation, usually found five hundred kilometres (three hundred miles) further north in taïga conditions, thrives. Reindeer lichen carpets the sandy soil.

How to See the Park

There are three good ways to explore the shape of the peninsula, and the plant and animal life on and around it. One is to see it from the sea. The sea trip can be taken on a cruise boat, which is privately operated from the wharf just north of the campground, at **Des Rosiers**. There are up to six sightseeing cruises a day, and up to five fishing trips, when you can jig for cod. I took the two-hour sightseeing cruise, which stays close to shore and goes to the tip of the peninsula, where the lighthouse overlooks all. From the boat, it's easy to see the geological structure of the soaring cliffs, to see the patches of orange lichen that colour them, and to see how they have become homes for sea birds, such as kittiwakes, black guillemots, common murres, double-crested cormorants and razorbills. The narrow beaches, formed of sheared-off rocks, produce nesting places for eider ducks. The harbour seal gives birth in the water surrounding the peninsula, and the grey seal arrives with its young already born. Huge white gannets fly overhead, no doubt wandering from Bonaventure Island, which can be seen in the distance on a clear day. An interpreter accompanies the cruise, and this helps with understanding, as well as simply enjoying, the beauty of the interplay between land and sea, and the life of both.

The second way to see the peninsula is to view the underwater life. Check the interpretive-programme timetable for the diving display, given twice a week at **Grande-Grave Beach**. Divers go down to progressively greater depths, bringing back characteristic plants and animals from each level. On shore, interpreters with aquaria receive the marine life, and explain in detail what is brought up and how it survives at its level. The divers explain, at the outset, how they are equipped and what they will do. This is a very popular item on the park's programme; many people are interested in the undersea life, but only a few are able to do this sort of diving themselves. The park welcomes divers, and is proud of the multitude of arctic species of plant and animal found so far south.

The third way to explore the shape of the peninsula is from its summit. Take the **Grande Montagne Trail**, which leaves from behind the **Grande-Grave Harbour** area and goes straight over the narrow neck of the peninsula, toward Des Rosiers Campground. In fact, you can walk from the **Cap Bon Ami** and Des Rosiers campgrounds all the way to the Grande-Grave Harbour, if you want a few hours' stroll. Parts are uphill, of course, over the spine of the peninsula, but the trail is good and there are plenty of lookouts from which to enjoy the scenery and catch your breath.

About a kilometre (half a mile) north from Grande-Grave, the trail follows the fluted edge of the highest side of the tip of the Gaspé. At each major turning, carefully fenced lookouts give a thrilling sense of being poised between the flower-strewn woods behind and the vast ocean in front—about 200 metres (650 feet) below, in places. Don't forget your camera!

Indian pipe, a saprophytic plant

People on the Land and Sea

Fishing, gardening and lumbering have been an integral part of the Forillon area for hundreds of years. People no longer live on park land itself, so there is no more gardening or lumbering, but they fish in the harbour of **Cap-des-Rosiers**, and from the quai at **Grande-Grave**. There is a wharf at Grande-Grave that is used largely for local boats to come and go. Visitors can picnic nearby, or drop a line over the edge of the wharf themselves. *Grève* is an old French word, referring to a pebble beach where cod were once dried. Pebbly beaches line the peninsula, and the beach there is larger than most, about 400 metres (450 yards) long. The park has preserved part of the little village that was once a centre of fishing and fish processing. You can go into those buildings that have been restored. The barn has been made into an informative display of the techniques and history of fishing in the area.

Here, you learn that the business side of fishing could be more precarious than being out on rough, cold seas. A system developed, where fishermen, who could not afford the equipment they needed, would borrow money or goods from merchants or fishing companies. The price of the loan would be set only *after* the last haul was in. Not surprisingly, income was never enough to allow people to pay off their debts, make enough profit to get through the winter, and be ready to fish the next year.

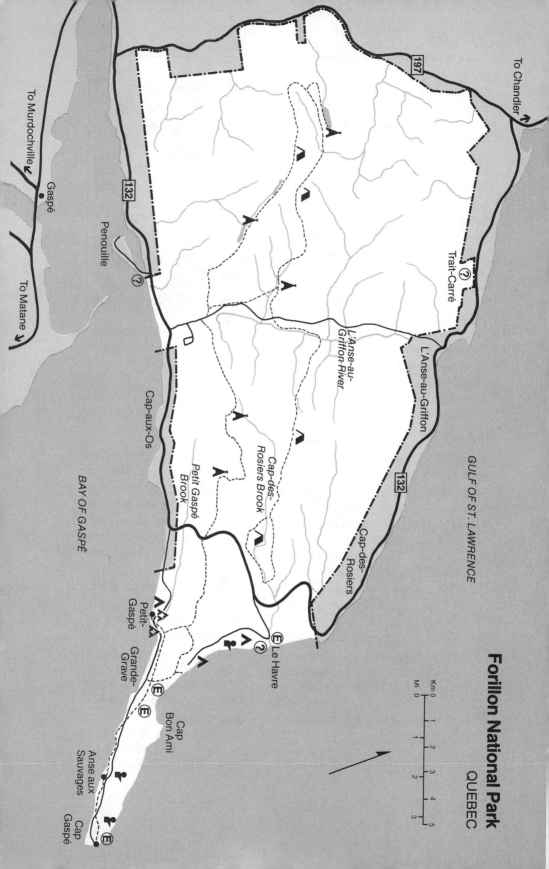

Forillon National Park
QUEBEC

This dispiriting aspect of fishing in the Gaspé is well documented at Grande-Grave.

Near the barn is the Hyman & Sons store, and its adjacent store-room. Both are now open to the public, and staffed by park interpreters. At the turn of the century, this store was the social and economic centre of the village.

Leaving the barn, you drive through the fields where haying was done, and then into the woods, which were the source of heating and building materials. The lumbering was done in winter, when logs could be more easily brought out, and the people were not busy with fishing or farming. A fascinating, scenic walk brings you much closer to at least some aspects of the former life of this area.

There is another walk, on the south side of the peninsula, that dramatically displays the hardships fishing entails, and the ingenuity that the people showed in meeting these obstacles. The road past Grande-Grave ends a few minutes' drive farther east, at **Anse aux Sauvages**. There is a wharf, still sturdy enough to walk on, an old cemetery, a picnic area with water and toilets, and an excellent pebble beach. It is a favourite place for scuba diving, and even for intrepid windsurfers.

But it's **Les Grèves Trail**, out to the lighthouse at the tip of the Gaspé peninsula, that is the route to follow, to experience more of the Gaspé way of life. The trail nears the cliff, overlooking the sea. The fields are thick with primroses and Queen Anne's lace, as you follow the mown track. Every few hundred metres, the ground seems to drop away beneath you, as the trail touches the border of a pebbled cove. You can look down in several places, and see the weathered remains of the stone-filled platforms and long ramps that were built to allow the transport of people, fish and even boats over the vertical cliffs to the land above. Even though these ramps must have lightened the load somewhat, there is something almost painful in seeing how much work had to go into their construction, and how terribly laborious hauling anything up (or down) must have been.

The trail that extends past these coves takes you out to the **Cap Gaspé Lighthouse**. The trail loops and, if you follow it all the way to the upper level (a ten-minute walk), you will be right in the middle of some of the park's boreal forest. It opens out suddenly onto the clearing, where the white-and-red lighthouse sits, booming out its warning on foggy days. You can be at the edge of the cliffs here, too, and it is an exhilarating experience to be at eye-level with the gulls and kittiwakes, which use the wind, howling up the cliff face, to keep tilting and soaring just a metre from you, but perhaps a hundred metres from the ocean below. It's a wonderful, and easily reached, destination, though the walk is about an hour each way.

Penouille Beach

Penouille Beach creates a striking contrast to the wooded mountains, white cliffs, and wind-and-sea-sculpted pebble beaches of the rest of Forillon. It is low, sandy and sparsely vegetated in some places, with rich mud flats in others. It is located at the southwestern entrance to the park, near an information centre, where staff can help plan a visit, give you maps and pamphlets, or sell posters and books on natural history. Visitors to Penouille park at this centre, and travel the two kilometres (one mile) to the point by propane-powered tram. The point has a snack bar, changing rooms and showers for swimmers, toilets and picnic tables.

The things to enjoy here are the low dune formations on the ocean side of the point, the eel-grass-covered salt marsh on the landside (very good for migrating shore birds), and the dry taïga vegetation in the middle of the spit. This combination is a very rare circumstance. Try to join an interpretive walk here; it's very worthwhile.

Park Services and Facilities

Interpretive Programme

There are two Information Centres, at Penouille near Cap-aux-Os, and Trait-Carré near L'Anse-au-Griffon, and one Interpretive Centre at the harbour of Cap-des-Rosiers. Here, you will find the schedule of interpretive events, other informative pamphlets, maps and books, and bilingual staff, who can discuss your interests in the park. There are four aquaria, with live specimens of the park's underwater fauna, and video displays are shown on a regular basis. The programmes are most often in French, but some are in English. The Information Centres, Interpretive Centre and Hyman Store are all wheelchair-accessible. At the Des Rosiers and Petit-Gaspé campgrounds, wheelchair access has been installed in the service buildings.

Camping

There are three areas for single tents or trailers, and one group campground. There is trailer-waste disposal facility in each, and all have water. **Petit Gaspé**, in the southwest, is the first campground to fill. It has 136 sites, in a beautiful, wooded area. Most of the sites are on split levels—one for the vehicle and one for the tent. This arrangement gives added privacy and is visually appealing. Excellent kitchen shelters and washrooms with showers are provided, as well as a small playground, and firewood. **Des Rosiers Campground**, at the north side of the park, has about two hundred sites, including forty-two with hookups. It is situated on a large, sloping

Limestone cliffs, seen best from a boat

field, with the ridge of the peninsula rising behind it and the ocean bordering its front. It is an easy walk to the beach, and to paths leading to the tip of the peninsula. This campsite boasts excellent showers, washrooms and kitchen shelters. Firewood is available. The amphitheatre is in the middle of this campground, and the Interpretive Centre is close by. The quai, for taking boat tours, is a short drive or easy walk from here.

Cap Bon Ami Campsite is a few minutes' drive further along the peninsula, on the road that goes past Des Rosiers. This is a small area, reserved for tent camping only. There are earthen platforms for tents, and cars can park between the sites. There are kitchen shelters, toilets and showers, picnic tables, and a broad field for playing games. The campground is very close to the mountains rising behind, and close to the sea and to the trails up to the peninsula tip. There is a picnic area and lookout near it, for day visitors. Nearby, a spectacular lookout overlooks bird-nesting cliffs and the picturesque Cap Bon Ami.

Group Camping
Reservations are necessary for this site, near **Petit Gaspé**; write to the Superintendent.

Other Accommodation, Gas, Food and Supplies
Both north and south of the park are small villages, which have motels and private campgrounds, small grocery and camping-supply stores, and

Grey seals basking at the foot of Les Falaises

gasoline stations. Often, these stores or motels have information on the park, especially its schedule of interpretive events.

Recreational Services

Swimming   Swimming is supervised at the point of Penouille, but unsupervised everywhere else. People often wade at other pebble beaches as they stroll or picnic. The water is cold, but not intolerable.

Scuba Diving   The park encourages scuba diving, because of its varied underwater habitat. This is one of the few places in the National Parks system where arctic-water plant and animal life can be seen. In summer, water temperatures in most areas vary from 8° to 19°C (46° to 60°F) at the surface, and 2°to 3°C (35°to 37°F) at eighteen metres (sixty feet).

Winter Use   There are plenty of opportunities for cross-country skiing and snowshoeing. Beginners are encouraged to use the **Des Concessions Trail**.

Camping is allowed there, also. A warming shelter, firewood, a stove and dry toilets are provided, but there is no water, so bring your own.

There are much longer and more strenuous trails in the interior of the park; La Cèdrière is one. There are three warming huts and toilets. Le Castor and Le Ruisseau are also good trails. The three trails interconnect.

Fishing Fishing is free, and no licence is necessary to fish from the various oceanside wharves. No quotas are imposed. Mackerel is the usual catch. For trout fishing in inland streams and lakes, a National Parks fishing licence is required, and can be obtained from wardens, or at the entry kiosk. There are fairly small quotas for trout.

Further Reading

Forillon National Park by Maxine St-Amour (Douglas & McIntyre, 1984)

FOR MORE INFORMATION

The Superintendent
Forillon National Park
Box 1220
Gaspé, Québec
GOC 1RO

Phone (418) 368-5505

KOUCHIBOUGUAC

NATIONAL PARK

Kouchibouguac* National Park offers a wonderful opportunity to appreciate a maritime plain. Its land slopes gently to the sea, and twenty-five
kilometres (fifteen miles) of white, dune-edged beaches protect warm
lagoons and rich salt marshes. At first, Kouchibouguac seems an unimpo-
sing place, remarkable only for its beautiful beaches. Perhaps because no
part of the plain is higher than thirty metres (one hundred feet), the visitor
tends to think of the park as a place that's simply good for swimming,
bicycling or picnicking. It's not immediately apparent that this is a place
of rich natural history and spectacular change. In fact, Kouchibouguac has
one of the most dynamically changing ecosystems in the whole range of
national parks: the chain of barrier islands lining its eastern border forms
constantly shifting dunes, reefs and lagoons.

The barrier islands are formed and changed largely through the
power of the sea. The action of waves, particularly during storms, tears the
sand from the land and from the sea bottom, and throws it up into ridges,
which you can see on a stroll along the beach. The crests of the dunes are
the result of further shaping by winds and longshore currents, which shift
the fine sand exposed as the barriers are built up from underwater. Three
major island dunes, North Kouchibouguac, South Kouchibouguac and
North Richibucto, have existed for about 2,500 years. They are migrating
shoreward over the centuries, driven by the wind. Although these dunes
are permanent, their shape is constantly changing.

This island system is not an isolated land form; it has important
effects on the character of the area behind it, because the barrier calms and
controls the effects of the sea on the land. Water that slips around the ends
of the islands, through inlets, does not scour the sandy bottom, or disturb
the many marine plants and animals. Rather, the sand is more stable and,

*Pronounced KOOSH-uh-BOOG-oo-WACK

near the edges of the tidal flow, mud can build up. Nutrients collect, seeds take, and molluscs and fish feed and shelter in the salt-tolerant plant life, in the fairly stable mud, and in the warm, sluggish water.

The rivers and streams that cut through the plain, flowing to the sea, unite at this special place. The fresh water meets the tidal lagoon water, mixes with it, and is partially held in the lagoons by the barrier islands. As a result, the sea water is diluted in the slowly flushing lagoons, and thus plants and animals can survive in the estuaries at the river mouths, and in the nearer parts of the lagoons. There are also salt-water marshes in some places, with the grasses that waterfowl love to visit and breed amongst. A big storm can radically change the shape of the islands and the life of the lagoons, estuaries and salt marshes beyond. But, as one part is lost, another is built, so the story is one of change, not destruction.

The forest and fields in the interior of the park have been moulded by people, as surely as the coastal area is moulded by the sea. The forest was logged and burned repeatedly, in the last few hundred years. The tall white pines were cut for ships' masts; other trees were taken for ship-building and construction. Occasionally a white pine was spared, because it was gnarled or distorted. Along the Claire Fontaine Trail or Ruisseau Major, it's possible to see several huge white pines, each with a quirk or kink in it. Fields were cleared for domestic animals to graze, or for crops to be grown. Both the forest and the cleared areas are being allowed to return to their natural state. They are rich and varied, and will be fascinating examples of change for many years to come.

Bogs compose twenty-one percent of the total area of the park, though they are accessible only at Kellys Bog. The Maritime plain underlying them is very flat and dense, and does not let water drain through it. High humidity and a low moisture-evaporation rate in this area produce just the right conditions for bogs to form. There are raised bogs, whose sole source of water is rain and snow. They build up layer after layer of sphagnum moss and small shrubs, and become gently domed in shape. Kellys Bog is more than five metres (eighteen feet) deep in sphagnum moss, and the condensed layers of it that have become peat.

How to See the Park

The Barrier Islands, Beaches, Lagoons and Salt Marshes

Most visitors' first destination is **Kellys Beach**. A large parking lot, snack bar, changing rooms, showers and toilets are part of a complex in the wooded area behind the beach. Paths to the beach are all boardwalk, to protect the fragile plant life and shifting sands. The five-minute walk starts in a narrow band of woods, where warblers, thrushes and flycatchers

may be seen, or owls heard at night.
(A wheelchair could be taken here,
with little difficulty.) Woods give
way to the grasses of the salt marsh,
where savannah sparrows abound.
This is the place for the sharp-tailed
sparrow, as well. Then comes the
first stretch of lagoon, running parallel to the beach. The boardwalk
floats across the water, a marvel of
sturdy construction, as it rises and
falls with the changing tide. It then
leads people to the start of their
beach walk, on the sheltered side of
the **South Kouchibouguac Dune.**
The boardwalk ends at the ocean
side of the dune. In the summer,

Kellys bog: arethusa orchid and pitcher plants

you can see gannets and eiders flying and feeding, not far out to sea. The
dune ridge is covered with marram grass, the primary colonizer of this
sandy, shifting environment. In slightly more stable areas, the searocket
and bayberry are taking hold. Down on the beach itself, there are kilometres of firm, clean sand to walk on. The ocean water is warm enough for
swimming in summer, but the lagoons are several degrees warmer and
much calmer.

Bird life is very rich on the less-visited bars and islands, well within
sight of this main island. Thousands of terns and gulls nest at **Tern Island,**
just at the south of the South Kouchibouguac Dune. A pair of binoculars
helps, but isn't essential. You can also see some of a herd of grey seals
basking on the quieter islands and beaches. They come in about mid-May,
and stay until mid-October.

Local fishermen sometimes take visitors into the Northumberland
Strait, the waters bordering the park. Such a trip certainly adds to the
enjoyment and understanding of this intricate ecosystem. Ask at the
Information Centre for help with locating a boat.

It is possible to canoe in the lagoons, though wind in the afternoons
can be a problem in some areas, and canoeists should be well protected
against insects, cold and wet (in case of swamping).

The Forests

There are excellent walks in both the north and south of the park. (The
Kouchibouguac River is the customary dividing line between north and
south.) In the north, the 3-kilometre (1.8-mile) **Claire Fontaine Trail** is
well-marked and easy. It rounds a wooded point, which juts out into

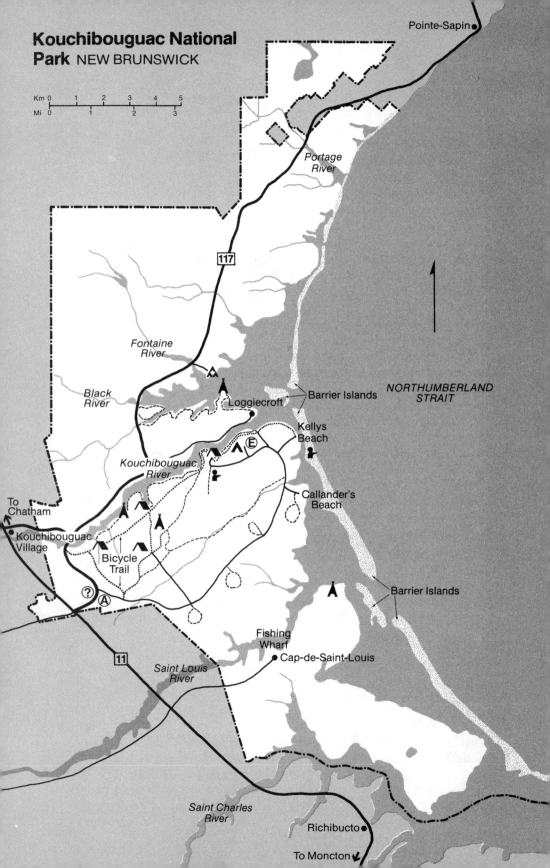

Kouchibouguac Lagoon. Here, the forest is typical mixed Acadian birches, white pine and several other kinds of conifer. The ground is fairly open, with trilliums, trout lilies and bunchberry. We also saw a couple of clumps of the saprophytic Indian Pipe, at the edge of the path.

There are several open areas, with benches, that overlook either the stream side or the lagoon side. The loop trail begins and ends in a bog area, with kalmia, lots of fungus, and several very damp spots. Short stretches of boardwalk are provided.

Beaver Trail is about halfway along the road between the Information Centre and the campground. This very short loop trail provides a fascinating example of change in the Acadian forest, as it is affected through altering water levels. The beavers have built a lengthy crescent of dams, and the pond formed has killed a number of big, old trees, but makes an excellent environment for water-tolerant bushes and trees, such as alder. The pond and swampy areas are also great habitat for aquatic insects. All this, in turn, means excellent breeding and feeding areas for birds. Canada warblers and American redstarts nest in the thickets at the border between dried and drowned forest, in the company of the common yellowthroat, magnolia, Tennessee and yellow-rumped warblers. Dead trees in the middle of the pond are havens for several kinds of woodpeckers. Thrushes and vireos patrol the slightly drier forest edges, and kingfishers and kingbirds swoop over the water to feed. I saw five species of butterfly, and four of dragonfly. Also plentiful was the rather eerie phantom cranefly, which loves moist, weedy areas. It is black, except for the joints of each of its three-centimetre-long legs, which are a luminous white. As it bobs and wobbles along, often all you can see are these spots of white, as the body holding them together is hardly visible.

The Fields

Most of the fields lie east of the main road to the campground. The best way to see them is by bicycle. Bikes can be rented at Ryan's Landing, though many people bring their own. The park is steadily upgrading its bicycle trails, which stretch for many kilometres along the edges of woods and ponds, or through the fields. There are picnic areas at Pattersons, Middle Kouchibouguac, Sandstone Gardens, La Source and Petit-Large. Trails start at the **Major Kollock Creek Bridge**, at the eastern edge of the campground, or at several places marked from the main road.

The Bogs

Kouchibouguac is such a dynamic environment that even its slow-moving features change quickly. This is true of **Kellys Bog**. Bear in mind that most bogs in eastern Canada have existed for approximately 8,000 years. But at only 4,500 years of age, the sphagnum and peat in this bog is deeper than much older bogs. It is a raised bog, forming a huge, low, inverted soup-bowl of sphagnum moss, spread over four square kilometres (one and one-half square miles). Visiting the bog is easy—just drive or walk two kilometres (one mile) past the campground, toward **La Source**. There's parking for cars and bikes. Then walk to one of the gems of the park's interpretive programme, the boardwalk into the middle of the bog. It is self-guiding, with colourful, informative signs along the way.

The first part of the trail is through the narrow band of woods sur-rounding the bog. This moist, densely treed area is excellent for warblers. Just as the woods open onto the vast bog, there is a viewing tower with a wide, spiral staircase and several flat areas to rest and look out from, on the way up its three storeys. The view from the top encompasses the whole bog. Looking straight down, the scarlet of the pitcher plants and the pink of the rose pogonia orchids stand out against the golden sphagnum surface.

The boardwalk leads you past small ponds, where common bladder-wort nod. These are carnivorous plants, as are the more common pitcher plants and sundew. The bladderwort's submerged leaves have little blad-ders, which quickly suck in any tiny, aquatic animals that bump against them.

At the far end of the boardwalk, there is a partially enclosed area with benches on three sides. It's a good place to stay for a while, and enjoy the atmosphere of the bog. My nephew and I stayed there most of one night, hoping a moose would come to graze or drink at one of the little ponds nearby. No moose appeared, but we heard coyotes and owls from the woodland edge. A deer came, too, and thoroughly frightened us with its loud snorting, sounding out of the blackness of 3:00 a.m.

Park Services and Facilities

Interpretive Programme

The interpretive service here attempts to bring the programme to the visi-tor, rather than trying to assemble visitors at fixed locations. There are schedules posted in French and English at the campgrounds, Information Centre and Kellys Beach. These programmes are presented in the language posted, but the staff is largely bilingual so, if you miss a programme in one language, it'll be sure to appear, at another time, in the other. Most pro-grammes are given under the big, yellow umbrella at the Kellys Beach boardwalk area, or from other selected places on the beach. There was a very pleasant campfire programme when I was there, a good mixture of song, story and natural history.

Parks Canada

The constantly shifting barrier islands protect the salt marshes inland.

Camping

On busy July and August weekends, there is often a line-up for camping sites. On these days, names are taken when visitors arrive, and places are given out in the early afternoon. Once you've given your name, you can leave to enjoy the park, and return at the appointed time to hear the names of those who will have places called. It usually pays to wait.

There are two main campgrounds in the park. The largest one is **South Kouchibouguac**, with 219 sites. There are no hook-ups, but there is a trailer-waste disposal area.The sites are beautifully designed for space and privacy—set well back from the road, with shrubs and some trees screening each site. The tent area is smooth lawn, not too natural but very comfortable. There are tables, fire rings with cooking grates, and firewood is supplied near the entrance. The large and handsome kitchen shelter is equipped with big wood stoves, sinks and washrooms. Clean, hot showers are available in one area, and large washrooms with sinks and hot water in four places. This campground has a marvellous adventure playground, set in a huge field. **Côte-à-Fabien Campground** is the other main camping area, with twenty-one drive-in sites and nine walk-ins. This campground is located between the Black and Kouchibouguac Rivers, and is quite removed from the main activity areas of the park. For those who are really wanting to get away from it all and have a very "natural" park experience, this may be the place for you. It overlooks one of the lagoons, and you can start your day with a saltwater splash and wind up the evening eating some freshly dug clams, while watching the sunset.

Canoeing at Ruisseau Major

Primitive Camping

There are three places, with room for four tents each—**Sîpo***, **Petit-Large** and **Pointe à Maxime**. These are accessible by canoe, except for Petit-Large, which can be reached by bicycle or hiking. They have dry toilets, firewood and water. Register at the Visitor Reception Centre. There is a minimal fee.

Group Camping

There is a group area, with kitchen shelter, firewood, toilets and pump water. Write to the Superintendent for reservations.

Other Accommodation, Gas, Food and Supplies

There are several small towns at either end of the park, and halfway along its length. Richibucto is the largest. There are motels and a good selection of private campgrounds, which are very close to the park and all its activities.

     The surrounding communities of Kouchibouguac, Pointe-Sapin, Saint-Louis-de-Kent, Richibucto and Rexton have grocery, hardware, and department stores, service stations, credit unions and banks.

*Pronounced Seeboo

Recreational Services

Swimming There is supervised swimming, from mid-June through Labour Day, at Kellys Beach. Swimming is unsupervised at Callander's Beach, which has big fields for picnicking, and a kitchen shelter.

Boating and Canoeing There are many kilometres of lagoon and river waterways. A publication by a local group on canoe routes in the area, and the park's own air-photo mosaic depict these routes. Rowboats and canoes can be rented at Ryan's Landing, near South Kouchibouguac Campground. Motor boats are permitted on the major rivers.

Bicycling The park is unique for its extensive development of bicycle trails, and a great deal of it is best seen from a bicycle, given the distances. Bikes can be rented at Ryan's Landing.

Winter Use The park emphasizes cross-country skiing and snowshoeing. Maps, showing trails and warm-up shelters, are available. An annual marathon, and other community events, are held in winter. The terrain is not rugged, and there are many places to go. Winter camping can be arranged for groups; contact the Superintendent.

Fishing Fishing is not a popular activity in the park. To do it, however, you must purchase a National Park fishing licence (not required for shell-fish). It is sometimes possible to arrange for deep-sea fishing expeditions with local fishermen; cod, mackerel and flounder are the catch.

Bird-Watching The park is very good for shorebirds and pelagic species (seen from a distance). It is one of the few breeding places of the endangered piping plover. The park is protecting the nesting area, but talk with the interpreters about other areas where you might catch a glimpse of this tiny bird.

FOR MORE INFORMATION

The Superintendent
Kouchibouguac National Park
Kouchibouguac, New Brunswick
E0A 2A0

Phone: (506) 876-2443/876-2446

FUNDY

NATIONAL PARK

In the last eight years, since I first visited Fundy National Park, it has undergone some of the most significant changes of any of the parks in our national system. Overall, its rich forests, dramatic shoreline, and lakes, rivers and bogs, are much more accessible to the visitor. There is a new network of trails in the back country, and this links up many of the familiar, shorter trails. Along with bringing nature closer for the visitor, the park has greatly enhanced its role in providing a safe haven for several species of wildlife which, until very recently, had not been seen in the park for many years. The American martin, the peregrine falcon and the Atlantic salmon are now regulars in the park. Any staff can tell you the story of the park's efforts to reintroduce these species. You aren't likely to see the shy martin, but there are places where you can see the "hacking box," where the peregrines were cared for as chicks, and then released. In autumn, you may see the salmon, as they return to their home river to spawn.

How to See the Park

There are a number of ways to become familiar with Fundy Park. Camp, drive the car trails, explore the walking trails, utilize the many brochures and signs, talk to the interpreters. In the summer, there is an extensive programme of interpreter-guided walks and slide-show presentations, geared to all ages and taking in a wide variety of the park's features, over a two- or three-day visit.

The Tides of the Bay of Fundy

The park is famous for the extreme tides of the Bay of Fundy. They are exceptionally high and low for two main reasons. One is that the usual expanse of free-moving ocean water is squeezed into a long, funnel-shaped bay, so the contrast between the highest point of the tide and the lowest is very great. The other reason for the tidal extremes is a phenomenon called resonance: the water in the nearly enclosed area of the bay sloshes back and forth down its length about every thirteen hours. The water is also subjected to the gravitational pull of the moon, which exerts maximum force every twelve hours and twenty-six minutes. The two forces roughly coincide, and effectively build on each other to reinforce Fundy's tidal extremes.

You can witness this phenomenon in several places. The **Headquarters Campgrounds** are beautifully situated on a cliff, at the eastern edge of the park. Here, you overlook the village of **Alma**, which sits at the edge of a small river that has its own small salt marsh, and a little mooring area of boats. Just by standing at the most eastern campsites, the wash of the water over the flats can be observed. A few minutes' walk or a two-minute drive to Alma will put you on the beach of the bay itself. You can walk out on the flats, at low tide, as far as a kilometre (half a mile), but remember the tide comes in at a rate of one and one-half metres/minute (almost five feet/minute), so don't leave your shoes too far away.

Herring Cove is another good place to learn about intertidal life. An interpretive display helps, if you've left your brochure behind and haven't joined a guided group. **Point Wolfe** provides another opportunity to be close to the ocean's changes. Look for signs to the **Wolfe Point Trail**. It's a wonderful walk to take.

Of course, you needn't be right on the beach to appreciate the beauty and fascination of the tides, and of the bay itself. Trails such as **Coastal**, **Dickson Falls**, **Devil's Half Acre** and **Coppermine** all have dazzling vistas of the bay, or spine-tingling views down to the rocks and shore far below. The park has constructed some amazing catwalk sections on some of the trails. They take you where you couldn't have gone otherwise, yet are completely in harmony with the surroundings.

The Forests

Of the eight different types of forest region in Canada, the Acadian occurs over most of the Maritime Provinces. An Acadian forest has both evergreens, such as red spruce and balsam fir, and hardwoods, such as red maple or white birch. It also features bogs, where glacier movements have scoured out depressions in which water from rain or snow now collects. These depressions are slowly filling with mosses and other plants that, in time, die but don't decompose. Very slowly, in the cold, acid water, they build up a peat bog.

Some areas of the Maritimes will have only the coniferous forests, or may be largely boggy, or predominantly hardwood. What is so distinctive about the narrow coastal area that borders the Bay of Fundy is that it has all three types of habitat. Each has characteristic patterns of plant and animal life, which can be seen quite clearly by following selected interpretive trails.

Dickson Falls Trail is self-guiding; interpretive signs help you understand the distinctive features of this coastal forest. It is quite easy walking along the catwalks, in some places. It takes you to the foot of the low, but beautiful two-tiered falls.

This tamarack may have taken 100 years to reach its one metre of height

Devil's Half Acre is part of a foggy, red-spruce forest. Here, you see the coastal forest precariously clinging to its foothold on the rugged, steep hillsides sloping to the sea. The trees aren't safely settled in, as they are at Dickson Falls. Trailside signs describe the various legends about how the ground at Devil's Half Acre came to resemble the aftermath of a giant battle: boulders thrown about, and gaping crevasses and cracks. What seems to be fact is that a lower layer of slippery shale is covered by relatively soft and water-permeable sandstone. Over the millenia, both have tended to buckle under the strain of being perched on the edge of a very steep slope to the sea. Years of freezing and thawing of ground moisture, with its attendant forces of expansion and contraction, have helped create this startling landscape.

The park has made this area accessible through the construction of a very convoluted railed stair and bridge system, without which there would be no way to traverse this intriguing place. When the mists from the sea below begin to rise, the trees and mossy wooden walkways take on the mood of a Japanese scenic painting. It is then very clear how this pathway is a true complement to the rugged natural setting.

Hardwoods and broadleaved forests are found mainly in one zone of the park, the middle uplands, about three kilometres (two miles) from the headquarters. The beautiful **Maple Grove Trail** is accessible by car, along the **Hastings Auto Trail**. The trail is mostly among the trees but, since the predominant ground cover is a wide variety of ferns, you can easily see into the many light-filled clearings, where deer graze in the early

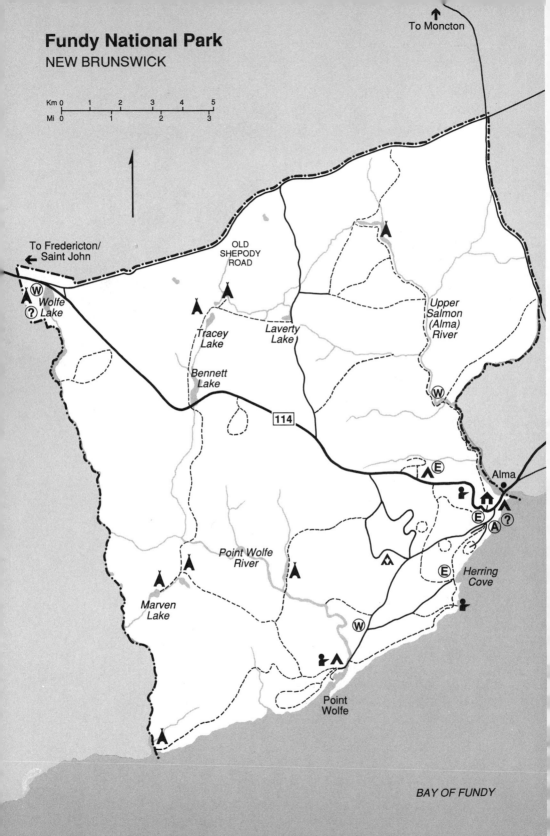

Fundy National Park
NEW BRUNSWICK

Km 0   1   2   3   4   5
Mi 0   1   2   3

To Moncton

To Fredericton/
Saint John

OLD
SHEPODY
ROAD

Wolfe
Lake

Tracey
Lake

Laverty
Lake

Upper
Salmon
(Alma)
River

Bennett
Lake

114

Alma

Point Wolfe
River

Herring
Cove

Marven
Lake

Point
Wolfe

BAY OF FUNDY

morning or at dusk. Listen for the songs of woodland birds, such as the purple finch. In contrast to the lushness of the coastal woods and the ruggedness of Devil's Half Acre, this is a quiet, spacious place, somehow restful in its familiarity, for a visitor from more southern parts of our country.

Raised Bog Habitat

A peat bog is a beautiful place, but walking in it can present problems. What looks like solid ground is really a huge mat of sphagnum moss. At Fundy, on the **Caribou Plains Trail**, the problem is solved. After a brief walk from the parking lot, through beautiful and increasingly moist woods (watch for many pink lady's slipper orchids in June), help is thoughtfully provided. First, you can make use of bridges here and there. Then, as you suddenly find yourself out in the open area of the main bog itself, there is a solid, winding boardwalk just centimetres off the sphagnum moss mat. The boardwalk extends into the midst of the bog, with a side branch or two to the lake. There's even a firmly anchored lakeside platform, where you have room to sit and eat your lunch with other hikers.

Once at the bog, it's worth making a really close examination of the pink-and-brown carpet of sphagnum moss, the basis of bog plant life. Often, where there are indentations a few centimetres across, you may see that most fascinating plant, the sundew. It looks like a collection of tiny, reddish tennis racquets with pink bristles radiating off the rim. There are drops of moisture sticking to the bristles. These globules are sticky, and insects that come in contact with them are easily trapped. The plant feeds on the insects by exuding an enzyme that dissolves the protein of the insect's body to release nitrogen, which can then be absorbed.

Taller than the sundew is the Labrador tea bush, which appears either in small clumps or as an extensive carpet. It grows about half a metre high and, in June, has beautiful, white, flower clusters. The pink flowers of the swamp laurel provide a lovely colour accent to the paler pink of the moss.

A striking red globe—two to nearly six centimetres (one to two inches) across—hanging from a stem ten to twenty centimetres (three to eight inches) high, signals another well-known bog resident, the pitcher plant. It grows singly or in groups, sometimes a number of groups together, sometimes widely scattered. The flower of the pitcher plant towers above its rosette of curved red-and-green leaves, or "pitchers," that collect water. Deceptively, this water is not the direct source of the plant's nutrition. The pitcher plant, too, is carnivorous. Insects and spiders are attracted by the colour of the pitcher and the glandular secretions on its lip, and fall into the water. Downward sloping hairs in the pitcher prevent the insects from climbing up and out. The victims are dissolved by enzymes and, as they are absorbed, they provide the plant with needed nutrients. The pitcher plant doesn't always have its bloom to draw your attention, so keep looking for the clumps of pitchers in among the moss. They'll be there.

On the bog, the tallest plants are the trees, but even these are miniatures—often no more than a metre tall. There are a number of ten-centimetre tamaracks here and there. On hummocks of drier land, a few trees, Labrador tea bushes and a few bog laurel may form a plant island, within a sea of mosses and sedges. One can begin to understand the often-times-slow process of change in nature, and the limited growth potential in a peat bog, when one learns that a tamarack or black spruce, less than a metre tall, may have taken a hundred years or more to reach that height. The same plant, in deep, rich soil somewhere else, could be thirty metres high.

In the bog, insects abound, as do amphibians. And birds hunt insects over the bog and its lake; swallows swoop ceaselessly.

The Caribou Plains Trail is 3.4 kilometres (2.5 miles) long, about half of it over the bog.

Human History

The original inhabitants of the Maritime provinces were the Maritime Archaic Indians, and then the Micmac and Malecites, who hunted and fished, settling briefly here and there, as they followed their food supply. In the 1500s, French fishermen came to the area, as did Basques from Spain. Then, in the 1600s, came missionaries and fur traders, most of whom only passed through the rugged Fundy area, on their way to some-where else.

While a number of French people settled in the Maritimes, which they called Acadia, few lived in the park area. Further European settle-ment came with the growing demand for timber; for buildings, for ships and eventually for pulp. Logging and improved agricultural implements made some farming possible, although the soil was not rich or deep enough to support many people. But prosperity was bought at a heavy price. The area was logged without any attempt at conservation, and the sawmills polluted the fishing in the nearby rivers and inshore. Today, with the park's protection, the salmon are recovering and the trees have a chance for a natural lifespan.

The best evidence of farming in the area is at **Matthews Head**. A trail there criss-crosses the now-deserted fields. The farm was started in 1865, and supported a family for a generation. Eventually, it became a go-vernment-run experimental potato farm. Now it is a stretch of beautiful fields, where deer feed and bobolinks float over them, singing in the wind.

Boats beached by the retreating tide

For other traces of earlier human settlement, follow the self-guiding **East Branch Trail**, or hiking trails like **Coppermine** and **Goose River**.

Park Services and Facilities

Interpretive Programme

Unlike many of the national parks, Fundy does not have a central visitor centre. But there is an interpretation office in the assembly hall at the headquarters area, and there is a varied schedule of talks and tours given throughout the park itself. A check of any campground bulletin board, from mid-June through September, should give you a week-by-week picture of the schedule.

A central attraction of the interpretive programme is the evening slide shows and animations presented, in the two outdoor theatres. The largest of these, in the headquarters area, is built into a hillside and overlooks a picture-perfect pond. The other theatre is nestled in a forest clearing, within walking distance of Chignecto Campground.

There are a number of guide books and informative brochures on the park's natural and human history, and on trails and other interesting places to visit. These are available at any campground registration kiosk. The Fundy Guild, a non-profit cooperating association, has bookshops at

Toad and three-leaved false Solomon's seal

the eastern and western entrances to the park, at the Information Kiosks. They have an excellent selection of books and gifts. They also publish a number of very attractive books and pamphlets for adults and children.

Camping

There are three main campgrounds and sixty-four fully-equipped chalets in the park, plus a number of primitive campsites for those hiking the back country. In winter, part of the Headquarters Campground is kept open for tent camping. The roads there are plowed; washroom facilities are open.

All campgrounds have toilets, showers, and enclosed kitchen areas where you can cook on wood stoves and eat at picnic tables. Each campground has a well-equipped children's playground. **Headquarters Campground** is lawned and treed, with one edge overlooking Alma Harbour and the tidal marsh at the mouth of the Upper Alma River. **Micmac Group Campground** is located in what was once farm fields. It has a lot of rolling open space, with occasional fruit trees and some treed field edges. Reservations are required for groups. **Point Wolfe Campground** is lawned and treed, and is very near the Point Wolfe River. It is a few minutes' walk to the beach and to the start of a number of interesting trails. **Chignecto North Campground** has wooded sites, and is located up on the plateau portion of the park, near several trails.

Other Camping

There are several private grounds in the village of Alma, just a couple of minutes by car from the eastern park entrance.

Other Accommodation, Gas, Food and Supplies

There are several modest, well-kept motels with and without housekeeping facilities, in and near Alma and towards Albert. There are two bed-and-breakfasts, and I expect the number to increase. There are thirty-two chalets near the park headquarters, and a similar number two kilometres (one mile) west on Highway 114. The facilities are park-owned, but privately operated. Each chalet has two double beds, full kitchen facilities and utensils, and full bathroom. You bring your own food. To reserve chalets, call (506) 887-2808 or 887-2930.

There is a concession-run restaurant, a five-minute walk from the assembly hall. It serves standard Canadian fare. The town of Alma, just down the hill from Headquarters, on Highway 114 east, has two small grocery stores, a bakery, and several small restaurants. There is a gift shop, selling park mementos and regional crafts, across the large lawn from the assembly hall. Alma gift shops specialize in regional wares.

There are no gas stations in the park, but several in Alma and nearby Albert.

Recreational Services

An extensive sports area is located within a few minutes' walk from the assembly hall.

Hiking Fundy has extended its hiking trail system considerably, and it is well worth your while to contact the staff, even before you visit, to find out about the back-country opportunities in particular. The most interesting back-country experience is hiking the fifty-kilometre **Fundy Circuit**. It

Parks Canada

Another way to see the tides of Fundy and the bay beyond

takes about four days, if you do the entire trail, though you can join it from a number of places and do day hikes, or camp in one of the primitive campsites by a lake or along a river. The park has an excellent trail guide for the Circuit and the many other, shorter trails. It gives elevation profiles, distance, average times, and trip highlights. Some of the shorter trails have their own interpretive booklets, which tell you about the natural and human history of the area in which you are walking.

Golf   There is a beautiful nine-hole course, with a pro shop for last-minute golf equipment needs. Fees are modest.

Tennis   There are three paved courts, adjacent to the Cluhouse Restaurant. Equipment can be rented in the golf pro shop.

Swimming   Aside from the beaches, most of which are perhaps better for wading, there is a heated salt-water pool open throughout the summer. It is a ten-minute walk downhill from the assembly hall. Bennett Lake and Wolfe Lake have swimming beaches, and the water is comfortably warm by mid-June.

Boating   Canoeing is possible at Wolfe and Bennett Lakes. Rowboats can be rented at Bennett Lake. No motor-driven boats are allowed in the park, though they are used in the bay waters.

Fishing Fishing is allowed in the park. Salmon and trout are the goal. You buy a National Parks licence at the entry (good for all national parks in Canada). Information on seasons and limits is available there.

Winter Use There is increasing emphasis on cross-country skiing in the park. Thirty kilometres (eighteen miles) of groomed trails loop through the back country, over old horse trails, roads and paths. Some of the more gently rolling interpretive trails can be used, too. Snowshoeing can be done nearly anywhere, but the opportunity to follow the interpretive trails in the winter is very appealing. There is a good brochure outlining winter activities in the park, and giving several phone numbers for up-to-date information on conditions.

Further Reading

Fundy National Park, by Michael Burzynski (Douglas & McIntyre, 1985)
Fundy, Bay of the Giant Tides, by Michael Burzynski and Anne Marceau
    (Fundy Guild, 1984)

FOR MORE INFORMATION
The Superintendent
Fundy National Park
Alma, New Brunswick
EOA IBO

Phone: (506) 887-2000

PRINCE EDWARD ISLAND

NATIONAL PARK

On an early summer Saturday morning at Prince Edward Island National Park, I went to the beach near my campground and walked alone there, seeing no other people for hours. Later in the day and farther up the beach, I wandered through the crowds of people baking themselves in the sun, swimming, or playing on these same warm, pink sands. The contrast was great, but both experiences pointed out the main joy of Prince Edward Island National Park—there is something of the beach environment to suit nearly anyone.

This park is a narrow, broken strip of land, forty kilometres (twenty-five miles) long, that runs along the northern shore of Prince Edward Island. A drive along the Gulf Shore Parkway—or a bicycle ride along its pathway border—can bring the central feature of the park, its dune system, very close. On the north side of the road is the Gulf of St. Lawrence. As far as twenty kilometres (twelve miles) out, the water is no more than fifteen metres (fifty feet) deep, which makes for warm water and gentle waves. Sand bars parallel the coast, playing their part in bringing in sand for the beaches and dunes that build up.

As dunes become established, marram grass gradually takes hold on the sand of the gently sloping southern, or bay, side. This grass sends down roots more than a metre deep, which hold the sand in place against the buffeting of the wind and water. The longer grass grows on a dune, the more fresh water and organic matter can collect there and, eventually, seedlings from other plants, such as the fragrant bayberry or the wild rose, take root. Trees, such as the white spruce, begin to do the same, though they never reach more than a metre or two in height. Nearer the road, in the protected and fertile areas, bushes and trees can grow taller, further contributing to water retention and soil development. Then seeds that have been wind-borne can take root, fringing both edges of the road, in many places.

Farther inland, to the south, are older dunes, which are now totally covered with mature spruce forest, rather than the earlier mixture of small bushes and scrubby trees. But the wind and salt water leave evidence of their power at the first row of tall trees rimming the forest to the north: they are shorter and their branches twist to the south, like a flag blowing steadily in the wind. This is an example of *krummholz*, or "twisted wood." At a certain point in their development, the trees can no longer withstand the constant, searing salt wind, but their skeletons provide a protective wall, enabling succeeding spruce to grow.

How to See the Park

Dunes and Beaches

The dune and beach system in Prince Edward Island National Park is varied in character. Most of the beaches are backed by dunes. The few that are not, are bordered by the steep, red, sandstone cliffs that provide the basic material for the dunes formed elsewhere. It is wonderful to walk along the cliff tops, to overlook the edge of the sea at places like **Orby Head** or **Cape Turner**, both in the western section of the park. The ragged cliffs provide homes for some nesting sea birds, such as the black guillemot, easily recognized by its rapid flight, black body with white wing patches, and bright-red webbed feet trailing behind.

As for the kilometres of dune-backed beaches, you can choose from eight busy, supervised swimming areas, dotting the length of the park. Alternatively, you can walk alone by the sea, nearly anywhere along the considerable distances that separate these swimming beaches. Numerous sheltered bays have quiet beaches like **Cavendish Sandspit Beach**, or you can overlook a bay like **Rustico**, while walking along grassy meadow edges.

Frequently-held beach walks with interpreters will enhance your awareness of the dune-beach environment. I went to one where we all were asked to collect objects from the beach. We brought them back to the interpreter, who identified most of them and explained a bit about the interrelationships among the assorted plants and animals. Some beach walks are held specifically for bird-watching. Several of the evening talks in the campgrounds concentrate on the changing nature of the dune-beach environment. At one of these talks, children and adults obviously enjoyed examining fistful of red-stained dune sand, passed around in a big bowl. We watched a slide-tape show on dune formation, and learned a number of facts—for example, it takes a twenty-kilometre-per-hour (twelve-mile-per-hour) wind to blow grains of sand down the beach.

We also learned how easy it is for dunes to be damaged by random walkers, and how important it is to walk alongside the dunes on the beaches, rather than on the dunes. To get to the beaches, there are established boardwalks through the dunes, which minimize dune destruction.

Woods and Fresh Waters

The beauty of Prince Edward Island National Park isn't confined to sand and sea. South of the beaches, on the landward side of the Gulf Shore Parkway, are long, narrow stretches of forests, broken now and then by

An earth-star fungus and grasses on the inner dunes

meadows and fresh-water ponds. Walks along the **Bubbling Spring Trail** or the **Farmlands Trail** are short, easy ways to see how the forests have overtaken old dune lands or more recent farm fields. Some of the fields are still open and, in mid-summer, thyme scents the air, berries are ripe for picking, and wild roses decorate the path. Bubbling Spring Trail leads you past a marsh overlook, and then dips back into the woods. A beautiful spring flows at the top of the trail, and the pink sand bubbles up like a cool cauldron. On this walk I saw the Black-backed Three-toed Woodpecker, a rarity that compensated for the mosquitoes.

The wind sweeping down from the north is responsible for the dune beach development, and for the subsequent fresh-water-pond creation. All along the south side of the park are small barachois ponds. The word, *barachois*, is uniquely Acadian, and it means *barricade*. Where there is a salt-water inlet in the shoreline, or where a fresh-water stream has formed an inlet, sand may slowly build up until the open end is choked off (except, sometimes, for a narrow outlet going to the sea). No more salt water comes in, the fresh water from rain and the existent streams or springs slowly fills in the land-locked bay, so a rich new environment for fish, plants, insects and birds evolves. A great place to see this phenomenon is on the **Reeds and Rushes Walk** to Dalvay Pond. I went with the interpreter-guided walk, on which we crossed the now-wooded bay-mouth bar and dipped nets at the pond for its inhabitants. We poured them into holding trays and jars the interpreter had supplied, and examined them closely. Everyone loved dabbling around in this miniature world.

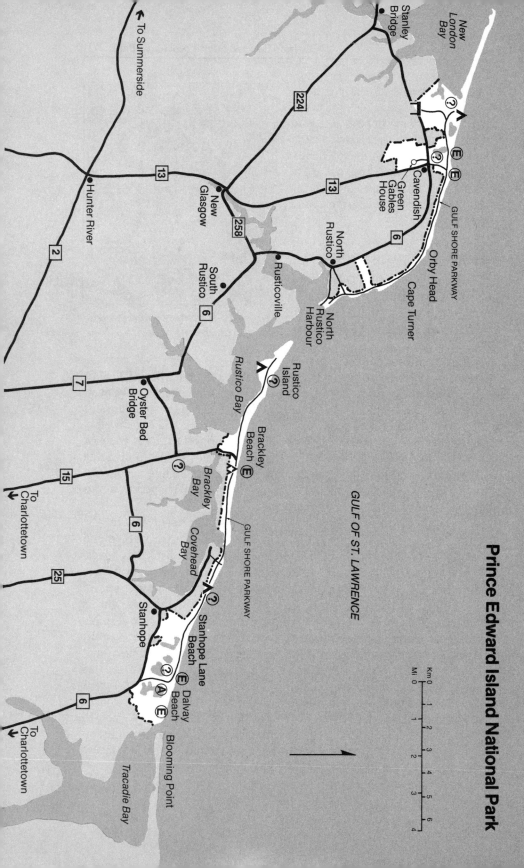

Prince Edward Island National Park

GULF OF ST. LAWRENCE

To Summerside

New London Bay

Stanley Bridge

Cavendish

Green Gables House

GULF SHORE PARKWAY

Orby Head

Cape Turner

North Rustico

North Rustico Harbour

Hunter River

New Glasgow

South Rustico

Rusticoville

Rustico Bay

Rustico Island

Oyster Bed Bridge

Brackley Beach

Brackley Bay

Covehead Bay

GULF SHORE PARKWAY

Stanhope

Stanhope Beach

Stanhope Lane

Dalvay Beach

Blooming Point

Tracadie Bay

To Charlottetown

To Charlottetown

224 · 13 · 2 · 258 · 6 · 7 · 15 · 25

Km 0 1 2 3 4 5 6
Mi 0 1 2 3 4

Human History

Until this part of the Prince Edward Island coast was made into a national park, in 1937, most of the land behind the dunes was used for farming. Bases of old earthen fences can be seen on the **Farmlands Trails**. The remains of small pits are there, too, which some enterprising residents made for stashing illicit rum barrels, during Prohibition days.

But the sight that means the most to a literature buff is **Green Gables House**, near Cavendish, in the western area of the park. Here is the home that provided the setting for Lucy Maud Montgomery's *Anne of Green Gables* stories. Montgomery herself did not live in the house, but it was the home of beloved relatives who always made her welcome there. A tour of the house, and a guided walk with an interpreter through the beautiful birch and maple woods, along a stream that the trail crosses repeatedly, will bring Anne's world very close to the visitor of today. Since the area of the house, **Balsam Hollow Trail** and **Haunted Woods Trail** are on fairly high ground, it has the additional distinction of being the only woodland walk relatively free of mosquitoes in the summer.

Park Services and Facilities

Interpretive Programme

There is an active and innovative summer programme. The schedule is available at entry kiosks, and on bulletin boards throughout the park. Exploring the park is quite easy. There are several self-guiding trails, with easy access to the woods and beaches. The roads through and around the park are wide and gently rolling—great for leisurely drives. Bicycling is a favourite activity in the park and surrounding countryside.

Camping

There are three campgrounds in Prince Edward Island National Park, with over five hundred sites in all. On the western side is Cavendish, a lightly wooded site. It is very heavily used, as it is right across from a supervised beach; interpretive outdoor theatre and picnic grounds are there, also.

Stanhope and **Rustico Island Campsites** are in the eastern section of the park. Stanhope is a bustling, wooded site, across the road from a supervised beach. Rustico Island, which faces Rustico Bay, has wooded and meadow sites. It is the quietest campground, and the last to fill up at busy times.

There are a variety of individual site facilities; Cavendish and Stanhope offer three-way trailer hookups, Rustico Island does not.

The transition from dunes to grass, to forest

The main season is mid-May to mid-October, though there is a winter camping area at the **Stanhope Lane** picnic area. It has a pit privy, water pump and tree cover.

No reservations are taken: all camping is on a first-come, first-served basis, with a maximum two-week stay.

Other Camping

There are an estimated 1,500 campsites in the area bordering the park, all along its length, so you should be able to find accommodation within a few minutes' drive of the park, even at the busiest season.

Other Accommodation, Gas, Food and Supplies

There are numerous hotels and motels near the park, and even a couple of concessions within the park. For further information write to Prince Edward Island Department of Tourism and Parks, Visitor Services, P.O. Box 940, Charlottetown, P.E.I., C1A 7M5, Canada. Dial "Information" in Area Code 902 for toll-free numbers from your home area.

There are fast-food stands at the Brackley, Stanhope and Cavendish supervised beach centres. A souvenir gift shop is open at the Green Gables House area.

There are stores near the park, and a full range of food, gasoline, camping supplies, etc., is available in the villages surrounding the park. There are small stores and gasoline stations scattered along the many access roads to the park.

Recreational Services

Swimming There are seven supervised beaches in the park. Guard season is mid-June to Labour Day.

Bicycling Bicycling is especially good in the park, because one-metre-wide strips are reserved for cyclists on either side of the Gulf Shore Parkway, running the length of the park. The land outside the park is rolling farm country with narrower roads, but it is heavily used for bicycling.

Boating Rowing and canoeing are allowed in the fresh-water lakes and ponds. Power boats are not permitted. You can charter ocean-going sightseeing or fishing trips at Tracadie Harbour, North Rustico Harbour and Covehead Harbour.

Tennis Three double courts are available in the park, at Dalvay, Brackley and Cavendish.

Golf Green Gables golf course, in the Cavendish area, is an extremely beautiful and popular eighteen-hole course. Daily fees vary somewhat by time of day and season.

Lawnbowling There is a green at Dalvay, on the east side of the park. No fee is charged.

FOR MORE INFORMATION

District Superintendent
Environment Canada
Parks Service
Prince Edward Island National Park
Box 487
Charlottetown, Prince Edward Island
C1A 7L1 Canada

Phone: (902) 672-2211/566-7050

KEJIMKUJIK

NATIONAL PARK

Fresh water, forests and people have always been the key elements of Kejimkujik National Park. Recently, the scope of the park has been extended to include a Seaside Adjunct—a twenty-two-square-kilometre segment of rugged coast on the south shore of Nova Scotia, near the community of Liverpool. Access to the Adjunct is limited but, over time, it may play a larger role in the visitor's experience of the park.

The typical fresh-water pattern of this part of Nova Scotia is one of many irregularly-shaped lakes, dotted with islands. There is little variation in elevation, so the many streams and rivers twist and turn over the thin, easily eroded soil, as they slowly make their way to the sea. Rivers and lakes make up about twenty percent of the park's 381 square kilometres (147 square miles), and the biggest lake of all is the park's namesake, Kejimkujik. This island-studded lake, and the meandering Mersey River, dominate the visitor's experience of the park.

Rainfall in Kedge* is high: it averages 150 centimetres (59 inches) a year, giving the park a very warm, moist summer. The rain is essential to maintain the levels of lakes and streams, for few are spring-fed. The richness of the plant life in bogs and meadows, and in coniferous and hardwood forests, depends on the high level of rainfall, because the shallow, nutrient-poor soil of the area could never support such abundance with a lesser supply of water. However, as the interpreters point out, acid rain may soon become a source of great harm to the plant and animal life.

The slow-moving streams, which flood regularly in the spring, and the numerous shallow lakes, are often edged with bog areas. These provide special habitats for animal and plant life. So, too, does the one true marsh in the park, at Grafton Lake.

The forest of Kejimkujik is the Atlantic uplands variety of the Acadian type. In the lowest and least well-drained parts of the park, the trees are typically black spruce, tamarack (larch) and perhaps some balsam

*The usual abbreviation of Kejimkujik is Kedge, pronounced ked-gee.

297

fir. In somewhat dryer and higher areas, there are the red spruce, balsam fir and occasional white pine of the softwood forest. Where the soil is deeper and better drained, hardwoods, such as maple, birch and oak, thrive. While there a few strands that are purely of one sort or the other, it is most striking to see those groves that are predominantly beech or fine eastern hemlock. Trails lead to these areas.

The woods and rivers provide excellent homes for deer, rodents (including beaver, muskrats and voles) and many amphibians. The forests are the home of a great variety of birds, particularly woodland warblers. The northern parula and black-throated green are very common. Birdwatchers stand a chance of seeing the black-backed woodpecker and the huge pileated woodpecker. The barred owl, too, is a resident. The forests are also the northern range for southern summer visitors, such as scarlet tanagers and great-crested flycatchers.

In the mixed-wood areas, which cover three-quarters of the park, an abundant variety of plants can be found. The spring flowers are splendid. There are special sights, like the orchids; calopogon, spotted coral-root and rattlesnake plantain. The galingale plant is here, too, very far north of its usual range. The cancer root flourishes in a few special places; you may find it on the Grafton Lake trail in early July.

People have played an important role, for thousands of years, in the area that is now Kejimkujik Park. Micmac Indians lived here, at one with the life-giving waters and forests. They fished and hunted, using the waterways as canoe highways, portaging where necessary, camping where they wished.

The Micmacs almost disappeared during the nineteenth century, when Europeans pushed into the area. The newcomers came mainly in search of timber for buildings and for boats. The whole area has been heavily logged in the last two hundred years or so and, with a few exceptions, all of the woodland has been seriously disturbed by protracted logging and burning. A few old, but small, stands of hemlocks and hardwoods have survived unscathed. In the late 1800s, a minor gold rush occurred, and remains of shafts and waste material can be seen here and there.

By the turn of this century, Kedge was a sport-hunting and fishing centre, but this use, too, slowly dwindled.

Today, people seek not to exploit Kedge, but to preserve it. Thousands of visitors a year can now enjoy a part of our country that is allowed, as much as is possible, to live by its own natural laws once more.

How to See the Park

There are, roughly, two ways to see the park: first, through the independent wilderness experience, by hiking or canoeing in the undeveloped areas of the park (ninety percent of it); and second, by camping in the developed sites, and being guided by interpreters in an appreciation of the park.

Independent Wilderness Experience

There are 140 kilometres (84 miles) of hiking trails. Most of that distance is taken up in trails that circle the perimeter of the park, with spurs leading from them into the interior. There are primitive campsites along the way, with tent pads, fireplaces and toilets.

Cancer root along a woodland trail

For the experienced canoeist, there are many kilometres of wilderness routes, including twenty-three portages, ranging from a few metres to over two kilometres (1.2 miles) in length. As many of the lakes are large and shallow, especially Kedge, they can get very rough, when it is at all windy; experience and caution are expected of the canoeist. Primitive campsites are provided for canoeists, too.

Waterproof, tear-resistant, marked, aerial maps and government topographic maps are available, for the back-country explorer. The park's map lists routes, portages, distances, etc., but not in much detail. Check with staff for any recent brochures describing canoe routes.

There are several embarkation points, with parking lots, for both the wilderness hiking trails and canoeing routes. Some primitive campsites, such as those at Big Dam trailhead, are within a few hundred metres walk from parking, and it is possible for a visitor to them to experience something of the wilderness life, without having to do a lengthy hike or canoe trip.

Guided Appreciation of the Park

Most visitors rely, for their experience of the park, on the varied programmes offered by the interpreters. The developed campsites and the interpretive programmes are very much family affairs. Special attention is paid to children's interests, and there are specific displays for them, although adults are not ignored.

Begin your exploration of Kejimkujik at the Visitor Reception Centre. There is a very attractive, sixty-seat theatre in the Centre. There

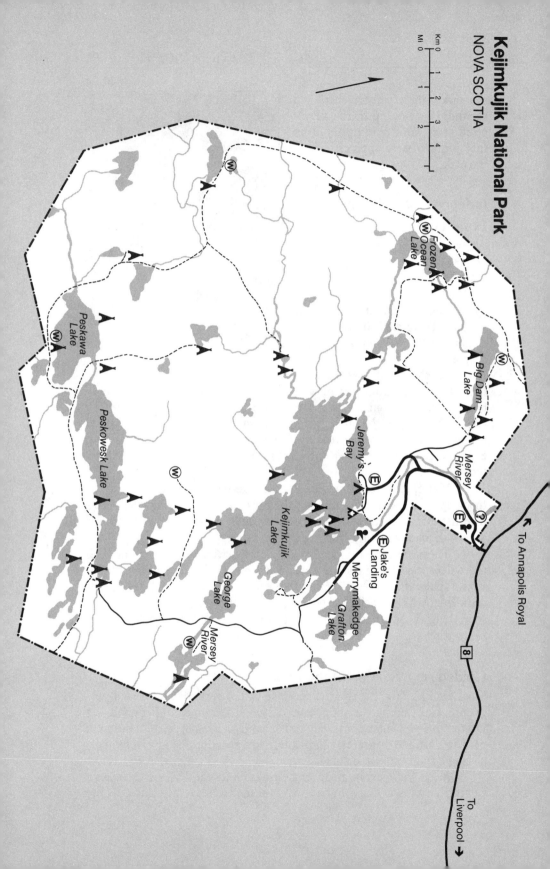

are several excellent, multi-projector slide shows. One introduces the park to the new visitor. Another is about canoeing on Kejimkujik Lake, and a third tells about those rare plants and animals in the park, which are usually found much farther south, but are protected here, in this northern outpost.

Once you've left the Visitor Centre, there are five ways of participating in the interpretive programme: interpreter-guided walks; interpreted walks or "paddles" near the shores of the lakes or streams (canoes may be rented); illustrated talks in the evening; interpretive displays at the Visitor's Centre; and numerous free pamphlets. The interpretive walks and paddles link the key elements of Kejimkujik. For the waters of the park, any interpretive event that goes along the Mersey River or to any lake is relevant. I went on a guided walk along the Mersey, and learned about its sources: why it curves as it does; how it floods; what the characteristic shoreline trees and grasses are; which animals make their homes right in the river; how islands are formed and changed over time. At one point, the interpreter literally plunged right into his topic, as he rooted around in the water to find rocks that harboured aquatic insects.

There are also four self-guiding trails, and they are well worth your time. One is the very short (.3 kilometre) **Mersey Meadow Trail**, which leads you along the edge of the Mersey River. The trail is a combination of boardwalk, paved trail and high-quality gravel. It is wheelchair accessible. There are large, colourful signs here, especially appealing for children. One of its features is a spotting scope, situated to give a good view over Mersey Meadow.

The **Mill Falls Trail** is also very short, and attractively signed. It, too, follows the Mersey River, and is accessible from three places along the road to Jeremys Bay. A distinctive feature of this walk is the fern life along the trail. The park has prepared a booklet that identifies the kinds of ferns you will find at twelve points along the way. If you haven't given ferns much thought up to now, you may be surprised at how interesting they can be, with easy guides like this.

Beech Grove Trail is just across the river from the Visitor's Centre. It is two kilometres long, with eight interpreted points along the way. The park has gone high-tech here, and provides visitors with a small, portable, cassette player (complete with earphones), which is keyed to the eight stops. The narration tells about the birds, plants and animal signs to be seen, and plays some local bird songs, as well. The tapes come in English, French and German. Guidebooks to the birds and flowers are available for this walk, too. Because of the richness of this environment and the fun of using the cassettes, you can easily spend an hour and a half on the trail.

A trail that shows some of the human history of the area is the **Gold Mines Trail**, located along the Peskowesk Road. The trail is three

When the river floods, it clears the shoreline of trees and large bushes

kilometres long. It has a series of interpretive signs, which tell about the gold-mining efforts that went on in the park area from the 1880s until 1939. Old trenches and shallow pits show the traces of the mining activity, and the signs tell about the local rock types, where gold occurred, and how the prospectors went about finding it.

After taking guided tours of the river, why not walk on your own to a similar habitat, such as **Rogers Brook Trail**. It's quite a revelation; now you *understand* what makes up the habitat around you!

The **Grafton Lake Walk** crosses the only true marsh in the park. The marsh was artificially created, with the damming of the lake fifty years ago. Cancer root is plentiful by early July, as are northern parula warblers. I saw beautiful, white-flowered waterlilies, and the crisp water shield was floating on the water. On partially submerged stumps, tiny islands form, providing perfect habitat for plants like the sundew, which is found more often in bogs.

For an appreciation of the special areas of the forest, the **Hemlocks and Hardwoods Hike**, beyond the Big Dam parking lot, is ideal. This is a longer walk than some in the park, but it is quite easy and within the scope of people of all ages. The park usually has a guided event along this trail, which takes a leisurely three hours, with all the stops to explore the rich environment in more detail.

For a better understanding of human involvement in the Kejimkujik area, the **Micmac Memories Walk**, or a guided tour of the small farmlands area, will show you some of what remains of the Indian and early settler experience. If you want to be alone, try paddling from Jake's Landing, just a little way up the Mersey, in the quiet of the evening. You'll be travelling, for a little while, just as people have done here for thousands of years.

The Seaside Adjunct

This coastal section of the park is about twenty-five kilometres southwest of Liverpool, off Highway 103. It takes in the tip of the Port Mouton peninsula, but has no official name of its own yet. There are two spectacular white sand beaches, tidal flats, salt lagoons, and salt marsh areas. The inland terrain is rugged, with a mixture of forest types. Bogs and ponds are common in some areas. It is a particularly good area for bird-watching, especially for fall migrations of shorebirds.

Access is limited, in that motorized vehicles and motorboats are not allowed in the area. There are two access points for walking into the area. One is a gravel road, five kilometres long, from Southwest Port Mouton to the shore on Black Point. The other is an old cart track from the community of St. Catherines River, which has been upgraded with boardwalks in the wet sections. This track is two kilometres long. There are no visitor facilities here, so pack in, and haul out your picnic, hot drinks and rain gear, and be ready for some wonderful views of the coast and the plant and animal life of the ocean, shore and forest. Fall and winter are particularly good for sea ducks, loons and grebes, and harbour seals are here year round, with their largest numbers occurring through fall.

Park Services and Facilities

Interpretive Programme
The park has a number of information newsletters, guides to trails, an excellent bird-watching pamphlet and checklist, a schedule and description of the guided walks and talks, and brochures about the main park and winter activities. There are bulletin boards at the campsites, Visitor Reception Centre, snack bar, etc., with the most up-to-date information on evening programmes and other activities offered. It is wheelchair-accessible.

Camping
There are 329 developed campsites at Jeremy's Bay, which is open year-round. It is subdivided into three sections. Each section has washrooms with flush toilets and hot- and cold-water sinks, faucets for water between every few campsites, well-equipped playgrounds for children, and an unsupervised beach. Trails lead from section to section and these, in turn, link up with some of the shorter hiking trails. Clean, tiled showers are available in one building, serving all campsites. It is a short walk or drive from the campsites themselves. You can purchase firewood there, which may only be used in the grates provided. This rule applies to both wilderness and developed campsites. There are no electrical hook-ups. A trailer-waste disposal depot is situated across the road from the showers. Several sites, and the washrooms, are handicapped-accessible.

Primitive Camping
There are forty-two wilderness campsites that you can reach by hiking or canoeing. There is a minimal fee in the summer, and you must register at the Visitor Reception Centre.

Winter Camping
A winter campground is located in one loop of Jeremys Bay campground.

Parks Canada/K. Pesplarque

Observation Tower

Facilities include hot and cold running water and toilets, fireplaces and free firewood. You can trailer- or tent-camp here.

Group Camping
Write to the Superintendent for information about reservations.

Other Accommodation, Gas, Food and Supplies
Very near the park, from Maitland Bridge to Caledonia, are three canteens and a restaurant, plus five food stores and several camping-supply outlets. There is an inn only three kilometres from the park, which is open year-round. Several local families offer bed and breakfast, and there are four

craft outlets near the park, as well. Write to the Superintendent for a list, and/or contact the Nova Scotia Department of Tourism (Area code 902). Within an hour's drive are the towns of Lunenburg, Bridgewater, Liverpool, Annapolis Royal and Bear River. They have motels, lodging houses, supplies, etc.

Within the park, there is a snack bar, which carries a few basic groceries, at Merrymakedge Beach. Gasoline is not available in the park, but there are several stations within ten or fifteen minutes' drive, along Highway 8.

Recreational Services

Swimming   There are a number of clean beaches, with unsupervised swimming, at each campground. There is a supervised beach at Merrymakedge, which visitors are encouraged to use. This beach area, and the trail beside it, are wheelchair-accessible.

Boating   Power boats are allowed on Kejimkujik Lake, with a 15 km/h speed limit. Canoes and rowboats may be rented at Jake's Landing, or you can bring your own. The Jake's Landing area is handicapped (and wheelchair) accessible. The park encourages canoe use by handicapped people, because it is an excellent way for visitors, who otherwise would not be able to do so, to get right out on the waters of the park and see the wildlife in the most natural setting. This part of the lake is sheltered, and all the equipment is available right there.

Fishing   There is good trout fishing in spring, with the season ending August 31, to conserve fish stocks. The park encourages catch-and-release. Otherwise, perch is the most usual catch. A National Park licence is required. You can buy it at the Visitor Reception Centre, where you can pick up the summary of anglers' regulations for the Atlantic Canada National Parks.

Winter Use   The amount of snow for cross-country skiing varies a great deal, from year to year. In good years, there is excellent cross-country skiing and snowshoeing along the wider trails. The park grooms four cross-country ski trails, about eighteen kilometres in total, and there are a number of non-groomed trails that are excellent, as well. There are wood-heated shelters at Merrymakedge Beach, Jim Charles Point and Mill Falls.

FOR MORE INFORMATION
The Superintendent
Kejimkujik National Park
Box 36
Maitland Bridge
Annapolis County, Nova Scotia
B0T 1N0

Phone: (902) 682-2772

CAPE BRETON HIGHLANDS

NATIONAL PARK

Northern Cape Breton is often associated in people's minds with the Cabot Trail, which wends its way in a loop, encompassing much of this scenic area. However, it is less common for people to realize that almost half of the Trail, 106 kilometres of its northern arc, is an integral part of Cape Breton Highlands National Park. This park offers wonderful opportunities to view rugged coastal vistas, ramble through forests and barrens, walk along magnificent beaches, and visit the charming small communities that are interspersed along the Trail, on private land adjacent to the park. Day trips are popular, but there is so much to explore in this park that you'll want to take much more time.

The park has six well-equipped campgrounds: some quiet, some crowded; some protected by woods, others exposed on windy ocean beaches. Short, self-guiding walks are accessible directly from the Cabot Trail. Longer walks lead up plunging river valleys, over the windswept highlands, and along wave-battered shorelines. Spring comes very late here: nesting birds are everywhere in the woods and even on the barrens, and the July visitor can see flowers that have long faded farther south in Canada.

The diversity and grandeur of the Cape Breton Highlands is due to its distinctive geological history and its geographical location, the north-ernmost point of Cape Breton Island, jutting out into two cold seas—the Gulf of St. Lawrence on the western shore and the Atlantic Ocean on the east. The Highlands are the most spectacular part of the Maritime Acadian Highlands, one of the forty-eight Natural Regions in Canada. The Highlands are a huge plain that, long ago, was lifted to 532 metres at its highest point, though the average elevation at the margins of this plain is 350 metres. It is tilted higher on the western side. The stress of this upward movement created long cracks in the earth's crust, which became straight steep-sided valleys, carrying rivers to the sea. The river mouths form inlets or coves between the massive headlands that project into the ocean.

Soil on the high central plateau is very thin, and supports tundra and heath plants and animals. On the lower eastern side of the park, and all along the valley sides and floors, forests can grow—boreal forests in the higher, more exposed areas, mixed hardwood and softwood forests in the more protected areas. The growing season is short at this northern latitude, but the ocean moderates the climate and provides a great deal of moisture. As a result, plant life is luxurious, if not greatly varied.

The coastline itself is very imposing, with many of the huge wooded headlands dropping precipitously to the sea. Other headlands reach far out into the water, and have been eroded nearly to sea level, and scoured clean in some places, by the power of the sea.

How to See the Park

Bogs and Barrens

To the early settlers of the Cape Breton Highlands, who were interested in the land for farming or grazing, the plateau may have seemed barren. But, if you like kilometres of misty vistas, Labrador tea plants waist high as you walk among them, pink granite outcroppings covered with pearly grey reindeer lichen or soft, green lichen, then the barrens are a rich source of life and beauty.

I drove the short, rocky road to **Paquette Lake**, and then began walking along the wide **John Dee Lake Trail** into the barrens. About ten minutes' walk along, I took a narrow trail off to another small lake. Reindeer lichen, heath plants and tamarack trees clung to the thin soil and occasional granite outcroppings. After reaching a slight crest in the trail, I began to descend to a wet, boggy area. Here, fewer bushes grew, but their place was taken up by vast beds of sphagnum moss, some of it extraordinarily pink. There were tiny lakes here and there; at one, a greater yellowlegs began diving repeatedly in the mist over me, calling loudly and whisking past my head, in a desperate attempt to distract me from its nest. I kept walking, since there was no way to tell where the nest was, so no way to be sure of avoiding it, but I stepped carefully, hurrying to pass by.

As I continued the gradual descent, there was a narrow, deep stream, and after fording it on some old logs someone else had left as a makeshift bridge, I came out onto a very wet open meadow. Surely one of the special areas in the park, it was sewn with dozens of orchids! White-fringed orchids and the brilliant pink arethusa were everywhere I looked. After revelling in their beauty a while, stepping carefully to photograph them, I headed back, for the mist was thickening to cloud, and the trail becoming harder to find. (In fact, it is a very good idea to stick to well-marked trails. It is astonishingly easy to become confused about directions in this kind of terrain.)

There are several trails that can take you onto the barrens, and one self-guided boardwalk, the **Bog Trail**, which is right by the Cabot Trail at **French Mountain**. This short trail is an enchanting miniature of the barrens further inland, which are more enticing, perhaps, to hardy and experienced hikers.

Bunchberry carpets the forest floor in spring

Parks Canada

The Forests, Rivers and Mountains

From the Cabot Trail in July, it seems as if everything in the park that isn't ocean is lush forest. It's hard to tell that there's more than one type of tree growing there; variations in the shades of green, or the occasional white gleam of a birch trunk, are the only clues. Of course, in autumn the contrast is clear between the brightly-coloured deciduous trees, such as the maples, and the green of the conifers.

Any of the walks or drives up the valley sides and onto the plateau will reveal the progression from deciduous forests, near the valley floors, to the evergreen forests, higher up. The **Acadian Trail**, from behind Chéticamp Campground, is an excellent way to cross through this whole sequence and return, in three to four hours. There are spectacular views of the interior of the park, of the Chéticamp River Valley and Chéticamp village, and also of the flatlands and barachois ponds that border the ocean, before it stretches out off to the horizon. Barachois ponds are formed when sand dunes or reefs build up at the mouths of freshwater streams. The dunes dam the fresh water in ponds, which are a little brackish and very rich in plant and animal life.

Franey Trail, near Ingonish, has sweeping views of the ocean and shoreline, and this is one of its main attractions. However, it is also a good opportunity for another magnificent experience of the forest, rivers and highlands of the eastern part of the park.

For a gentle walk that leads to a woodland lake, try **Jigging Cove Trail**, just off the Cabot Trail, a short drive from the Black Brook day use area. You can walk around the lake in less than an hour, enjoying the

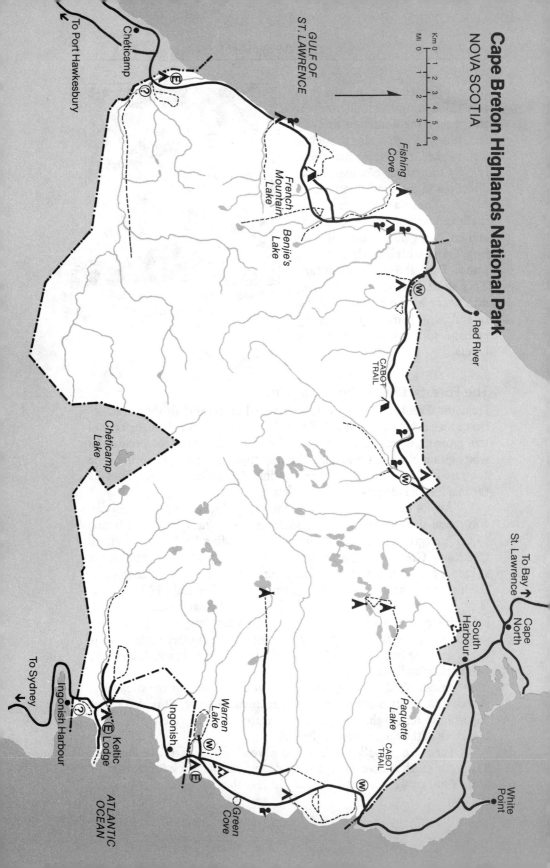

mixed forest, the dark lake, and its beautiful vegetation. Birdwatching here is really rewarding. I stood in one place for about five minutes, making squeaking noises to attract the birds' attention. There were seven species of warbler and four other bird species surrounding me in seconds!

At **Benjie's Lake**, a short trail in a higher, more boreal woodland will bring you to carpets of spring flowers. The highlight of the walk turned out to be a mother moose and two calves, which startled me as I came around the bend in the narrow, tree-lined trail. We watched each other for several minutes, as I photographed them in the evening mist. Then they turned and were gone, so quickly and quietly that only the trace of their tracks furnished proof they had been there.

For woodland rivers and streams, try the **Corney Brook or MacIntosh Brook** trails. Both end at waterfalls. The valleys of both brooks are rich and well drained, and support mature deciduous forests, with maples and other hardwoods. Spring flowers are a treat, and these are the areas to visit to see the changing colours of autumn.

Another favourite visitor site, nestled in a mature deciduous forest, is **Lone Shieling**, a few minutes' drive east of the MacIntosh Brook trail-head and campground. The loop trail from the parking lot is only .8 kilometres long, and is level, except for two places, which have staircases. The shieling is a reproduction of Scottish sheep crofters' huts. This lone shieling was erected in 1942, to commemorate the Scots heritage of so many Cape Bretoners. But, for the nature buff, the setting of the shieling is striking, indeed, for the deciduous forest here has never been cut, and some of the trees (sugar maple, yellow birch and beech) are over three hundred years old.

The Shoreline

Cape Breton Highlands National Park has a number of places where the visitor can walk, at one with the sea and the shore. The northwestern **Chéticamp** area has more precipitous shore edges, with the giant, high headlands plunging to the sea, so walking is often along ridges and crests overlooking the ocean. The **Skyline Trail**, which begins at the **French Mountain** parking lot, is not along the shore itself, but runs along the top of a three-hundred-metre coastal headland. The trail offers one of the best "overviews" of the rugged western coast of Cape Breton. At sea level, near the Chéticamp area, there are two very good places to experience the shoreline environment up close. One is **La Bloque** beach and picnic area, which has interpretive signs telling about the life of the small Acadian fishing community that existed there at the turn of the century. The other is **Le Buttereau Trail**, near the Grande Falaise picnic area. This is a short (1.9 kilometres/1.2 miles) trail, part of it near the shore and the other section going slightly inland, where the Acadian settlers had their fields and pastures. Interpretive signs give some of this history. There are views of the Chéticamp River, the Gulf of St. Lawrence, Chéticamp Island, and pillar rocks offshore.

On the Ingonish side of the park, the elevations are lower and the land slopes more gently to the sea. Here, you can walk at your leisure in areas like **Green Cove**, where trails right by the ocean take you through mushroom-studded forests, over low headlands that seem more like Scottish moors, and onto spurs of pink rock, washed by ocean waves. Another gentle but spectacular walk is that at **Middle Head**, which starts at the Keltic Lodge. The trail goes all the way to the tip of this peninsula. There are great views of the coast here, and the bird life is rich. **Coastal Trail** is another good opportunity for a shoreline and forest experience.

Park Services and Facilities

Interpretive Programme

The park has a rich, and quite complex, interpretive programme, because overnight visitors are concentrated at the opposite sides of the park, and there are an enormous number of people who visit for a few hours only, as they drive along the Cabot Trail. Also, the strong Acadian and Scottish traditions of the area call for programmes that interpret the park in both French and English. (Interpreter-led programmes are given in the language in which they are advertised, and signs and brochures are in both languages.)

The core of the summer interpreter-led programmes is the nightly slide shows, given in the Chéticamp and Broad Cove outdoor amphitheatres. Interpreters are also stationed, at various times, at the major lookouts and exhibit sites along the Cabot Trail, to talk with visitors about the highlights of the site.

There is also increasing involvement of local people in interpretive and recreational programming. The Park Cooperating Association (Les Amis du Plein Air—friends of the outdoors) sponsors Scottish Acadian Concerts, which feature Cape Breton music and dance. They also put on nightly lobster and crab "boils," in July and August, at Broad Cove campground. (Prices vary, according to supply.) Just check at the Visitor Centres at Chéticamp and Ingonish, to get the latest information.

There are eight roadside exhibits along the Cabot Trail, and six selfguiding trails. These trails tend to be short and easily accessible. Interpretation is through trailside signs. **MacKenzie Mountain** lookout is wheelchair-accessible, as is **Lakie's Head** lookout, and the Bog self-guiding trail. More wheelchair-accessible sites are being added regularly—check with park staff for an update.

Parks Canada

Middlehead Peninsula

The greatest single source of information on all aspects of a visit to the park is the Chéticamp Visitor Centre. It is wheelchair-accessible. The Centre focuses on what can be seen along the Cabot Trail, including its natural and human history. Staff are there to help you learn about the park and decide how best to spend your time and energy, for whatever length of stay you plan. Among the many exhibits, there is a photo album showing colour pictures of each hiking trail, which is a big help in planning your time. There is also a hiking trail brochure that is keyed to numbered items on the main park map. There is a large topographic relief map of the park here, and cyclists find it particularly useful. There is a Family Corner, which has games and displays that invite children to become directly involved with their environment. There is also an excellent nature bookstore (including postcards, posters,etc.) in the Centre, run by Les Amis du Plein Air. It specializes in Nova Scotia and Cape Breton Island publications. Les Amis publish a series of booklets on the park, and they also sell a cassette tape to take with you in the car, as you navigate the Cabot Trail. It is keyed to major sites along the way. If you do not want to buy it, you can rent it at one of the Centres, and return it to the other one at the end of your drive.

The Ingonish Information Centre is the place to start your visit at the eastern entry to the park. It is not as large as the Chéticamp Visitor Centre, but there are staff to answer your questions, a smaller nature bookstore, a copy of the hiking trail photo album, and information on non-park visitor facilities in nearby locations.

Parks Canada/F. Williams

Dense forests clothe the headlands on the Franey Trail

Camping

Because the two sides of the park are quite distinct in natural setting, it is a good plan to camp first on one side, and then move for a time to the other.

The campsites of this park are among the most luxurious in the national system. Of the six developed campsites, **Broadcove** (256 sites) and **Chéticamp** (162 sites) have many sites with three-way trailer hook-ups, showers in the washrooms, separate dishwashing areas, and kitchen shelters with woodstoves. Broadcove has a wheelchair-accessible campsite and washroom.

Chéticamp is the least crowded, the most wooded and the quietest of the campgrounds.

There are four campsites without any trailer hook-ups, but they do have water, washrooms, fireplaces, and kitchen shelters with woodstoves. Ingonish has ninety unserviced sites. It is the first campground to fill up, especially as the weekends approach, so come mid-week and/or early in the day. The others are **MacIntosh Brook** (ten sites), which is in cleared woodlands; **Corney Brook** (twenty sites), which is near the beach on the west side; **Big Intervale** (ten sites), which is cleared woodland and about halfway along the Cabot Trail. These three campsites are prized as rest-stops by cyclists.

Primitive Camping

There are two wilderness campsites, with fireplaces and pit privies. Most are in the interior of the park, and have been set up particularly for people fishing. **Fishing Cove Campground** is along the coast, and **Lake of Islands** is on the plateau, quite far into the interior of the park. Both require a permit. Check with staff at the information centres for permits and information on trail conditions.

Group Camping

There is a group campground at **Marrach**, and by **Robert Brook** at the Chéticamp Campground. Write to the Superintendent for information about your group's camping there.

Both of these campgrounds are near hiking trails and near water, whether it be ocean, rivers or lakes.

Other Camping

Private campgrounds are situated south of the park, along the roads that lead into either side of the park.

Other Accommodation, Gas, Food and Supplies

Keltic Lodge is a provincially-run resort located in the park, in Ingonish. There are motels in the small towns bordering the park, at either edge and in the small villages scattered along the Cabot Trail.

The park itself does not provide gasoline, food or supplies, but you will find them at the towns at Chéticamp and Ingonish, and in several of the villages along the Cabot Trail. You are never more than half an hour away by car from a small, but sufficient, supply of gas, food, camping material, souvenirs, local crafts, film, etc.

There is a restaurant at Keltic Lodge in Ingonish. In the towns, you'll find snack stands, small cafes and full-fledged restaurants in most communities along the Cabot Trail.

Recreational Services

Swimming   Ocean swimming is supervised at beaches at Ingonish Beach and Freshwater Lake. Unsupervised ocean beaches are at North Bay, Broad Cove, Black Brook, and just north of Chéticamp Campground at La Bloque Beach. You can swim in fresh water, north of Ingonish at Warren Lake. There is also ocean swimming outside the park, on the Chéticamp side.

Fishing   Two main species of fish are caught in the park; Atlantic salmon in the Chéticamp River, and Eastern Brook trout in the lakes and rivers that go to the sea. Also, most streams have a good run of sea trout. Ask staff at the entrance, or any warden, for a National Park fishing permit and information on seasons and limits.

Golf   Ingonish offers an eighteen-hole highlands course, run by the Canadian Parks Service. There are daily, weekly, seasonal and twilight fees, and special junior rates. A clubhouse provides refreshments, equipment rental and sales, and a golf pro gives lessons.

Tennis   There are three free hard-surface courts at Ingonish Beach day-use area. Players rotate every forty-five minutes, on the honour system.

Winter Use   Like most of the National Parks, Cape Breton Highlands is rapidly expanding its winter access. There is a Winter Activities bulletin available from the park, which lists a wide variety of activities—snow-shoeing, winter camping, tobogganing, skating and cross-country skiing. Cross-country skis can be rented from the Chéticamp Visitor Centre, from January to March, and there are a number of groomed and ungroomed trails in the park. The bulletin lists their length and degree of difficulty. There are also good cross-country opportunities outside the park, especially in the Cape North area (which was the site of the 1987 Canada Games cross-country events).

Bird-Watching There is a wide variety of habitats and bird life within the park, but visitors who wish to see the offshore birds, such as puffins and razorbills, should follow signs outside the park, for boat charters to the Bird Islands near Bras d'Or, about an hour south of the Ingonish entrance. Park staff carry a supply of the relevant leaflets, if you have missed the signs. These trips are an extension of the park experience, even if they aren't actually within its boundaries.

Whale-Watching There are several whale-watching tours offered in the park vicinity, leaving from Chéticamp, Pleasant Bay and Bay St. Lawrence. There are good chances of seeing whales and, in any case, the chance to see the park area from offshore is well worthwhile. Contact the Nova Scotia Department of Tourism, inquire at the park information centres when you arrive, or check at the various shops or other tourist facilities along the Trail for the brochures they are sure to carry.

FOR MORE INFORMATION
The Superintendent
Cape Breton Highlands National Park
Ingonish Beach
Cape Breton, Nova Scotia
B0C 1L0

Phone: (902) 285-2270, or
      (902) 285-2691 (Ingonish)
      (902) 224-3403 (Chéticamp)

The Nova Scotia Department of Tourism can provide information about all of Cape Breton. The department has several toll-free numbers: from within Canada, phone (800) 565-7166; from Maine, phone (800) 492-0643, and from elsewhere in the United States, phone (800) 341-6096.

GROS MORNE

NATIONAL PARK

Rugged, glowering mountains and long, pearly beaches are quite unexpected in this part of Canada, but Gros Morne National Park* has these and more; steep-sided fiords, trout and salmon streams, bog-engulfed lakes. Nestled in the grandeur of this setting are several small fishing and farming enclaves. Walking along lobster-trap-laden wharves or dodging the occasional sheep on the roads, you get a sense of how, for the past five thousand years, people have made their living on this land at the edge of the sea; fishing the sea and the fiords, and gardening or hunting in the forested slopes.

The geological history of this particular combination of fresh and salt-water fiords, coastal plain and mountains, makes Gros Morne an essential link in the preservation plan of the Canadian parks system. Since some of the rock formations exist in only a few other places in the world, Gros Morne is now a World Heritage Site—a location considered to be of exceptional interest and value, not just within this country, but throughout the world. In places, rock from the depths of the earth's mantle is exposed right beside rock that originated in the earth's crust. There are other sites where you can clearly see the filigreed graptolites from the Ordovician period.

The park's variety of terrain and rock composition came about largely through two related processes. One was glaciation, where the tremendous weight of the debris-filled ice rivers cut out fiords. The other force was "re-bound," when much of the area lifted out of the water (as it is probably still doing). Land that was already exposed rose after the glaciers melted, when their great weight was no longer pressing down. The sea was then able to shape this raised shoreline: the rivers cut down through the uplands, into the gorges left by the retreating glaciers, and frost cracked and splintered the rock on the bare surfaces of the uppermost

*Gros is pronounced locally as "gross."

mountain areas. The last glacial retreat began about fifteen thousand years ago, but the Gros Morne lowlands were not ice-free for another five thousand years or so.

How to See the Park

To see as much of this park as possible in a visit of a few days, it's helpful to envision it as three levels, stairstepping upward to the east. First, there is the sea and its meeting with the land; second, the long, low coastal plain, with its forest, fiords and bogs; and third, the rugged uplands of Gros Morne itself and other mountains, in the northern part of the park, and the Tablelands in the southern part. At each level there are places especially accessible to visitors, so that they may best enjoy and understand each area.

The Coastline

Within fifteen minutes of entering the park from its southeast gate (the one nearest the Trans-Canada Highway), the role of glaciation, in forming parts of the coastline, becomes very evident. For about sixteen kilometres (ten miles) the road skims past a deep fiord, **Bonne Bay**. The fiord opens to the sea in the west, and its arms dip south into steep highlands. It was gouged out of bedrock by glacial tongues and, when the icy flow retreated, the sea came to fill in the steep-sided trough left behind.

The views are spectacular. If you can take one of the boat tours run by an operator out of **Rocky Harbour**, at the mouth of the bay, you will get an even better impression of its expanse. For a shorter ride across the bay, to the charming village of Woody Point and to the Tablelands and Lomond Campground, sometimes there is a small car ferry from **Norris Point**. It's a brief ride, but excellent for seeing the blue bay and its enveloping mountains, with a village or two tucked into its more sheltered areas. Ask at the Park Information Centre about whether it is in service when you visit.

A quarter of an hour's ride from the Woody Point landing is the **Green Gardens Trail**. It has two trailheads, along Highway 431. The park recommends taking the Long Pond Road trailhead route, which start 11 kilometres from Woody Point. There is a 4.5-kilometre hike to the coast, so you can come back the same way, in one day. It is possible to continue on the route and make a loop back to the other trailhead, at Wallace Brook, but the trail is not maintained to the standards of the Long Pond route, so be sure to check with park staff about trail conditions, if you decide to make this more rigorous trip. The Green Gardens Trail takes you from the barren, plant-poor environment near the road, down into an increasingly lush wooded valley and, finally, out to the cliff-top meadows of Green Gardens, at the edge of the rugged coast. There are sea stacks, and a giant sea cave accessible at low tide, and small coves and waterfalls scattered along the shore. There are two primitive campsites along the coast, for those who are prepared to pack in and pack out all their equipment and supplies. (The Visitor Centre provides free backcountry garbage bags.)

Heading straight north from Norris Point through the park, the coastline road soon offers an opportunity to see how the local people related to their environment. A few minutes past the turnoff to the park information building is Rocky

Flowers find a foothold on Green Point Cliffs

Harbour, where life goes on for many people as it always has in Newfoundland's villages. The fishing boats come and go, and a fish-processing plant sometimes wafts its characteristic odours over the nearby area. At the beginning and end of the lobster season, traps are piled high along the wharf, either just before being taken out to sea, or ready to be stored away for next year.

A rocky coast wouldn't be complete without a lighthouse. Gros Morne provides one at **Lobster Cove Head**, just north of Rocky Harbour. The light is now automated, but the keeper's house is open to the public every day, from mid-June to late September. One room is a reproduction of how the lightkeeper's den might have been at the beginning of this century. There is a theatre, with an audio-visual display about the environmental forces that shape the rugged western shore of Newfoundland and, by the time you visit, there will probably be a major new exhibit, telling the history of the area for the last 4,500 years. It describes the traditional lifestyles and harvesting of marine resources, from the prehistoric camps of Maritime Archaic Indians and Dorset Eskimos, to the seasonal fishery on the French Shore in the 1800s, right through to today's rapidly changing lifestyle. And you can enjoy all of this in a context of the sea crashing on the rocks, sometimes throwing its spray as far as the gnarled trees clinging to the upper levels.

About halfway up the park's length, **Green Point**, just beyond the Green Point Campground, offers two places to visit that are hidden by the bluffs bordering the main road. Descend along the gravel road (park at the junction with the highway, if your car isn't totally dependable on steep, gravelly hills), and discover the first of these places, a working fish camp

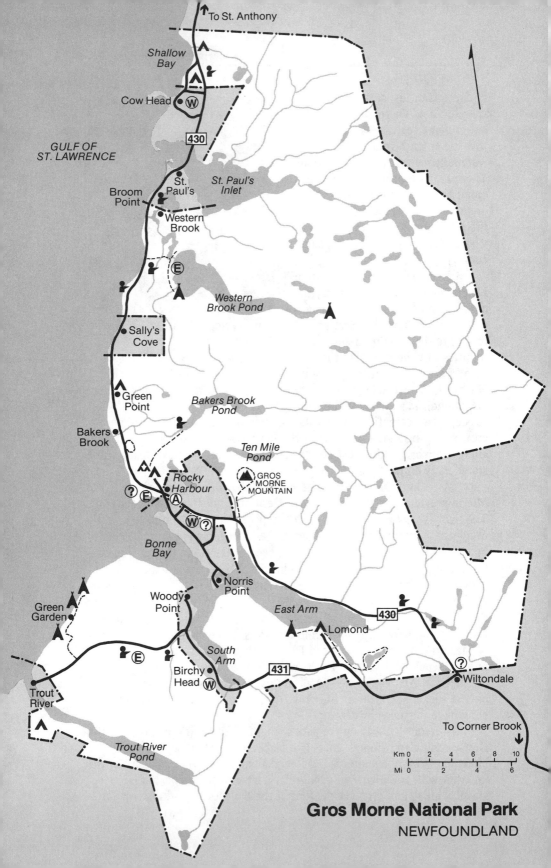

Gros Morne National Park
NEWFOUNDLAND

on the cobbled beach. In the summer, the people who make much of their living by fishing come from miles around to the sheltered cove, where they can pull their boats up on the narrow beach, dry their cod on wooden platforms, and camp out in the row of small cabins there. The lucky visitor can buy fish or lobster right on the spot. Lobster season ends during the first week in July, though, so plan accordingly.

A little further along the shore, at Green Point, is another very different place to visit. A few minutes' walk north along the beach, layer upon layer of geological history spreads out before your eyes. As you come around the headland, walk along the level, tide-pooled slabs of rock; the low cliffs to the right are composed of sedimentary layers, thrown up vertically by the slow but huge earth movements that shifted rocks 450 million years old. At one sharp indentation of the cliff line, there is a clear demarcation of the Cambrian and Ordovician periods. The layering is particularly easy to see, because it is standing on its side and has, therefore, eroded unevenly. After every few layers, there is a space of clear surface before the next layer takes up, rather as though someone had stood a thick-paged book on its side and begun to bend the pages slowly, with a few at a time sliding out of the fingers' grasp. Textures range from pockmarked to rippled, dimpled, smooth or jagged. Colours are a fan of subtle greens, yellows and greys. Be sure to take one of the guided walks here at Green Point, to get the fascinating facts about what you are seeing.

The drive farther north passes the first real dune area of the coastline, at **Western Brook** picnic ground. Several picnic tables, a cook shelter and washrooms are provided here.

The salt water of Bonne Bay and of the Gulf of St Lawrence, as it spills over the narrow beaches, is not within the park boundaries, although the visitor has easy access to it. However, near the north end of the park you come to **St. Paul's Bay**, which lies just outside the park boundary. This bay, too, is glacially carved, but its sides are not as steep as the other fiords. Much of it is edged with salt-marsh flats. Basking seals are not an uncommon sight on the sand bars, and the bird life is rich: migrating shorebirds, especially, abound.

Park near the bridge or in the tiny hamlet of St. Paul's, and walk along the crooked point of land that forms the inlet's lower edge. The sheltered beach is long and flat, with barnacles and beached shells, wood and seaweed; a favourite place for blue mussels and razor clams. The narrow channel out to sea is called a "tickle"—a deceptively mild term, for the sea rushes in and out with the change of tide, at alarming speed. Caution forbids walking too close to the edge at those times, but there are safe slopes, turning into pastureland, nearby.

At the end of the point, the land is no longer the park territory, and you see again the local use of the coastline, where scattered sheep or horses graze. The horses are free-roaming, although they still have nominal owners, who once used them for logging. The wind-scoured gulf side is a good place to see coastline plant colonization. The tasty sea-rocket grows here, alongside the silverweed (*Potentilla anserina*), which spreads its bright red runners to grasp any solid place to put down roots. You may find, as we did, an old jaw of a whale—the lower one—stretching about 2.5 metres (8 feet) long, flowers growing in its shadow of protection from the wind. Local people sometimes offer visitors boat tours of St. Paul's Inlet and, even though this is not a part of the park, it is likely that park staff can tell you if the tours are available, and who to contact.

As you continue your drive along Highway 430, rocky beaches and salt flats give way to long stretches of white sandy beach, edged by dunes or flower-dotted grassy fields. This landscape stretches for many kilometres at **Shallow Bay**, at the northernmost part of the park. Here, you can picnic in one area, or camp in another. Alternatively, you can hike beyond the campground, walk through a narrow band of forest that begins past the small bridge over the Stanford River, and cross the dunes to the beach. The park has built walkways across the dunes, from the campground and from the picnic area. Using them is very important for protecting the fragile dunes from the wear and tear of thousands of footfalls.

To view a remarkable aspect of the Gros Morne area, though it is not actually within the park boundaries, just walk south from Shallow Bay, along the water towards Cow Head, the low point of land jutting into the ocean. The point is one huge rock, and it contains the renowned **Cow Head Breccias**. Close examination shows a light-coloured rock face, with one type of sedimentary rock engulfing rough-edged chunks of another rock. There are fossils, too, embedded here and there. Breccias do occur elsewhere in the park, for example at Green Point, but this is where geologists first came to understand what appeared to be a paradox: how could there be, in this cold northern climate, rocks laden with fossils of animals that could live only in shallow warm seas, together with fossils of species that lived only in deep water? The answer is that, long ago, these rocks were part of the edge of the shallow shelf of the continent, which stretched far into what was then the sea. Occasionally, underwater avalanches would occur at the edge, and tonnes of the shelf, with all its living and sand-entrapped dead animals, would plunge suddenly down the slope, to the depths of the sea. These fragments would then be layered, over the millennia, with other debris, and compacted into a breccia. The ongoing movement of the huge plates that make up our earth's crust slowly raised these areas, and moved them to where they are now. Thus, Gros Morne's Cow Head Breccias have made an essential contribution to the theories of plate tectonics and continental drift. There are always naturalist-guided tours of the breccias. Check your *Tuckamore*, the park information guide, to see if any are scheduled.

Wild horses, Lomond Campground

The Coastal Plain

The coastal plain was once a shallow shelf, submerged by the sea, but the re-bound after glacial retreat lifted it to its present level, the second level of the park. Now it slopes up slightly inland, and then changes dramatically into the highlands. This narrow band of plain contains a world of its own. Soil has settled there; moisture can collect in considerable amounts; streams flow gently from the lakes gouged by the previous glaciers. Here, you can appreciate a special feature of Gros Morne, which is a meeting place of three ecological zones: temperate, boreal and arctic-alpine. Two of these zones can be distinguished on the plain. Lower elevations are temperate, with mixed woods of birch, red maple, black ash, eastern white pine and even the most northern examples of the choke cherry. Robins, jays, chickadees and warblers of many sorts abound. As the elevation increases slightly, the boreal forest dominates, with its balsam fir, black and white spruce and white birch. Moose, lynx, snowshoe hare, red fox, beaver and otter all live in this habitat. Heavy annual precipitation and a low evaporation rate result in moist soils. The soil is water-retaining and relatively level, so there is a wealth of bogs, lakes and meandering streams here.

There are three good places to visit, if you want to enjoy the fiords, woodlands and bogs of the lowlands. The first is the **Lomond** area, at the south end of the park. The easy walk, from beyond the Lomond Campground to Stanleyville, passes through the temperate zone forest that

Old forest skeletons emerge from the dunes

characterizes the lower reaches of the plain. At Stanleyville, you can see traces of a sawmill, and the gardens and orchards of the previous inhabitants.

The second location worth visiting is **Berry Head Pond**. A short walk, on the road north of the Berry Hill Campground, leads to a typical freshwater lake of the area. It has beaver dams and irises, marsh marigolds and bog orchids growing tall by the lake. A large, raised bog spreads out from three sides of the lake. Bogs are rarely as accessible as this one. The wetter part is traversed by a narrow boardwalk. Look out for the tussocky growth of sphagnum moss, bog laurel, Labrador tea and the carnivorous sundew and pitcher plant. The whole walk is very easy, and can be done in about an hour.

The third place to visit lies further north, and offers one of the most exciting experiences of the park—the hike to **Western Brook Pond**, and a boat ride on it. "Pond" is the rather modest local term for the massive, land-locked fiords that slash through the park. Western Brook Pond is, in fact, sixteen kilometres (ten miles) long and three kilometres (two miles) wide at its western, widest edge, and it is about 150 metres (500 feet) deep. However, it stretches into some of the highest of the upland areas so, as it narrows quite suddenly, it is enclosed by sheer cliffs nearly 800 metres (2,600 feet) high! The lower slopes support some trees and shrubs, but higher up the cliffs are nearly perpendicular, and only the gulls can cling to tiny cracks and shelves. Waterfalls sheet down, sometimes turning to mist curtains in the wind, at their upper heights.

To see all this you have to take a boat ride, a service which is usually offered by local residents in the summer. The Visitor Centre will have the telephone number for reservations.

The enjoyment of Western Brook Pond begins with the walk-in. The three-kilometre-long trail starts in the temperate, mixed-forest, lower area of the coastal plain, slowly moves through bands of bog, and continues through more mixed woods, more bog, then boreal forest areas, with beaver ponds and streams. The damp areas have a wide boardwalk. A camera is an excellent companion, as are binoculars. You may spot a beaver. Warblers are common in the boreal stands; at your feet are orchids, cloudberries, known locally as "bakeapples," and other flowering plants that thrive in the open, wet areas.

Even if the boat trip isn't possible, the hike is worthwhile. At the boat dock area, there is space to picnic and walk along the lakeshore or skip rocks across the water. Even farther along the trail is one of the park's "primitive" campsites at Snug Harbour, about another easy hour away, on the north shore of the pond. Water is plentiful: the pond has some of our world's cleanest fresh water. The beach is relaxing and the camping invigorating.

The Arctic-Alpine Areas

The third ecological zone to see at Gros Morne is arctic-alpine, and there are three places where this environment occurs. One of these places, the **Long Range Mountains**, which run from the north to the south of the park's eastern boundary, is not very accessible to visitors. The southernmost of these areas is the **Tablelands**, the plateau that makes up much of the southwest segment of the park. Access to it is on Highway 431, which turns to the left at Wiltondale, the hamlet at the edge of the park. It's easy to get there from Woody Point, too, if the ferry from Norris Point is operating.

The interpreter for the walk to the Tablelands called his programme "A Journey Towards the Centre of the Earth," a dramatic title that was borne out. The looming Tablelands are made of peridotite, a rock that is found in the mantle of the earth—the dense, but active, layer just below the earth's crust. As might be imagined, there are very few places in the world where mantle rock is on the surface, so this is a very special place and the rock has unusual qualities. It is made up largely of iron, magnesium silicates and chromite. The rock is very inhospitable to plant life, because it is low in nitrogen, phosphorous, calcium andother elements that plants need. Nevertheless, there is active plant life on the slopes of the plateau. Few species of plants can live without the usual nutrients, but on the dry, yellowing surfaces you'll find pitcher plants, sundews and butterworts, all plants that can extract nutrients from the animals they trap. Plants, such as alpine campion, balsam ragwort and Lapland rosebay, also manage to live because they can tolerate great amounts of magnesium. With a little rain now and then, and a crack in the earth to provide a holdfast, these plants can survive.

Peridotite is also interesting because, when it is exposed to water under very high pressure, or to heat, serpentine can be formed from this rock. Along the Winterhouse Brook at the base of the Tablelands, and at a few other locations, rocks show exposed sheets of serpentine, gleaming green in the light.

Gros Morne, the park's namesake mountain, is the third arctic-alpine area, located about one-third of the way up the main park road. The experience of hiking into its base, and then struggling up its face to the stark, rock-littered top will stay with you for a lifetime. The trail reaches more than 805 metres (2,600 feet) up to a flat expanse, where quartzite, shattered by water freezing and thawing on the chilly, windy surface, has created nine square kilometres (three square miles) of *felsenmeer*, a "sea of rocks."

In a few indented places, dust has collected and plants have taken hold. They exist in dwarf forms, such as the arctic willow and alpine bearberry, or they form compact cushions, as the diapensia and alpine azalea do. These cushions help them to resist the drying effects of wind, and to retain heat in their dense centres.

The views from Gros Morne are fantastic. Fiords and gulches, surrounding the mountain, cut sharply into the land around; other mountains rise as sharply in the distance. The coastal plain, with its mixed bogs, forests, lakes and streams, spreads out below, and the blue of the coast with Bonne Bay and the distant gulf accentuate the grey and green world all around.

It's an extremely rugged hike to the top, and it can take more than three to four hours each way. There is a detailed brochure on the hike, available at the parking lot at the trailhead. The first hour is spent on a fairly steady rise through the range of coastal forest types, and then up into the drier, sub-alpine heath. This trail is well marked and very well maintained; even children should find it quite walkable, if they go slowly. At the end of this part, near the base of the mountain, there are several jewel-like lakes and a refreshing rushing stream, an excellent spot for a picnic or exploring. The ground is even and dry, and there are plenty of places to walk near the base of the mountain.

If you choose to go to the top, you first have to scramble up a large and very steep scree slope. On top, a trail is clearly marked with rock cairns. This is a strenuous climb, but the view is marvellous. The park recommends that you ascend on the scree slope, and descend by the trail on the back side of the mountain. Half-way down, you will find a small lake with a rest stop and pit toilets. Unless you are sure your children are strong, patient hikers, you might want to stop short of the final push up the scree slope to the top.

The trail to Gros Morne's top is easy to follow, but requires hard work on the scree slope

Park Services and Facilities

Gros Morne is one of the newest of the National Parks, but it already has well-established visitor facilities, a wide range of trails for a variety of hiking experiences, and informative, extensive interpretation programmes. These programmes take place all over the park, but are coordinated at the Visitor Centre at Rocky Harbour. This centre is a beautiful building, with excellent displays and a good indoor theatre for evening presentations.

Camping

There are a total of 287 campsites in the park. None have electrical hook-ups, but the Berry Hill Campground has trailer-waste disposal facilities, and a water supply for filling storage tanks. All campsites are on a first-come, first-served basis. Firewood and cooking grates are provided, but bring your own hatchet and small saw. Most sites have picnic tables. At **Berry Hill**, 156 sites are situated in a densely wooded area, four kilometres (two and one-half miles) inland. The trees give a lot of privacy. The campground is equipped with hot showers, washrooms and toilets, excellent kitchen shelters with running water, sinks and sophisticated wood stoves. There are three sandbox and play areas for small children; one's very large, with a well-designed adventure playground. There is a trail to a good lookout point, leading from the back of the campground, and a trail leading around a small pond behind it. There are three bulletin boards, with information on the interpretive programmes.

There are six "walk-in" campsites on a small lake. Parking is about forty-five metres (fifty yards) away. These sites are more secluded, but the walk to the facilities is longer.

   Green Point campground has eighteen sites, nestled into the low, coastal tuckamore—the coastal border of windswept, gnarled trees. There is a kitchen shelter with a wood stove, and pit toilets. There is a central, pumped water supply. The campground is self-registering, with the staff collecting the slips each day. There's a low cliff here, but a stairway descends to the beach. The sea is too rough for swimming, but the beach is great for walking and enjoying the marvellous sunsets. Being so close to the Green Point fishing settlement, and the fascinating geology of the cove, is the real advantage of this quiet, modest campground. There is a bulletin board, with a park map and announcements of the interpretive programme. At **Shallow Bay**, fifty sites are located on a rather dull open field, but this campground is the nearest to the dunes and the wide, shallow beach that stretches for kilometres along the northern part of the park. It has an adventure playground for children. There are flush toilets and showers. Adjoining the kitchen shelter is a mini-theatre, for evening interpretive programmes. There is a kiosk for registration and information. The **Lomond** area (twenty-eight sites) is at the southern edge of the park, on the western segment near the Tablelands. It is four kilometres (two and one-half miles) east of Highway 431, on the road to Woody Point. The grassy field for camping leads down the east arm of Bonne Bay. Three of the sites are "walk-ins," overlooking Bonne Bay. The brief walk is through meadows thick with flowers. You can fish along the Lomond River, nearby. There is a kiosk for registration and information. There is also an adventure playground for children.

   Trout River campground has thirty-three sites, overlooking Trout River Pond. There is an adventure playground, kitchen shelters, pumped water and pit toilets. There is a kiosk for registration and information. There are plans for boat tours on Trout River Pond, so check with the kiosk, to see if they are happening.

Group Camping

There is group camping now, at Berry Hill campground. Write to the Superintendent for information and reservations.

Other Accommodation, Gas, Food and Supplies

The villages of Rocky Harbour, Cow Head and Woody Point have motels. There are private campgrounds near Woody Point and Rocky Harbour, on private land. Most communities provide gas, food and supplies. There are guest homes now in Woody Point, Rocky Harbour and Cow Head, and guest cabins in Rocky Harbour, Trout River and Wiltondale (near the southeastern edge of the park). The Superintendent should have listings, or contact the Newfoundland Tourism Department (call telephone information for Area Code 709).

Recreational Services

Playgrounds   There are adventure playgrounds at Berry hill, Lomond, Shallow Bay and Trout River campgrounds.

Swimming   There is no supervised swimming in the park, but there are many areas of shore and stream that are good for wading or swimming. Shallow Bay picnic area is the only area with changing rooms. The community of Rocky Harbour has an unsupervised beach on Rocky Harbour Pond, as well as a fitness park. Shallow Bay and Lomond day-use areas have unsupervised saltwater swimming. Both have changing rooms, and Lomond has outdoor showers for rinsing off. Trout River has freshwater swimming, with changing rooms. Two kilometres south of Berry Hill campground, on Highway 430, there is a new, indoor, twenty-five-metre swimming pool overlooking Rocky Harbour. The shallow bay, a marina and a whirlpool complete the picture. This facility is open from mid-June through Labour Day.

Fishing   This is a very good area for Atlantic salmon or speckled trout. Provincial fishing regulations are in force. Park staff can give information, as can the local businesses servicing visitors, motels, grocery stores, camping suppliers, etc. There is a small "fish camp" at Broom Point, just before St. Paul's Inlet. There is a summer cabin and fishing-supply store. They are staffed by local people, who can relate first-hand experiences of fishing along the coast. This site has been restored to the period between 1963 and 1969. The history, economy and technology of family fishing operations that were characteristic of the in-shore fishery are the story here.

Further Reading

Gros Morne: A Living Landscape by Pat McLeod (Breakwater, 1987)

FOR MORE INFORMATION

The Superintendent
Gros Morne National Park
Box 130
Rocky Harbour, Newfoundland
A0K 4N0

Phone: (709) 458-2417

TERRA NOVA

NATIONAL PARK

Terra Nova occupies almost 400 square kilometres (155 square miles) along the eastern coast of Newfoundland, and it is a great place to see the heritage of the Ice Ages. It is a park you can see, literally, from the ground up; from the deep fiords, to the sweep of bog and fen, upward to the boulder-strewn slopes, to the boreal forest clinging to the shallow soil, and finally up to the bald, windswept hilltops.

How to See the Park

Because much of the park is rugged, exposed, island-studded coastline, with hectares of mushy bog, it is not easily accessible to the visitor. However, there are at least one or two car roads and hiking trails to each of the key areas; the coastline, the bogs, the forests and the upland barrens.

In the last Ice Age (eight thousand to twelve thousand years ago), there was a massive ice cap in southwest Newfoundland, which sent out rivers of ice that gouged valleys, deepened rivers, and ground bedrock to a high polish. As it began to melt and retreat, it left behind a trail of sand, gravel, rocks and boulders, which had been bound up in its ice. The gouging and scouring action of these deposits resulted in the varied topography of Terra Nova.

The Coastline

There are almost two hundred kilometres of coastline in Terra Nova, with fiords, coves and tidal flats lining the southern, eastern, and part of the northern edges of the park. In places, the land's edge is highly sculpted with caves, cliffs and rocky stacks; elsewhere, there are sand and pebble-strewn beaches. To appreciate the beauty and variety of the coastline, take the shoreline trail that runs along much of inner **Newman Sound**, from **Buckley's Cove** to **South Broad Cove**. The trail can be reached from several roads off the Trans-Canada Highway, which runs the entire north/south length of the park, or it can be taken up near the Newman Sound Campground. A short drive or walk to the Day-Use Area, with its cooking shelter for picnickers and its gentle, sandy beach, leads you right to the path, at a point about halfway along it. This is a good trail for viewing the coastline, for wandering onto the beach at low tide, or for watching for boreal birds or flowers in the forest through which it weaves.

The shore area is rich in plant and bird life. Look for shore birds, ducks and geese in spring and fall. Bald eagles and ospreys nest in the park, and can regularly be seen from this trail. Rare birds, storm-tossed or straying off-course from their homes in Greenland, Britain or Europe often take refuge here. (The park has excellent bird-watching books available; ask for them at the Information Centre.) You can stop near the wharf area to view **Pissing Mare Falls**, far more elegant than its name. At the wharf you can watch people fish, or try it yourself.

The Fresh Water

Fresh water flows in many narrow swift streams, slows down in numerous ponds, and remains still in the bogs and fens. Here, too, the Ice Age has left its imprint. Some of the streams were cut out by the melt water from the retreating ice, long ago. Some of the lakes and bogs were scraped out by glacial action, or built up when coarse soil was compacted by glaciers, so that the torrents of rain could not drain off rapidly. Slow drainage and high moisture collection are ideal conditions to form the bogs and fens that cover over fifteen percent of Terra Nova.

For a good look at some of these wetlands, take the **Ochre Hill Ponds Loop Trail** (keep your eyes open for the curve back to the road!), or keep going past the Ochre Hill Ponds up to the Ochre Hill Lookout (not to the Fire Tower Lookout—that's another trail). Here, you will walk on a gravel and boardwalk trail, through sphagnum-based bogs or sedgy fens dotted with little islands of tiny, twisted tamarack trees or spruce. The bogs give way to a stream littered with jagged boulders, which have most intriguing lichen patterns. All along the way you can see pitcher plants, as well as pink sheep and bog laurel, and sundews trapping insects.

The trail also weaves in and out of the boreal forest that edges the bog and pond system. Eventually, you reach a lake, with water that is clean, but coloured brown by the tannic and humic acids that seep in from the surrounding bogs. This trail can be taken all the way to the overlooking Ochre Hills. The view from there reveals bogs spreading in nearly every direction. The bogs at Bread Cove Meadow, to the south, are the most fascinating. They look like half of a drowned coliseum, with the concentric half-circles of water forming the remaining tiers of seats.

Sandy Pond Trail takes you on a delightful walk around this fresh-water lake. Start just past the swimming beach, for a leisurely hour's walk through forest, past little marsh edges of the lake, one boggy area, and over the stream that connects it to the main canoe route of the park. There's an old dam at one end, made entirely of hewn logs. The scenic mix of water, shoreline, forest flowers and other vegetation makes for a splendid walk.

Arethusa orchids on the edge of a bog

The Forests

The forests of Terra Nova are boreal, supporting only the kind of trees that can grow on thin soil, at low temperatures, with a very short summer. Predominant trees are black spruce and balsam fir. The coastal walk along **Newman Sound**, and the Malady Head and Newman Sound Campgrounds offer fine opportunities to enjoy the boreal forest, with its bird sounds in the early mornings and evenings.

But my favourite place was on a short hike to **Malady Head**. This trail is hard to find. It begins near campsite 62, in the Malady Head Campground. The kiosk operator should be able to provide instructions on how to get there and where to park. Then comes the quiet, intense experience of a true boreal forest. There is a special smell, and a softness to the feel of the air. The trees are bare of needles for about half their lower length, due to the limited sunlight penetrating through the upper branches. The stubs of old branches, and the trunks themselves, are draped and pasted with old man's beard, a wispy, pale-green lichen that hangs down in triangles. Old man's beard does not harm the trees, and indicates that the air is clean, for it cannot survive in even low levels of atmospheric chemical pollution.

The forest floor is the familiar tumble of moss or laurel-covered rock-jumble, depending on the slope and dryness of each little area. Many varieties of moss thrive here in the humid environment, sphagnum being one of the most common. Another type of moss is called "step-moss," and deserves a careful look. Each year, it grows a small, new, feathery beard above the previous season's growth, making the whole mass look very thick, and feel very soft.

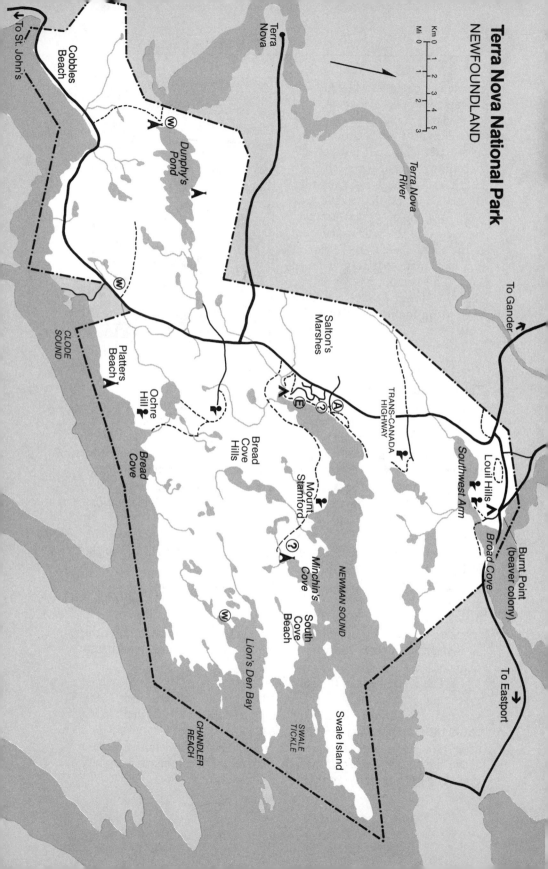

Terra Nova National Park
NEWFOUNDLAND

Km 0   1   2   3   4   5
Mi 0   1   2   3

To St. John's

Cobbles Beach

Terra Nova

Terra Nova River

To Gander

Dunphy's Pond

CLODE SOUND

Platters Beach

Ochre Hill

Bread Cove

Bread Cove Hills

Salton's Marshes

TRANS-CANADA HIGHWAY

Southwest Arm

Louil Hills

Broad Cove

Burnt Point (beaver colony)

To Easport

Mount Stamford

Minchin's Cove

South Cove Beach

NEWMAN SOUND

Lion's Den Bay

CHANDLER REACH

SWALE TICKLE

Swale Island

The Barrens

Coasts, bogs and forests give way to barrens. At transitional levels, there is pearly-grey caribou lichen in puffs and rolls, interspersed with the occasional hearty tamarack or low-growing spruce. Some of these black spruce trees send out their lowest branches in a wide circle, and keep their tops less than a metre (three feet) tall. You can see this kind of plant life on the slopes leading to the **Ochre Hill Fire Tower Lookout**, and to the **Ochre Hills Lookout**. But, at the top of both lookouts, the altitude and winds have conspired to prevent even this much vegetation taking hold. As at **Malady Head** and **Louil Hills**, there is just exposed rock, remoulded through the ages, with the occasional glacial erratic breaking its profile. The lichens on the rocks are marvelous, and tenacious berry shrubs stretch out low from rock cracks, and hold on tight.

Park Services and Facilities

Interpretive Programme

The park has an active interpretive programme of guided walks, evening presentations, children's programmes and special events, during the summer season. There are outdoor theatres and campfire circles at each campground. Times and places of park programmes are posted on the campground bulletin boards, and listed in various park publications available at the kiosks and Visitor Centres. Ski events and school and special group tours are available on request in the fall, winter and spring.

Camping

There are two large campgrounds in the park. **Newman Sound** is the larger of the two, with large, clean flush-toilet facilities, hot showers, kitchen shelters, laundromat, playgrounds and a grocery store. The setting is sparsely forested, with gravel pull-ins and a picnic table at each of its 387 sites. **Malady Head** is smaller and quieter, with only 165 sites. It is more densely treed than Newman Sound, and has clean flush-toilet and shower facilities. There are no electrical hook-ups at either site, but both have a trailer-waste disposal facility. Campfire pits are available at each campsite, at Malady Head only.

Primitive Camping

There are four back-country camping areas, with pit toilets and picnic tables, for the use of hikers and canoeists. Sites are free, but you must register. Park staff can provide you with more information on these.

Parks Canada

Bread Cove Hills, a glacially scoured area

Other Accommodation, Gas, Food and Supplies

The park has twenty-four kitchenette cottages, run by a private concession. These are near the park administration area, and just a short walk from Newman Sound Day-Use Area. Write to the Superintendent for information.

There are gasoline stations at each end of the park, and a concession-run grocery, with a wide variety of food and other small camping supplies, near the Newman Sound campground. The villages in the area have grocery and hardware stores and gas stations. Charlottetown lies near the central area of the park; Terra Nova and Eastport are about sixteen kilometres (ten miles) outside its boundaries. Traytown is the closest village to the park—about two kilometres (one mile) beyond Burnt Point.

Recreational Services

Swimming There is supervised swimming at Sandy Pond, 10:00 a.m. to 6:00 p.m., seven days a week, from June until Labour Day weekend. Changing rooms and a snack bar are provided.

Canoeing You can rent canoes and kayaks hourly, daily, or weekly in the summer, at Sandy Pond. Waterproofed aerial photo maps of the park, for canoe routes, are sold at a moderate price.

Fishing   There is fishing in a number of ponds and streams. A park permit is required. However, salt-water fishing from the park wharves does not require a licence. Ask any warden, or at the information kiosk, for further details.

Skiing   Cross-country skiing is a popular winter activity in the park. Groomed ski trails are open at Newman Sound, Twin Rivers Golf Course and Sandy Pond.

Golfing   The scenic Twin Rivers Golf Course is located at the southern end of the park. Currently a nine-hole course, the remaining nine holes are under construction. Club rental and dining facilities are available at the clubhouse.

Boat Tours   Regularly scheduled trips/boat tours leave several times daily from Headquarters Wharf, between mid-June and Labour Day. Special adventure and education programmes are available throughout the summer. Group rates are available. Call (709) 677-2327 (May, June and September) for information.

FOR MORE INFORMATION

The Superintendent
Terra Nova National Park
Glovertown, Newfoundland
A0G 2L0

Phone: (709) 533-2801

ELLESMERE ISLAND

NATIONAL PARK RESERVE

Ellesmere Island National Park Reserve is located at the northernmost tip of the western hemisphere. ("Reserve" status means that, though the area is governed by the National Parks Act, it remains for the land claims of aboriginal people to be resolved for it to achieve full park status.) Ellesmere is surely the ultimate northern experience in the Canadian parks system, and quite likely there are few experiences to compare, anywhere in the northern hemisphere. The park reserve was established in 1988, and the land set aside is 39,500 square kilometres of the north of Ellesmere Island. The reserve protects a representative part of the Eastern High Arctic Glacier natural region.

Ellesmere abounds with glaciers. Icefields, as much as 900 metres thick, cover the Grantland Mountains at the northern part of the park. Several of the peaks in the Grantland Range are over 2,500 metres high. Along the coast, there are many valleys, cut by glaciers, sweeping to the sea. Within the park is Lake Hazen which, at eighty kilometres in length, is the largest lake north of the Arctic circle. It is an area especially rich in wildlife, because there is more moisture there. Moisture is a major issue for this rugged place, because it is actually a polar desert, with an anuual precipitation of only six centimetres!

Plant and animal life is rich, with the landscape carpeted, for the few weeks of summer, with dwarf willow, bright Arctic wildflowers, and colourful lichens and mosses. Musk ox, Arctic wolf and fox, bears, caribou, and many nesting birds are easy to see and easy to approach and photograph.

There is evidence of human use of the area as long as four thousand years ago, a use that has continued sporadically to this day. Along with the artifacts of aboriginal people, there are a number of sites with remains from Arctic explorers, who used the tip of Ellesmere as their jumping-off place, en route to the North Pole.

Visiting Ellesmere Island Park Reserve is expensive, and requires that the visitor either be very knowledgeable about travel in the High Arctic, or use the services of the tour companies that are licensed to operate in the reserve. The park has a very useful information handout about visitation, including lists of licensed outfitters, what conditions to expect, what to bring, associated costs, etc. Because the season for visiting is very short—mostly July and August—and there is a great demand for transportation and guiding services, you must plan very far in advance for your trip. And once on your way, the conditions of northern travel may throw your carefully planned schedule very far off. I'm sure that, for the adventurous soul, the trip would be worth any amount of inconvenience.

FOR MORE INFORMATION

The Superintendent
Auyuittuq/Ellesmere Island National Park Reserve
Canadian Parks Service
Pangnirtung, N.W.T.
X0A 0R0

Phone: (819) 473-8828

Conservation and Natural History Associations

These are some of the groups that are involved in various aspects of national and provincial parks policy. Many have local chapters. Joining one or more of them is an excellent way to become better informed on parks-related issues, and to affect local and national policy on the protection and use of our natural heritage.

National Parks Cooperating Associations
Many parks have very active cooperating associations. The associations aim to increase constructive interaction between local people and the park, and to encourage local participation in park activities and policies. Many of the associations operate bookstores, and assist in park interpretation.

Canadian Parks & Wilderness Society
#1150-160 Bloor Street East
Toronto, Ontario
M4W 1B9

The purpose of the association is to promote the use and management of national and provincial parks in a manner that will contribute to the education, inspiration and well-being of the public; to encourage expansion of national and provincial parks systems, and preservation of places with outstanding natural or historic significance.

Canadian Nature Federation
453 Sussex Drive
Ottawa, Ontario
K1N 6Z4

The purpose of the Federation is to educate the Canadian public about the value of wildlife and other natural resources, the interdependence of wildlife and wildlife habitats; to be spokesman [sic] for nature in national and environmental and conservation issues; to support public education and environmental action programmes of local and provincial naturalists' clubs and federations across Canada. The Federation also publishes *Nature Canada* magazine.

Federation of Alberta Naturalists
Box 1472
Edmonton, Alberta
T5J 2N5

Ecology North
P.O. Box 2888
Yellowknife, Northwest Territories
X1A 2N1

Federation of British Columbia Natuarlists
1367 West Broadway
Vancouver, British Columbia
V6H 4A9

Federation of Ontario Naturalists
355 Lesmill Road
Don Mills, Ontario
M3B 2W8

Manitoba Naturalists Society
#302-128 James Avenue
Winnipeg, Manitoba
R3B 0N8

Natural History Society of Prince Edward Island
P.O. Box 2346
Charlottetown, Prince Edward Island
C1B 8C1

New Brunswick Federation of Naturalists
277 Douglas Avenue
Saint John, New Brunswick
E2K 1E5

Newfoundland Natural History Society
Box 1013
St. John's, Newfoundland
A1C 5M3

Nova Scotia Bird Society
Nova Scotia Museum
1747 Summer Street
Halifax, Nova Scotia
B3H 3A6

Saskatchewan Natural History Society
Box 4348
Regina, Saskatchewan
S4P 3W6

Union québécoise pour la conservation de la nature
160, 76 Street East
2nd Floor
Charlesbourg, Québec
G1G 7H8

Yukon Conservation Society
P.O. Box 4163
Whitehorse, Yukon Territory
Y1A 3T3

Special Aids for Birdwatchers

Canada Birding

This bulletin has taken the place of *Birdfinding in Canada*. It is published monthly. It contains information on birdwatching hot-spots across Canada, up-dates of life lists of active birdwatchers, discussions of rare-bird sightings, etc. It is very enjoyable and useful. It has good material on the national parks, when they are discussed. For more information write to:

Blake Maybank
333 Bayview Drive
Site 14A, Box 43
R.R. #4
Armdale, Nova Scotia
B3L 4J4

Birding in Atlantic Canada: 3 volumes, by Roger Burrows

These books give detailed information on birdwatching locations, and are good for information on accommodation, etc. in areas referred to. Volume I is Nova Scotia, Volume II is Newfoundland, Volume III is L'Acadie, which includes P.E.I., New Brunswick and maritime Québec. They are available from:

Jesperson Press, Ltd.
26A Flavin Street
St. John's, Newfoundland
A1C 3R9